IN DEFENSE OF SOVEREIGNTY

M. & J. Walzer
March 1964
Cambridge

IN
DEFENSE
OF
SOVEREIGNTY

Edited by W. J. Stankiewicz

PROFESSOR OF POLITICAL SCIENCE

UNIVERSITY OF BRITISH COLUMBIA

New York

OXFORD UNIVERSITY PRESS

London 1969 *Toronto*

To all students of politics
who have grasped the limitations
of contemporary empiricism and the value
of speculative thought

CONTRIBUTORS

Stanley I. Benn (born 1920): Senior Fellow in Philosophy at the Institute of Advanced Studies, Australian National University; co-author (with R. S. Peters) of *Social Principles and the Democratic State*, London, 1959 (Amer. edition, *The Principles of Political Thought*, 1964).

Kenneth C. Cole (born 1898): Emeritus Professor of Political Science at the University of Washington, Seattle, Washington.

Karl W. Deutsch (born 1912): Professor of Political Science at Harvard University; author of *Nationalism and Social Communication*, 1953, *Political Community at the International Level*, 1954, *The Nerves of Government*, 1963, 1966; co-author (with others) of *Political Community and the North Atlantic Area*, 1957.

F. H. Hinsley (born 1918): Reader in the History of International Relations at the University of Cambridge and Fellow of St. John's College; author of *Hitler's Strategy*, 1951, *Power and the Pursuit of Peace*, 1963, 1967, *Sovereignty*, 1966; editor of *The New Cambridge Modern History*, Vol. XI (1870–98), 1962.

Hans Kelsen (born 1881): Jurist of international renown; Professor Emeritus at the University of California (Berkeley); author of *General Theory of Law and State*, 1945, *Principles of International Law*, 1952, *Collective Security Under International Law*, 1957, *The Pure Theory of Law*, 1967, and other books.

Jacques Maritain (born 1882): Philosopher of international renown; Professor Emeritus of Philosophy at Princeton University; author of *The Range of Reason*, 1942, *Existence and the Existent*, 1948, 1957, *Man and the State*, 1951, *St. Thomas Aquinas*, 1958, and other books.

K. W. B. Middleton (born 1905): Sheriff-Substitute of the Lothians and Peebles at Edinburgh; author of *Britain and Russia*, 1947.

W. J. Rees (born 1914): Senior Lecturer in Philosophy at the University of Leeds.

Georg Schwarzenberger (born 1908): Professor of International Law at the University of London; Director of the London Institute of World Affairs; author of *Power Politics: A Study of World Society*, 1941, 3rd ed., 1964, *A Manual of International Law*, 1945, 3rd ed., 1966, *The Fundamental Principles of International Law*, 1955, *The Principles and Standards of International Economic Law*, 1967, and other books.

Yves R. Simon (1903–1961): The late Professor of Philosophy at the University of Chicago; author of *Introduction à l'ontologie du connaître*, 1934, *Philosophy of Democratic Government*, 1951, 1961, *A General Theory of Authority*, 1962, *The Tradition of Natural Law*, 1965, and other books.

W. J. Stankiewicz (born 1922): Professor of Political Science at the University of British Columbia, Vancouver; author of *Politics and Religion in Seventeenth-Century France*, 1960; co-author (with J. M. Montias) of *Institutional Changes in the Postwar Economy of Poland*, 1955; editor of *Political Thought Since World War II: Critical and Interpretive Essays*, 1964, *Crisis in British Government: The Need for Reform*, 1967.

Ivor G. Wilks (born 1928): Professor of History at Northwestern University, Evanston, Illinois.

PREFACE

The theme of this symposium is apparent from its title: *In Defense of Sovereignty*. An anthology of this type, apart from serving as a university textbook, can play a new role—that of fostering an argument, or scholarly polemic, and perhaps bringing to a boil a discourse on one of the central concepts in political theory. I see my task as not only that of selecting and presenting papers, but also taking issue with some of the chief critics of the concept of sovereignty and taking a definite stand regarding its validity.

The papers collected in this book fall into two groups: one group opposes the concept of sovereignty and the other defends it. The reader will become aware that although there has not been any 'debate' on sovereignty, there have been prolonged—although inconclusive—discussions about the relevance of the concept to the modern world.

In the last two decades there has been a significant upsurge of interest. However, the ensuing discussion has been diffuse: most participants have never confronted each other. Hence, presenting the papers in form of a 'round table' discussion may help to clarify the nature of the debate and give substance to it.

It is not the purpose of this symposium to give a full account of the discourse on sovereignty since World War II, but to subject to critical scrutiny some of the most telling or typical statements. A further aim is to bring the merits and weaknesses of various arguments into focus; to draw conclusions from existing trends of thought; and to suggest new interpretations of the present role of the concept.

The concern with sovereignty largely reflects the current trend of the social sciences: an iconoclastic, value-free, empirical 'science'-directed orientation. But the degree to which scientism has affected modern thinking has inevitably involved a critical reaction which is bound to culiminate in a 'secondary' iconoclasm, this time in defense of philosophical thought and a system of values opposed to relativism.

How will the concept itself fare in these circumstances? Its future will depend on both the cogency of the arguments advanced by its advocates and the general revival of political theory. The latter, if it is to have any significance, must be consonant with the era of change. It must grapple with the major issue of relativism, which, under some interpretations, has thrown doubt upon the revelance of norms and ideologies to political analysis. It must aim at exactness when restating old concepts and must be capable of defending the importance of speculative thinking; that is, it must demolish the notion that speculative thought has become 'old-fashioned' and that 'research' (in the sense of merely gathering quantitative evidence) is an adequate modern substitute. The present defense of sovereignty is offered in the hope that it will contribute to a wider discussion and to the revitalization of a number of 'classical' concepts and issues pertinent to modern political philosophy.

I wish to express my indebtedness to Mr. Ian W. Peyman, who co-operated in the search for relevant papers and contributed substantially to the analysis; to Mr. Ronald C. Cooke, who made valuable editorial suggestions; also to the Dean's Committee on Research of the Faculty of Graduate Studies at UBC, which provided financial assistance. Acknowledgments are also due to Harcourt, Brace & World, Inc., for permission to include, in the Conclusion, a passage from *The Structure of Science* by Ernest Nagel.

W. J. Stankiewicz

University of British Columbia
December 1968

CONTENTS

Another question is "Where ought the sovereign power of the state reside?" With the people? With the propertied classes? With the good? With one man, the best of all the good? With one man, the tyrant? There are objections to all these.

Aristotle, The Politics

The importance of the doctrine of sovereignty can hardly be overrated. It was a formidable tool in the hands of lawyers and politicians, and a decisive factor in the making of modern Europe.

A. P. d'Entrèves, Natural Law

one

INTRODUCTORY

W. J. Stankiewicz

IN DEFENSE OF SOVEREIGNTY:
A CRITIQUE AND AN
INTERPRETATION

Is sovereignty still worth discussing, or is it simply a myth which prevents its adherents from recognizing the complexity of power relations in a society? Is it useful only to jurists, whose discipline requires an ordering idea, arbitrary or not, or does it express a principle of order inherent in the very definitions of society and government?

As a myth, the concept was for a long time accepted: 'Sovereignty is a legal fiction but a practical necessity.' But it was not immune to criticism, and has lately been subjected to particularly sharp attacks. There has been a tendency to link these attacks with the 'decline of political theory,' although their very intensity suggests that the claims of that theory have not been invalidated and that certain classical concepts—of which sovereignty is an outstanding example—still exert an influence which is sufficiently strong to cause a hostile reaction. One suspects that behind these assaults is the realization that sovereignty is not simply a myth, but a fact of political life which is inconveniently at odds with democratic assumptions of what ought to be. As will be shown later, there are certain aspects of modern democracy, paradoxically its relativism, which may ultimately validate the principle of sovereignty. Despite the claims made by the opponents of the concept, the present-day exercise of sovereignty is not far from what the classical theory postulated: the sovereign tends to be an unlimited, supreme, coercive power which has a will and expresses itself through legislation. What has happened is that the loss of support for values in general has once again made order the central value, as it was for Bodin and Hobbes.

Objections to the Classical Theory

The new critics have tried to discredit sovereignty on three grounds: semantic, empirical, and moral. The semanticist argues that the term has too many meanings; the empiricist laments that sovereignty—with its classical attributes—is impossible to identify and measure; the moralist claims that the concept conflicts with other values, particularly the principles of order.

The semantic objection that sovereignty has no single, precise meaning is an objection to the term, not the concept, and is of interest only because it reveals a failure to recognize that sovereignty is a set of logically related ideas—and not a simple, empirically verifiable condition. The semanticist—or the linguistic analyst like T. D. Weldon—is likely to see in all the conceptual problems of traditional political theory the results of confusion caused by 'purely empirical difficulties.' [1]

The empiricist objection rests on the assumption that all scientific concepts must be reducible to 'observation terms': a position that Hempel calls the "narrower thesis of empiricism." [2] The latter is the type of statement that many social scientists find irresistible: for the idea that science is based

1. A curious trap into which semantic analysis is leading some critics can be found in the yardstick which they apply in order to expose other people's 'sins of language.' This trap is the identification of *words* with *things*. The idea has been well expressed by Stuart Chase: "We are continually confusing the label with the non-verbal object, and so giving a spurious validity to the word, as something alive and barking in its own right." (*The Tyranny of Words,* New York, 1938, p. 9) Many semanticists seem unable to reach beyond the realm of things in order to demonstrate the applicability or non-applicability of words.

2. Carl G. Hempel, *Fundamentals of Concept Formation in Empirical Science,* University of Chicago Press, Chicago, 1952.

exclusively on a physical view of the universe and that all abstractions can be reduced to sense impressions offers the dazzling possibility that all sense impressions can be elevated to the level of science, and that every researcher can become a scientist simply by donning white overalls and recording the sense perceptions of himself and other human beings.

In fact, however, no general scientific concept having explanatory or predictive significance can be so obtained: not only because of the difficulty of formulating disposition [3] and quantitative terms, but also because empirical observation alone can yield nothing more than disconnected sets of sense data which are valueless to science because they were not collected on the basis of some hypothesis. In other words, scientific statements—unlike the results of sense perception alone—always imply a connecting theory. It is the original hypothesis which guides the selection of facts and the testing of the latter's significance. Thus, while empiricism can arrive at the concept of gravity (the conclusion that all things fall, which is a generalized description rather than a scientific principle), it cannot yield the concept of gravitation (a law in physics referring to the force which tends to draw all bodies in the earth's sphere to the earth's center), for data collection alone cannot provide a tested statement of the relationship between observed facts. What the empiricists fail to understand is that sovereignty is not a generalized description like gravity, but an explanatory principle like gravitation. It stands or falls on its logic, given certain assumptions, not on the accuracy with which it describes conditions at all times and places. In essence, sovereignty is a declaration that if order is to have certain characteristics, then an ordering body or sovereign having certain qualities must exist. The classical statement about sovereignty would be an empirically verifiable description of existing conditions only if order were the one thing man

3. As Hempel puts it, "A disposition term . . . designates not a directly observable characteristic, but rather a disposition . . . to display specific reactions . . . under certain specifiable circumstances." (*Ibid.* p. 24) The notion of sovereignty suggested by W. J. Rees in the paper included in this collection resembles a disposition term.

valued. In so far as man wants other things as well, the sovereign power is modified but not refuted.

The moralist objects to the 'absolutist' claims of sovereignty, particularly on the ground that they conflict with statements about law, obligation, freedom, individualism, and the like. In the main, the moralist says that one or more attributes of classical sovereignty are unacceptable because they conflict with other accepted notions of human relations. The moralist may be a federalist and object to the indivisibility attribute; or an upholder of government by consent and reject the coercive implications; or he may believe in natural law and question the unlimited nature of sovereignty in classical theory. If his objections refer to consensus, when questioning classical theory he points to the fact that the 'sovereign' in his own community lacks the attributes usually attached to sovereignty, for though 'sovereignty' makes an essential statement about order, the maintenance of that order requires an accommodation to other statements. Indeed, because the authority of the sovereign ultimately rests on recognition of the need for order, and because other values are felt to be parts of the order maintained by the sovereign power, the latter cannot violate the subsidiary orders without ceasing to be sovereign.

The problem raised by moralist objections becomes especially acute when particular sets of values—for instance, the democratic set—are held to constitute the main ordering principle in a state. If one believes in pure democracy, it is hard to believe in sovereignty in the classic sense. If one believes that the logic of the classical theory is essentially sound, it is hard to believe in democracy, unless the ambiguous and unsatisfactory notion of 'popular sovereignty' is introduced. Perhaps a complete reconciliation is not possible here. It appears that when the need for action in the face of an implicit threat of conflict arises, the logic of sovereignty prevails over the logic of democracy. Then—despite the moralist objections—in the clash between the statement of indivisible sovereignty and the federalist insistence on divisibility, the logic of sovereignty is victorious. On balance, democracy may be prone to this type of 'defeat'; the shortcomings inherent in its pronouncements about social order—in particular the anti-social nature of its individualism—may tend to produce conditions propitious for the full-fledged classical theory of sovereignty.

The claim that sovereignty must be unlimited appears to be one of the more objectionable attributes of the classical concept, for it would seem to place the sovereign beyond the restraints of the society's normative order. In fact, it does not do so, since the function of keeping order includes the maintenance of norms which are part of the social order. Nonetheless, the denial that the sovereign's primary responsibility is action in accordance with the common good or natural law—or even that 'relativist natural law,' the constitution—has historically been a major objection to the concept. The growth of relativism, however, has considerably reduced the force of objections. The relativist, whatever his particular interpretation of the source of norms, denies that any set of norms can be superior to any other and must in principle be as ready to accept those of a sovereign as those of the people.

Moralist Objections of Jacques Maritain: Absolutism and the Value-Order

Maritain's thesis, as expressed in the last paragraph of his paper "The Concept of Sovereignty," reads: "The two concepts of Sovereignty and Absolutism have been forged together on the same anvil. They must be scrapped together." He acknowledges that Bodin, the chief architect of the modern idea of sovereignty, "had . . . submitted the Sovereign to the law of God," but he argues that "the inner logic of the concept was to make Sovereignty free from every—even heavenly—limitation." What is this 'inner logic' which makes the authority of God's law irrelevant to the sovereign and which turns men like Bodin and Rousseau, who unquestionably denied that might is right, into defenders of absolutism?

The Essence of Sovereignty

Maritain's argument is that the concept of sovereignty requires that the supreme power "[transcend] the political whole just as God transcends the cosmos. Either Sovereignty means nothing, or it means supreme power *separate* and *transcendent* —not at the peak but above the peak . . ." To separation in itself he does not object ("there is no command without some kind of separation"); but he does object to a separation that is "one with the very *possession* of that right, which the people have supposedly given up entirely, so that all the essence of power—henceforth monadic, as indivisible as the very person of the Sovereign—resides in the Sovereign alone." Reasoning from the assumption that in sovereignty the supreme power is separate and transcendent, Maritain identifies sovereignty with absolutism and therefore sees it as incompatible with democracy.

But does acceptance of the concept necessarily imply an acceptance of absolutism? Is there room for democracy? Maritain's answer to the latter question is negative: "It would be simply nonsensical to conceive of the people as governing themselves separately from themselves and from above themselves." For Maritain this proves that the theory is absolutist. In fact, however, his argument shows only that the hypothetical right to self-government is incompatible with the theory of sovereignty. It is absurd to talk of anyone governing himself or of any group ruling itself, for there cannot then be any 'government.' If democracy requires the people literally to govern themselves, and if all other social orders are called 'absolutist,' Maritain is quite correct in his contention: sovereignty and absolutism are synonymous. But if we recognize that no democratic society has been characterized by true self-government, Maritain's objection can be challenged. He is simply implying that self-government in the full, literal sense is not feasible.

The Right to Self-government and the
Social Contract

Maritain assumes that self-government is a right "naturally possessed by the people"; from this assumption follows his rejection of sovereignty. His argument takes this direction because he mistakes the intent of sovereignty, seeing in the latter's contractual element a masked defense of absolutism. The argument of the classical theorists, however, makes it clear that popular sovereignty—the exercise of a hypothetical right—is impossible and an impossibility cannot be a right. The classical theorists clung to the fiction of a social contract because it was a useful method of preventing the argument for sovereignty from being mistaken for, or used to support, a case for absolutism. When the social contract element is included, the sovereign's function becomes that of keeping an agreement which ascribes rights to the governed. It is true that even without the contract some sort of natural law could still set limits upon the sovereign, but in that event there would be no way of knowing what the content of the law was, and whether the sovereign was observing it, and therefore no way of ensuring that he did comply with it.

The social contract thus played a definite role in the theory of sovereignty, though not the one assigned to it by Maritain. In the classical theory there is no place for a hypothetical right to self-government which is transferred to a sovereign. The theory maintained the fiction of a contractual transference of power, not because its adherents were absolutists, but because they were not. Compelled by logic to deny that the people can govern—to deny that they had such a 'right'—they invented the contract to ensure that the people would not become the hapless victims of tyranny.

The Missing Relation between Power, Obligation,
and Social Order

Maritain's evidence that the concept is applicable to but one kind of government is based on selected phrases from Bodin and his own analogy between the power of the sovereign and the power of God: "When Jean Bodin says that the sovereign Prince is the image of God, this phrase must be understood in its full force, and means that the Sovereign —submitted to God, but accountable only to Him—transcends the political whole just as God transcends the cosmos."

The trouble with this analogy—reminiscent of the concept of the Great Chain of Being, which tried to encompass a scheme of the universe and was current in Bodin's time—is that it does not represent his position or that of other classic theorists on sovereignty. The argument they advance is not that there is a continuity between social order and nature, but that there is a relation between power, obligation, and social order. The argument for sovereignty stands or falls on its ability to relate these three terms. It can be epitomized in the statement that order demands a power structure with a head (or supreme decision-maker) able to make ultimate decisions. Maritain's mistake is to argue that this supreme decision-maker is by definition absolute, a simple embodiment of power. But classical theorists were not discussing power alone. To them power was unintelligible unless related to a willingness to submit to that power. What cannot be ignored is the *function* of sovereignty in maintaining social order: it is this function which creates the obedience that makes sovereign power and its exercise possible. Only in one sense is the sovereign separate and above the people (absolute and unlimited): no one else has more power unless he replaces him as sovereign.

Adherence to a Value-Order Does Not Limit Sovereignty

If we like paradoxes, we can say that unlimited sovereign power is limited by its ability to fulfill its function, but if we prefer to avoid such a paradox and examine instead the nature of the 'limitation' we see that the concept of sovereignty, far from negating moral law, virtually demands it as a condition of its function.

When we begin thinking about the relationship between will, choice, and values, the paradox dissolves. Among animals 'will' may be said to exist without a corresponding value-order—their biological drives and the circumstances determine their choices—but among human beings sets of values are necessary to explain complex behavior, and essential to make 'will' meaningful. When we talk of human will we are talking of the value-order held by the individual. If it were possible for man not to have one—to be without desires or goals—he would be limited in his behavior, for he would be a vegetable. Behavior is limited by the absence of such norms, not by their presence. Only if we suppose that there is an essential incompatibility between the value-order that the sovereign must hold to fulfill his function as a sovereign and the one he holds as a biological individual, can we argue that adherence to a value-order limits the sovereign. In this sense sovereignty can be both unlimited and yet not above moral law. Maritain in order to be consistent does not have to reject the classic attributes of the concept.

THE NORM-POWER FALLACY OF STANLEY BENN

Benn's analysis of six distinct meanings of sovereignty, each of which has awkward difficulties of interpretation and application, is at first glance a damning criticism of the concept of sovereignty, for so "protean a term" as he puts it, can hardly be applied as a tool of analysis or be used without confusing both reader and writer. But his analysis is based upon Bodin's definition isolated from the context of its function, which for classical writers was the reason for postulating a 'supreme power.' Taking the concept of sovereignty to be "supreme power . . . unrestrained by law," and following Rees's analysis of the different kinds of power possible, Benn has no difficulty in showing that when 'legal power,' 'coercive power,' and 'influential power' are used in the analysis of traditional 'sovereigns'—such as the constitution, parliament, the state, and the people—the result is a set of disparate definitions which are either of no great use to political science or so manifestly unrelated to actual conditions in any known society that they might just as well not be used at all. As an exercise in logical analysis within the framework he has set himself, Benn's analysis has merit, but if his intention is to display conflicts in usage, his analysis is not successful. His arbitrary division of usage into that appropriate to normative studies and that appropriate to non-normative—a division that simply ignores actual schools of thought—and his disregard of historical developments would, if employed by the author of a dictionary, make every word in the language seem a mere jumble of unrelated impressions. The first step in examining any word which has several meanings, must be to identify the assumptions underlying its usage, and this is scarcely possible unless we order our material historically: 'supreme coercive power' is simply not contemporaneous with 'supreme political influence.'

Benn begins his discussion of 'the uses of sovereignty' by accepting the concept of legal sovereignty when the term refers to a supreme norm: "The judge called upon to settle a dispute sees law as a system of rules to guide his decision; and such a system needs criteria of validity determining which rules belong to it; it needs a *supreme norm,* providing directly or indirectly the criteria of validity to all other norms, and not itself open to challenge."

Is Sovereignty a 'Supreme Norm'?

Having established that a legal sovereign is logically necessary to a legal order, Benn raises the question of "whether there is a place in the political scientist's vocabulary for a 'supreme legislative organ.' " He concludes that there is "neither logical nor practical necessity for a legislative sovereign in every state, though there may be states in which such organs are discoverable." This is a rather surprising conclusion, for it would appear from Benn's statements about the positions of the jurist and the political scientist that in respect to normative orders they are looking at the same thing but from different viewpoints. (For the judge, "the law appears . . . as a body of given rules. . . . For the political scientist, however, law appears in the process of creation.") What makes

Benn feel that a shift from the static to the dynamic, from a narrower to a more comprehensive view, entails a loss of the logical necessity present in the narrower view?

He says: "A political scientist might significantly classify legislative organs in a legal order into superior and inferior (or subordinate), and he might arrange them hierarchically as a sort of reflection of the judge's hierarchy of norms." "But does it follow," he continues, "that the necessity which leads the judge to postulate a supreme norm is paralleled by a similar necessity leading the political scientist to postulate a supreme legislative organ?"

This method of posing the question seems misleading. The concept of sovereignty does not stand or fall on discovering whether there is a supreme legislative organ paralleling the supreme norm in a judicial order. The classical discussions of Bodin and Hobbes—which took a far different direction— derive much of their continuing interest from their capacity to bring together into a logical whole the state's normative order, its coercive power and the public's 'obligation' or readiness to accept the coercive element—and by accepting it, to give it in effect the power to be coercive. This view of sovereignty seems to have been widely recognized as late as the eighteenth century. Swift presents it in allegorical form in Part One of *Gulliver's Travels*. Gulliver, representing the Common Man, forms a pact or social contract with the King of the Lilliputians in return for security and freedom; he serves the King faithfully even though he is physically capable of demolishing him and his court. By serving, Gulliver makes the King "the most puissant Emperor" in a very real sense, but when the latter threatens Gulliver's life, he feels the contract has been broken, for him at least, and flees for his life. Evidently, Swift had read his Hobbes. It is a pity that Benn did not return to the same source before assuming that the concept is a simple assertion of power, analogous to the different kind of power exercised by a legal order.

Clearly, the term sovereignty could never have been applied to the 'supreme norm' if it had not already become a significant concept with reference to the political order as a whole. On

Benn's assumption—that the political scientist in employing the term sovereignty is simply drawing an analogy between the legal order and the political order—one is bound to arrive at the conclusion that the term might best be left to the jurists. But in the absence of the political scientist's use of the term, a jurist would not think of applying it to his supreme norm or ultimate point of reference: it makes no sense in pure legal theory to call a norm a power.[4]

Norm Not Synonymous with Power

Benn's analysis is less useful than it might have been because sovereignty for the political scientist is not a statement about supreme power alone. The classical theory in essence states that if there is to be order, there must be a supreme power; in other words, the norm—which when upheld by the

4. It is true that Hobbes himself has done so. His "instrumentall" powers are norms. To him "The Power of a Man . . . is his present means to obtain some future apparent Good." (*Leviathan*, Dent, London, 1965, p. 43) A definition of instrumental powers follows: "Instrumentall are those Powers, which acquired by [natural power] or by fortune, are means and Instruments to acquire more: as Riches, Reputation, Friends, and . . . Good Luck." When he speaks of "a perpetuall and restlesse desire of Power after power" (p. 49), he uses a tautology. Replacing the term 'power' with its definition, we can say that Hobbes is speaking of a "perpetuall and restlesse desire of 'means to obtain some future apparent Good' after 'means to obtain some future apparent Good.' "

Clearly, in the quotations above Hobbes does not use 'power' in its usual sense today. Nor does he argue that everyone has the kind of power-hunger that some modern analysts of power politics consider a universal trait of human nature. Thus, although he recognizes that such a trait exists, he seems to believe that only a limited number of men have this characteristic: "there be some, that taking pleasure in contemplating their own power in the acts of conquest . . ." (p. 64) It was essential for him to establish that man's desire for security was not accompanied by a desire for power in the abstract. He was also anxious to win a polemic point when implying that sovereign power was the sovereign or chief desire of men. Hobbes's subtle argument, however, escaped many of his commentators, who have imputed to him the notion that man has an innate desire for power in the sense of mastery over others. But such a hypothetical urge—if translated into effect—would make sovereignty, or any social order, impossible.

sovereign creates the obligation—is order, and supreme power is the instrument.

Bodin's definition of the sovereign as a supreme power misleadingly suggests that he has adequately described the sovereign, when he has, in fact, supplied only one of the essential attributes; but it is also clear from the direction taken by his argument that "supreme power unrestrained by law" is unintelligible apart from its function, which is the maintenance of order. Thus, by denying the possibility of dividing the sovereign power on the ground that "the soveraigne right and power of them being divided, find no rest from civill warres and broiles"; [5] by stating that law-making is an essential attribute of the sovereign; by asserting that "in all things wee desire and seeke after a convenient and decent order, and deeme nothing to be more ougly or foule to looke upon than confusion and broyle"; [6] and by opposing factions,[7] Bodin implies the importance of the sovereign in maintaining order. Bodin also makes the relationship explicit. He specifically declares that it is the maintenance of order that creates the sense of obligation, and not, as some critics of sovereignty have supposed, the sovereign's command, which logically cannot:

> The word of protection in generall extendeth unto all subjects which are under the obeysance of one soveraigne prince or seignorie; as we have said, that the prince is bound by force of armes, and of his lawes, to maintaine his subiects in suretie of their persons, their goods, and families: for which the subiects by a reciprocall obligation owe unto their prince, faith, subjection, obeysance, aid, and succour.[8]

Thus the statement about order and power in the classical concept is not a factual statement about society, but a logical statement, taking the form of an 'if-then' proposition—if there is to be order, then there must be a supreme power. Two im-

---

5. Jean Bodin, *The Six Bookes of a Commonweale* (ed. by K. D. McRae, Harvard University Press, Cambridge, 1962), pp. 194–95.
6. Ibid. p. 386.
7. Ibid. Book IV, Chapter VII.
8. Ibid. p. 69.

portant conclusions follow. First, because the concept is not
a statement about power alone, it cannot be replaced by empirical studies of actual power relations. Second, the two elements, sovereign order and sovereign power, are separate.
To identify the two, for instance by supposing that order is
merely an arbitrary exercise of sovereign power, not only leads
to the tautological assertion that the manifestation of a sovereign will (the exercise of sovereign power) is necessary to
the manifestation of a sovereign will (order or law) but also
causes some critics to suppose that sovereignty is a confused
concept which refers to two different things: a supreme norm
and supreme power.

Benn's method of posing the problem is unfortunate because it makes it appear that the real problem of sovereignty
is whether sovereign power can be limited by a normative
code. If the question whether a legislative sovereign can be
limited is essential to the concept, how could one possibly
speak of a legislative sovereign, who by the very fact of serving his function is certainly limited? Benn, intent on as close
an analogy to the legal sovereign as possible, argues that a
legislative organ "competent to legislate on all matters without the possibility that any of its rules might be invalidated
by reason or conflict with some other rule not of its own making . . . is not logically necessary to a legal order. A constitution might allocate fields of legislative competence between
coordinate organs, or place certain matters beyond the competence of any organ." The two points requiring discussion
are the apportioning of sovereignty and normative limitations.

The Apportioning of Sovereignty

There can be no doubt that in theory a legal order could
allocate power in such a way that no conflict would arise.
Each of the legislative powers established by the legal order
would have its own area of jurisdiction. Many written constitutions attempt to achieve this. But a constitution cannot
fully describe the actual system operating in a state, since the
allocation of powers cannot settle disputes about itself unless

it includes an allocation of power to some person or body higher than all others. In other words, a constitution can allocate powers in the way Benn suggests only at the cost of conflict: that is to say, at the cost of no longer being sovereign.

The real difficulty with the juristic conception of society is that it begins by assuming an order which includes all possible situations.[9] It does this by making all situations either illegal or not-illegal. Apart from the illusory nature of this comprehensiveness, the weakness of such a system is that it cannot make the decisions itself, for a legal code is not capable of making predictions. True, it can classify situations and assign them to particular legislative powers, none of them supreme, but because of the inevitable arbitrariness of such a classification, we cannot assume that everyone will understand the categories, and hence cannot assume that everyone will agree to the jurisdiction of a particular body. Conflicts will arise out of sheer confusion, and the society will eventually disintegrate because of its inability to take action under the 'rule of law.'[10] It is no service to the rule of law to insist that it can rule all by itself: classify, assign, predict, and settle all issues.

Benn has in the past recognized some of these difficulties by saying that the rule of law "might be highly inconvenient if the co-ordinate organs were operated by men of different opinions, and competition developed for the latest place." However, in suggesting that the inconvenience could be avoided by having the co-ordinate organs "operated by members of one highly disciplined political party, or by men who reached decisions by mutual agreement before legislation," he is no longer dealing with logical relations. If it is possible to

9. The political scientist is aware, however, that the comprehensiveness of the system is an illusion. For him, the largest class—things that are not-illegal, such as earthquakes, poverty, and disease—has been left out of account; and yet these are the very matters which demand the making of decisions.

10. One of the defects of egalitarian societies has been the assumption that the law can establish a workable system without an ultimate decision-maker. This has led, *inter alia*, to severance of the actual exercise of power from the rule of law.

suppose that such highly disciplined parties and mutual agreement can exist, it is clear that one does not need the concept
of law.

Normative Limitations

The essence of Benn's criticism of sovereignty is that if the
jurist is allowed to apply the term to what is a logical requirement of the system, its sense becomes confused when it is
applied in any other way: that is, the term is a necessary part
of the jurist's vocabulary but a misleading and unnecessary
part of the political scientist's, except when he is commenting
on the juristic position.

The juristic view of the law is a static one. As Benn says,
to the judge "the law appears, at any particular moment, as
a body of given rules." But the political scientist's view is
dynamic; to him "the law appears in the process of creation."
From this, it would appear that if the concept of sovereignty
is necessary to the jurist, it is also essential to the political
scientist, for both are looking at the same situation, though
from different standpoints: the political scientist's view differs
only in that it includes the decision-maker and the decision-
making function, as well as the norm on which the decision
is based. Without the existence of a supreme decision-maker
capable of deciding conflicts of opinion about new situations
and about whether action should or should not occur, the
same kind of disorder would ensue as in a static legal order
lacking a point of reference.[11] A practical legal order requires
a point beyond which disputes cannot be carried if order is
to be maintained. It is this difficulty that requires us to postulate a sovereign legislator in the state viewed dynamically.

11. Only by arguing that all possible new situations could be fitted into
    the static legal framework without dispute could one avoid this neces-
    sity. But if one could make such an assumption, one could also avoid
    the need for a legal sovereign. Theoretically, it is possible to con-
    struct a static legal order which is not a hierarchical order, but com-
    prises separate and equal categories into which all problems fit. But
    such a system cannot work because disputes about classifications do
    arise, since phenomena do not classify themselves.

Without one, necessary decision-making will not take place, for laws do not enforce themselves.

However, this is not Benn's position. He argues, instead, that the supreme norm of the static order prevents the hypothetically supreme decision-maker of the dynamic system from being supreme, since his competence as a decision-maker is limited by the norm. Thus he sees limitations of any kind as incompatible with sovereignty.[12] Obviously his reasoning must be faulty, if the situations we are considering are really one and the same, whether viewed statically or dynamically.

The difficulty seems to lie in the word 'supreme.' When arguing that the legal order requires an ultimate point of reference, Benn makes the word 'supreme' mean 'point beyond which no further appeal is possible,' but when arguing that a legal order containing such a point precludes a sovereign legislator, he shifts the meaning to 'omnipotent' or 'capable of deciding all issues without legal limitation.' Now the supreme norm is not omnicompetent. It is capable of deciding not all issues, but only one: a conflict between subordinate members of the order; that is, the supreme norm is limited by its position as a supreme norm. If we suppose that the concept of sovereignty excludes any kind of limitation, we have to conclude that not even a supreme norm can be called sovereign.

Sovereignty has, of course, been so defined, but if we interpret that which defines to be a limitation on what is defined, then no definition of any unlimited thing is possible. This was the problem that beset theologians confronted by the attribute of God's omnipotence and God's goodness, when the goodness was defined in terms of fixed laws. Some took the view that the attribute of omnipotence required that God be capable of reversing divine laws. Others saw the attribute of goodness as part of the definition of God, such that any change in its nature would entail God's ceasing to be God. In the case of sovereignty, it is possible to begin with omnipo-

---

12. Maritain makes the same point by reversing the position: beginning with the postulation of a supreme legislator, he concludes that this excludes a supreme norm.

tence as the only attribute and argue that this excludes all
other attributes. This can be achieved by logical application
of the concept of supreme power. On the other hand, if the
sovereign by definition has the attribute of omnipotence and
also that of serving a *function* in the social order, the inclu-
sion of the function can hardly be viewed as a limitation on
his omnipotence. Neither the fact of having a position in a
normative order nor the serving of a function in the social
order can in itself be considered a limitation on power. A
definition is not a limitation on the power of what is defined.

Kenneth C. Cole and
the Juristic Conception of Sovereignty

The title of Cole's paper is not 'Sovereignty,' or even 'Juristic
Sovereignty,' but "The Theory of the State as a Sovereign Juristic Person." It is this conception that he deals with, and
within these limits he is quite successful. He begins his analysis
by listing what he supposes were the reasons why jurists
adopted the concept of sovereignty and shows that the logical
difficulties are such that it cannot serve their purpose. He
argues that they should use some other term such as reason,
custom, or Sir Edward Coke's "artificial reason of the law,"
though he is not really interested in the precise nature of the
substitute. His task ends once he has exposed the impossibility
of there being a "sovereign juristic person."

The gist of Cole's argument is that the state does not have
the attributes of personality which juristic theory attributes
to it, and that to regard the state as a sovereign juristic person
does not accurately describe the real process of law-making.
He has, of course, no difficulty in establishing both propositions. However, he would appear to have scored a victory over
straw men, for in attributing personality to the state the jurists
are not attempting to describe the law-making process, nor are
they dependent upon an analogy between the state and the
human organism to defend their conception of legal authority.
The attribution of personality is for them a figure of speech

required only in a specific situation—when external relations of the state are under consideration.

Obviously, for jurists 'sovereignty' is a better concept than any of the substitutes suggested by Cole. They are aware of the logical power of the argument for political sovereignty, and also, of course, of the political sovereign's status in relation to law. If they did not persist in attempting to adapt the concept of sovereignty to their conception of the rule of law, the latter would become meaningless, and along with it, their own *raison d'être*. One of the flaws in Cole's paper stems from his very success in exposing the weakness of what he attacks: he does not really explain why jurists use the concept of sovereignty, despite the appalling difficulties it creates.

Sovereignty and Cybernetics: Karl W. Deutsch's Analogy Between the Sovereign and the Brain

One of the oldest ways of looking at the state is by comparing it with an organism. One of the latest is to liken it to part of an organism—the brain and neural paths. The new analogy may have the didactic advantage of drawing parallels between material that most people find rather uninteresting (abstract nature of the state) and what is currently interesting (brain seen as a machine); like the old analogy, however, it tends in unskillful hands to lose its character as a didactic device and to become an independent argument for a particular position, where the truth about the state is decided by truths about the body. This is especially likely to happen when the analogy is used to attack a certain view. Analogies are not arguments.

Because Deutsch uses neural analogies as arguments in themselves rather than as metaphorical aids, it is difficult to follow his line of thought. The jargon of cybernetics fused with that of the behavioralists produces a smog of words in which known landmarks disappear. As with all writings of this kind, one makes a guess and hopes for the best.

The first guess is that the following statement expresses Deutsch's view of an essential characteristic of sovereignty:

"If all important decisions are concentrated at one point, and if decisions made at that point tend to govern or override all decisions made elsewhere in the system, the performance of the system may resemble the situation of concentrated sovereignty, familiar from the absolute monarchies of seventeenth and eighteenth-century Europe." The difficulty here is that none of the key terms—"important decisions," "concentrated," "govern or override"—are explained or explicable in terms of the neural analogy. Furthermore, if one attempts to relate the material to history, as Deutsch suggests, one encounters the equation of something he calls 'concentrated sovereignty' with absolute monarchy. Is Deutsch equating absolute monarchy and sovereignty? If not, what is he doing? What does he mean by 'concentrated'? Is this a reference to the requirement in the theory of sovereignty that there must be an ultimate decision-maker, or is it a reference to the quite erroneous opinion that the sovereign must make all or most decisions?

"An even more essential characteristic of sovereignty is the absence of any recognized input channel of controlling or overriding information from outside the system," Deutsch continues. What does "controlling," "overriding," and "outside the system" mean? If we assume that he is pursuing the analogy between the brain and its sensory apparatus and government, he can hardly be saying that in the classical theory the decisions of the sovereign are *sui generis,* entirely uninfluenced by information from the society he governs. We certainly could not suppose such a thing if we have read Hobbes and Bodin; yet the writings of Deutsch almost compel this interpretation. How else can we account for his objection that "The emphasis on sovereignty may tend to divert attention from the very real limits that constrain the decisions of even the most powerful nation?" Deutsch seems to have assumed that the attribute of being 'unlimited' means that the sovereign must pay no attention whatever to conditions within or outside his society. His 'will' must be motiveless.

Improbable as this may seem, it is a fairly common position among those who detach sovereignty from its function. When sovereignty is interpreted as a statement about power rather than government, it is easy to suppose that 'unlimited' sovereignty means 'capable of making decisions without respect to anybody or anything else' and it is then possible to equate this with the child's-eye view of absolute monarchy. But no one who has carefully read the classical statements can believe for a moment that they are statements about power rather than government.

HANS KELSEN: THE JURISTIC CONCEPTION OF SOVEREIGNTY AND INTERNATIONAL LAW

Kelsen, working within a juristic framework, takes the discussion of sovereignty in a direction which is not easy to reconcile with that of the political scientist, who cannot assume, as Kelsen does, that the law of the state is a "coercive order," that the state can be defined as a "specific legal order," which is "identical with the law called its law," that sovereignty is "the quality of being a supreme power or supreme order" and that "to be sovereign seems to be incompatible with being subject to a normative order." It is not that a political scientist must necessarily disagree with all or any of these assertions, but that he cannot begin with them as axiomatic truths whose acceptance brings into question certain aspects of the concept of sovereignty. The problem of where a state gets the power which makes its legal order a coercive one, the oddity of regarding 'supreme power' and 'supreme order' as alternative ways of saying the same thing and the grounds for asserting that to be sovereign seems incompatible with being subject to a normative order raise questions for the political scientist which he must answer before proceeding further. However, if we recognize that, for Kelsen, the problem of the sovereignty of the state is no more than "the problem of the sovereignty of the national legal order in its relation to the international legal order," and that this is a problem because of Kelsen's set of assumptions and definitions, it is possible to accept his analysis as a valuable clarification of one aspect of a larger problem.

Importance of the Juristic Contribution to an Analysis of Political Sovereignty

How important is Kelsen's paper in other respects to an analysis of political sovereignty? Why, in fact, should a paper dealing with something that the concept of political sovereignty says does not exist—international law—be important? The classical concept denies that there can be an international law if there is no supra-national sovereign. Consequently, the jurists repeatedly return to the issue of national law and international law, even though their case for a juristic sovereign would be much simplified if they could simply ignore international law, as the advocates of political sovereignty do. But the jurists cannot of course do that. Essential to their case is the proof that international law is a meaningful concept and no less important than domestic law. Indeed, it is so important to them that many—but not Kelsen—inject a moral flavor into their discussion of the issue. Some jurists denounce the classical concept of sovereignty as a hindrance to international morality —and the rule of law—but beneath the moral outrage lies the necessity for proving that a legal order can itself be sovereign, and the only area where this can be proved is the one in which a political sovereign does not exist. Hence a logical and objective analysis of juristic sovereignty and international law, such as Kelsen's, is of great importance to the student of sovereignty.

International Law and National Law: Kelsen on the Pluralist View

Kelsen argues that two "diametrically opposed" theories attempt to resolve the conflict that arises when one is confronted with the definition of state sovereignty and the assertion that international law is "a legal order obligating and authorizing the state." The first theory, the pluralist view that international and national law are independent but simultaneously valid, Kelsen treats rather high-handedly. He begins his argument with the condition: "If we recognize that obligation and authorization of the state by international law means that the international legal order delegates to the national legal order the power to determine the individuals whose behavior forms the content of the obligations and rights established by the international law . . ." Reasoning from this condition, he has no difficulty in arguing that two norms A and Not-A cannot be simultaneously valid. This is certainly true if they derive their validity from the same source. Norms that cancel each other cease to be norms. But this is not the argument that Kelsen uses. Instead he argues that although the principle of contradiction applies only to statements describing norms and not to the norms themselves, and that because there exist alternative 'scientific' ways of describing the relation which escape any kind of contradiction, the pluralist conception is invalid. This argument is unacceptable. The contradiction arises from the condition just quoted: "If we recognize that obligation and authorization of the state by international law means . . ." etc. But if we refuse to recognize anything of the sort and argue instead that the validity of national law does not depend upon international law, and that they have different sources by our definition of sovereignty, then it is possible for the two laws to be simultaneously valid.

International Law and National Law: Kelsen on the Monist Views

Kelsen gives much more attention to monist theories of the relation between sovereign states and international law. These take two forms: one maintaining that international law has primacy; the other, that the state has. For those who regard state law as primary, international law exists only in so far as the state chooses to recognize it. For those who regard international law as primary, national law derives its validity from international law. The latter view causes some problems in view of Kelsen's declaration that sovereignty is "incompatible with being subject to a normative order." It is precisely this assumption which causes the difficulty. If we define sovereignty as Kelsen does and make his assumption about normative orders, the particular monist viewpoint asserting the primacy of international law seems to be excluded from consideration. It fails to accord with the assumptions made. On the face of it, the only possibility would appear to be the other monist viewpoint.

Kelsen, however, who is eager to defend the position that the two monist stands differ only as viewpoints, attempts to restore the balance by discussing some of the juristic difficulties raised by the assumption that national law is primary, the only assumption consistent with the definition of sovereignty and the assumption about norms. He argues that if international law is valid only in so far as a sovereign state proposes to recognize it, the sovereignty of only one state can be presupposed, for "the reason of the validity of the other national legal orders lies in the law of the recognizing state . . . As a consequence of the primacy of national law the other states must be regarded as subordinated to this national legal order which includes international law as part of it. Hence, they cannot be presupposed as sovereign." Plausible as the argument appears, however, it is apparent that the assertion of state sovereignty as primary within territory X makes no statement about who is sovereign outside the territory except for one important qualification: the state making the assertion of its own sovereignty within a territory is denying its sovereignty outside that territory. Although it may later enlarge its claims, at the moment of asserting its sovereignty in territory X it denies its sovereignty in Not-X territory. If it were to assert not only that international law was dependent on its own recognition of it but also that all other states were dependent on international law for their validity, then, and only then, could a state make a claim to universal jurisdiction and the dependence of every other state. Kelsen has apparently fallen into this discrepancy because of his juristic definitions. His definition of a state as a "specific legal order" pays insufficient attention to the territorial limitations of that order, which are only vaguely suggested by the word "specific."

Kelsen on the Misapplication of the Concept of Sovereignty

Kelsen examines some misapplications of the concept of sovereignty—deductions concerning the content of international law from one's assumptions about its relation to sovereignty. His position throughout is that no such deductions can be made, for him the two monistic interpretations are simply different ways of looking at the same thing. No doubt it is true that no part of the specific content can be deduced, but the kind of monistic interpretation one chooses would seem to matter. If international law has primacy, national laws in conflict with it will be eliminated, and this will have a very marked effect on the content of national law. If national law is primary, international law will become only a shifting set of accommodations. There will, in effect, be no content that can serve the function of law. Indeed, in view of Kelsen's definition of state law as a coercive order, it is exceedingly difficult to conceive the nature of international law, for it certainly cannot be coercive.

Kelsen's difficulties perhaps illustrate why some political scientists have insisted that 'law' is but part of a larger discipline. The problems he raises result from his assumption that certain ideas are 'primitive' terms that cannot be further reduced: they are axiomatic. But the political scientist, as a social scientist rather than a logician, must assume that none of his terms can be primitives. Where the natural scientist and philosopher must eventually arrive at certain irreducible assumptions,[13] the social scientist must accept the fundamental proposition of all science, namely, that all things are related. If he supposes, as Kelsen does, that propositions about the nature of the state, law, order, and obedience are irreducible, he detaches his discipline from the rest of science. This is what Kelsen has done in his analysis of the application of the concept of sovereignty to jurisprudence.

13. Such as: all things are, or are not, 'caused'; the self and its experience are, or are not, separable.

An Interpretation of Kelsen's Implicit Position

Kelsen's discussion of sovereignty, though not intended to refute any particular author, provides an interesting commentary on Maritain, whose two main points he rejects, one of them explicitly, the other implicitly. Maritain objects to the use of the concept because: first of all, it is incompatible with the kind of normative order that can be called 'natural law'; secondly, because it is unavoidably associated with absolutism. For Maritain, the term can be used with reference to only one kind of state, an objection which if upheld would certainly make it useless to political science. Kelsen, however, presents a strong case for continued use of the term, and in doing so disposes of a number of the most common objections: that the term is ambiguous; that it is incompatible with a normative order; that it is absolutist by nature, and therefore irreconcilable with any other form of government; that it is incompatible with international law and a world order; that it provides a defense for imperialism; and that it describes no real situation.

Kelsen achieves this by beginning with a definition of sovereignty which is derivable from the classic definition of 'supreme power.' Avoiding problems of *de jure* and *de facto* sovereignty by asserting that "to be sovereign seems to be incompatible with being subject to a normative order," he defines state sovereignty to mean "that the state is not subject to a legal order superior to its own national law," a position that is one of the two that can be taken. He points out—and this is important in view of the common objection that sovereignty does not describe an actual situation—that "sovereignty in this sense is not an apperceptible or otherwise objectively recognizable quality of a real thing; it is a *presupposition* . . ."

Ambiguities do not arise from a presupposition about state sovereignty unless one attempts to combine it with its alternative: the presupposition that international law is a "valid normative order" which "obligates and authorizes the state." If international law is conceived to be "a universal legal order, superior to and comprising, as partial legal orders, all national legal orders . . . , " the "sovereign," Kelsen observes, "is the international order [and] . . . It is therefore recommendable not to use the misleading term 'sovereignty of the state' when one assumes the primacy of international law."

The points we should notice here are that Kelsen is prepared to speak of a normative order as 'sovereign,' even though whatever coercive power it has must be delegated; also, that he is prepared to apply the term to normative orders that are purely coercive—normative, solely because they have been imposed. Thus he does not limit the term 'sovereignty' to a particular form of government or a particular assumption about norms. Choose whichever you prefer, he argues, and the term 'sovereignty' is a useful shorthand description for your choice. Ambiguity arises only when we try to keep a foot in both camps.

Because of his contention that either of the two possible presuppositions about standards are aspects of the same need for a starting point in considering society, Kelsen can dispose of several common objections (already mentioned) to the concept. The specific arguments he uses are not important here. The essential point is that if his contention is correct—namely, that the term 'sovereignty' is applicable to the only two possible fundamental assumptions one can make concerning the relations between societies, and that these two assumptions comprehend the two positions one can adopt about norms, which are that they are arbitrary and imposed or not necessarily arbitrary or imposed—the term 'sovereignty' can be applied to any form of government having any content.

K. W. B. MIDDLETON:
SOVEREIGNTY AS A 'LEGAL CONCEPTION'

Middleton's view that sovereignty is "a legal conception . . . a matter of political authority and not of political power" accords with the juristic view of the state and avoids the ambiguities that arise when 'power' is used in the twofold sense of "the physical and moral force at the disposal of a govern-

ment" and "the right of a government to exercise that force."
But unless we are very careful in interpreting 'legal conception,'
we may seriously limit the usefulness of the concept of sovereignty. In making the necessary distinction between coercive
power and authority, it is only too easy to separate the two
conceptually, so that any analysis of the state based on the
distinction becomes incomplete: a statement about power relations without regard to the source and nature of the power,
or about the legal order without regard to the observance
or non-observance of it. A concept of sovereignty useful to
political science in general must avoid this. Yet Middleton's
analysis virtually demands the limitation.

It is no more possible to discuss sovereignty adequately if
we limit it purely to the concept of authority, than if we limit
it to 'power.' The two must be related, if only because, in
the words of Middleton, "*de facto* supremacy ripens into
de jure supremacy, while the latter also attracts to itself the
former." Certainly there can be no logical objection to calling
sovereignty a legal conception. But if "legal conception" entails regarding 'power' and 'authority' as separate phenomena
as well as separable, we must be wary not to apply the term
to any description of sovereignty that is not strictly juristic.

Georg Schwarzenberger:
Sovereignty as an Abstraction from Reality

Schwarzenberger focuses on the problems of independence and
interdependence raised by the conflict between the facts of
sovereignty in international relations and man's desire for the
same kind of order and law between states as sovereignty produces within a state. He easily disposes of objections based
on man's desire for co-operation by arguing that sovereignty
is "a mere abstraction from actually operative rules" and that
no matter what man desires, the reality of the *lex lata* will not
change until other laws limiting it are in effect.

Despite the ambiguities of the concept, which Schwarzenberger attempts to reduce by means of a phenomenological
analysis of the actual situations comprehended by the term,

he feels that the concept cannot be rejected because the ideological issues it raises are perennial. These issues are supremacy and freedom; in law they are expressed by the terms 'jurisdiction' and 'discretion.' Schwarzenberger makes a case for sovereignty by arguing that whether one begins with the facts of sovereignty and proceeds to the questions of supremacy and freedom raised by the facts, or begins with the concepts of supremacy and freedom and carries on the discussion by means of other terms, one is in each case discussing what has been traditionally called sovereignty.

To what extent does Schwarzenberger's approach contribute to the defense of sovereignty? Appealing as his 'Let's-look-at-the-facts' approach may be, one wonders whether in the end it does support the concept; for sovereignty as a pure abstraction from reality cannot explain political phenomena. It becomes a generalized description whose sense changes with the situation.

Furthermore, though the approach provides an effective answer to the view that sovereignty is a pure fiction, there can be no doubt that the issues raised by sovereignty, such as supremacy and freedom, are in themselves much more than mere descriptions. They are premises, assumptions about the direction that man chooses (rather than is compelled) to follow. They have a permanence far beyond the immediate situation, for they are assertions about man's beliefs about what 'ought' to be, what is possible, and the steps necessary to realize his beliefs. No matter how rapidly man's knowledge of 'facts' accumulates, beliefs and values of this kind change very slowly, for the number of possibilities is very limited. Most were explored at the very beginning of man's intellectual history. If we detach sovereignty from this more permanent order in order to defend it against charges that it is inaccurate and ambiguous as a description, we abandon one of the very few fixed points in the field of social phenomena.

Juristic Defense: A Summing Up

The analyses of Middleton and Schwarzenberger provide— with certain reservations—a useful answer to those who would abandon the concept of sovereignty entirely. Both emphasize that the concept is the cornerstone of international law and international relations. Furthermore, as both jurists demonstrate by reference to the facts of sovereignty, it does not entail anything resembling what has traditionally been called absolutism. The facts of international relations show accommodations between states and self-imposed limitations, rather than attempts to extend power indefinitely or to claim the right to such power.

Another significant point about sovereignty is brought out by its position in international law: the absence of sovereignty —or rather, denying its existence—entails denial of the capacity for rational choice, because it means denying the identity of the willing agent necessary to rational choice. This point becomes clear when we ask whether international relations would be possible if they were conducted on the basis of 'fact' alone, namely, as relations between territorial governments whose characteristics would be dependent on the kind of things behavioralists are interested in: the patterns of authority, power structure, and the types of personalities involved in the governmental process. Relations would indeed exist—things would happen between such units—but (notwithstanding the claims of the behavioralists) nothing predictable would and hence no course or policy could be rationally chosen. No meaningful treaties would be possible, for a change of government in a state so conceived would entail a change in the parties to the treaty; and no long-range interest could be considered because the units involved would, by definition, be temporary. Under such circumstances, all acts would be expedients, and the future would be at the mercy of chance, not influenced by reason. This principle—unmistakable in international relations—also applies to internal sovereignty. We must know who is who and what is what, if we are to make rational choices. So long as we pretend that the people are in some way the government ('popular sovereignty') or that government is simply a power struggle rather than a power structure with a necessary relation to the community, we cannot make rational choices. All of us, government and governed, become the victims of circumstances.

IVOR WILKS'S LEGAL SOVEREIGN

Wilks's contribution to the discussion of sovereignty is his suggestion that the 'must' in the assertion "there must be a sovereign in every state"—for which even Kelsen has given only an intuitive 'proof'—is a special case of a situation which Goedel has proved formally. The point is indeed valuable, but we should not accept it without reservation, since the concept that Wilks is discussing is the legal, not the classical, sovereign. If we attempt to apply his argument to the political sovereign or the classical theory, we are faced with an obvious difficulty: the sovereign cannot be located. Yet a 'sovereign' in Wilks's sense must be identifiable, because it is a fundamental assumption. It is both the initial premise and the ultimate standard. Since this standard is arbitrary, there is no point in challenging or changing it. Consequently, if the political sovereign also falls into this category, the objections raised by Maritain are valid. A state with such a sovereign would be Hegelian.

W. J. REES'S ANSWER TO BEHAVIORALIST OBJECTIONS

Rees's analysis of sovereignty is important not so much because he examines the multiple meanings of the term but because he recognizes that sovereignty resembles 'dispositional' terms. He demolishes a number of behavioralistic objections based on the fact that sovereignty seems to describe situations that are not readily observable. In his view, sovereignty may legitimately embrace such concepts as coercive power, authority, and influence because it analyzes the concept of power. Yet his argument, in the form in which it is presented, does not quite satisfactorily answer the behavioralist objection that these three things are observably different phenomena, which ought therefore to be discussed with the aid of different terms. The fact that all three can be included in the general term 'power' does not alter the case.[14] Only if the theory of sov-

---

14. Similarly, a study of veins and arteries, frying pans, and ocean liners cannot be defended on the grounds that all are comprehended by the term 'vessel.'

ereignty, not the term, permits unification of the three concepts, are we justified in applying the term to each form of power separately. Classical theory does link coercive power and authority, but does not appear to say anything about influential power; the latter's role consists of describing one of the elements in decision-making, whereas classical theory focuses not on the process of making decisions but on the question of why the results are recognized as binding on members of the community and how they can be enforced.

'Influential sovereignty' would also seem a doubtful component of the larger concept because it is the only one of the assumed trio which requires us to speak of 'most' rather than 'supreme.' As Rees himself says, "The most serious objection which might be raised against the retention of this concept is that it is . . . never possible to determine its strength." But when pointing out that "The determination of degrees of influence is a job which economists, historians, anthropologists and politicians have often to undertake, and which they often undertake quite successfully," he really misses the point of the behavioralist objection. For only behavioralists are equipped to deal with questions of degree. If 'degree' creeps into the concept of sovereignty, it must be left to the behavioralists. Apparently they do not want the concept.

Yves R. Simon's Transmission Theory of Consent

Yves Simon's argument is that the transmission of power by the people during an election suspends their exercise of power and that spurious transmission of power, or denial that the power is suspended, destroys the essence of government and becomes in effect an act of rebellion. This argument is of major importance, for it solves some of the most perplexing problems of democratic theory.

The difficulty is that the concept of consent of the governed, as interpreted by strict egalitarians, makes government one of man's more suspect inventions, something to be hedged about with restrictions and constantly questioned by all responsible citizens, since "eternal vigilance is the price of liberty." The view that the governing body is by nature a special interest group at odds with the public interest, or likely to become so, has long supplied weapons for the 'conservative' and the libertarian, both of whom seem to suppose that they can continue in an ordered community without a strong ordering power. Much of the hostility to politicians, and of lawlessness and apathy, also stems from this paradoxical view, since the public, recognizing that government is not as amenable to pressure as the egalitarian theory requires, comes to see the government as an alien body. Hemmed in by restrictions on its power, attacked by both starry-eyed 'idealists' and pressure groups, and frustrated by public apathy, the government has had only limited ability to take action. Yet the complex, megalopolitan societies of today need more government not less, and the consequently increasing discrepancy between what simple egalitarian theory demands and what is actually happening has exacerbated the problems of government.

Simple egalitarianism has also raised difficulties for supporters of sovereignty. The theory of sovereignty requires a supreme power, but the theory of democracy seemingly requires that this power be the people or some charter accepted by the people, neither of which makes sense in terms of the classical theory. It is not possible to be one's own government or to have supreme power over one's self, nor can a constitution be a government. These obvious difficulties help to explain why so many democratic theorists have been suspicious of the concept of sovereignty: it cannot easily be fitted into the democratic pattern.

Simon rescues theorists from such difficulties by accepting consent of the governed in a special sense. For him, power is transmitted unconditionally, and is held by the government during its tenure of office. Organized opposition, as in Hobbesian theory, is rebellion and destroys the social order. 'Consent of the governed' for Simon does not mean what many, perhaps most, have supposed it to mean.

There are, however, certain aspects of Simon's view which give cause for alarm. The first is connected with one of the advantages of the theory: its justification of current democratic practices. Despite the egalitarian-consent theory, the bulk of government policy is normally decided without much attempt to discover whether the public 'consents' or not. Most legislation affects the people only indirectly; moreover, its precise effect cannot be estimated by even the best-informed segments of the population so that the question of obtaining, or not obtaining, their 'consent' simply does not arise. Other legislation and policy which obviously do affect the public directly —and in some cases conflict with their immediate interests or values—are made necessary by factors to which the government, to be a true government, must accord primary importance. All this does not mean that public wishes are habitually ignored by legislators and policy-makers. The egalitarian-consent theory has undoubtedly induced many legislators—out of a sense of duty rather than self-interest—to take public wishes into account. The crux of the matter is that Simon's theory denies that the legislator has any such duty. Under his Transmission Theory of Consent, it becomes wrong—because it is a matter of self-interest, the fear of not being re-elected—for a legislator to do so.

What is likely to happen when both law-makers and the electorate feel that deliberate attempts to influence the government are not evidence of public spirit? Attempts to influence legislation will not cease, of course, but the quality of the influence will change as will the identity of those open to influence. The genuine 'idealists' will leave the scene and the corrupt will acquire much more power than they have at present.

Another difficulty is that democratic theory, by its very nature, denies that any values exist apart from those created by self-interest and personal taste. It is inexorably relativistic. If a democratic government is freed from the necessity—however limited—of taking majority tastes and interests into account, what is to replace the latter as policy determinants? No doubt economic realities and the facts of international relations will continue to shape a good deal of policy, but what will decide the government's approach to divorce reform, law reform in general, poverty, disease, social justice, and other 'problems?' These are problems, incidentally, not because they are facts but because our value-order says they are problems. If the pressure from those who regard them as problems is removed or very much reduced, there will be little or no reason for the government's attempting to do anything, for it will have no basis for deciding whether something needs to be done.

On the other hand, it is possible to conclude that Simon's position might result in a more rational approach to values. A government freed from the necessity of supposing that 'majority wishes' are equivalent to 'the good' might be compelled to develop a non-relativist value-order—or listen to those who suppose that one is possible. Thus, Simon's position, like Plato's, could lead to either utter stagnation in government or a rebirth of the mind.

F. H. HINSLEY'S HISTORICAL APPROACH

Hinsley's approach to the concept of sovereignty, to which he has devoted a full-length study,[15] while open to the behavioralist objection that it depends on a speculative reconstruction of facts rather than on the facts themselves, answers several objections to the theory of sovereignty.

While ostensibly tracing the development of the concept in different societies throughout history, Hinsley has in reality set himself the task of answering the view that sovereignty is no more than a piece of armchair philosophy, an attempt to defend absolutism, which cannot live up to its claim to express a necessary condition of political order since it has occurred only sporadically in political philosophy and never as an actual condition of a political order. Critics of the concept have asked why, if it is a necessary concept, it was known to the Romans but not the Greeks, who were more philosophically minded; known in Europe but not Asia or Africa; known to Renaissance, but not medieval, Europe. Hinsley's answer to these questions provides a strong rebuttal of the charge that a concept prevalent in certain periods and places has no relevance today.

15. F. H. Hinsley, *Sovereignty*, Basic Books, Inc., New York, 1966.

In essence, Hinsley's position is that the concept of sovereignty is a "restatement of the permanent problem of deciding the basis of government and obligation within a political community." [16] It cannot be irrelevant to the society which debates it. Throughout his book, he states explicitly that several preconditions are necessary to the development and acceptance of the concept of sovereignty. These are: the rise of state forms; identification of the claims of the state with the needs of the community; and a view that the law of the body politic transcends any external dictates. His main point is that the concept of sovereignty has never been a mere abstraction.

Hinsley's argument, which succeeds admirably in explaining the relation between political concepts and political conditions, has important consequences when we come to consider the recent history of political theory. Together with repeated attempts to decry sovereignty, there has been a tendency to analyze the problems of government solely in terms of power. But this approach to the facts of political orders in operation today has left a serious gap between government and the governed, and between society and the state; it has also led to a persistent decline in the sense of obligation felt by the governed and to a growing lack of purpose, a mere maneuvering for power, on the part of government. The harmony of interest which Bodin and Hobbes sought by developing a logical theory of sovereignty needs now to be revived; the conditions required to make the concept relevant are again present. It is perhaps possible to ignore this fact, to assume that somehow society produces working accommodations without the help of concepts. But in the light of Hinsley's historical survey it is hardly possible to argue that the concept of sovereignty is irrelevant to modern political analysis. Emerging sharply from his discussion is the conclusion that the concept is debatable only when it encompasses factors existing within a society. If it seems less accurate than descriptions of actual power relations, this is because it says a great deal more. It is a unifying theory, not a simple description.

16. Ibid. p. 26.

two

THE
PHILOSOPHIC
ATTACK

Jacques Maritain

THE CONCEPT
OF SOVEREIGNTY

I · The Point at Issue

No concept has raised so many conflicting issues and involved XIXth Century jurists and political theorists in so desperate a maze as the concept of Sovereignty. The reason for this is perhaps the fact that the original, genuine philosophical meaning of the concept had not been, from the very start, sufficiently examined, tested, and taken seriously by them.

In the same measure as crucial practical problems dealing with international law developed, the controversies about State Sovereignty, considered in its external aspect (relations between States), grew deeper and more extended. The question was posed whether the international community as a whole is not the true holder of Sovereignty, rather than the individual States.[1] In some quarters, even the very notion of Sovereignty was challenged.[2] Such was the stand taken first by Triepel, then by several other international lawyers like Edmunds [3] and

From *Man and the State* by Jacques Maritain (The University of Chicago Press, Chicago 1957), pp. 28–53. Copyright 1951 by The University of Chicago. Reprinted by permission of The University of Chicago Press.

1. Cf. Robert Lansing, *Notes on Sovereignty* (Washington: Carnegie Endowment for International Peace, 1921), chap. ii, "Notes on World Sovereignty." Reprinted from the *American Journal of International Law,* January, 1921.
2. Cf. Hymen Ezra Cohen, *Recent Theories of Sovereignty* (Chicago University of Chicago Press, 1937), pp. 82 ff.
3. Sterling E. Edmunds, *The Lawless Law of Nations* (Washington, D.C.: Byrne & Co., 1925).

Foulke.[4] Yet that challenge to the concept of Sovereignty remained only juridical in nature, and did not come down to the philosophical roots of the matter.

My aim in this chapter is to discuss Sovereignty not in terms of juridical theory, but in terms of political philosophy. I think that the grounds for doing so are all the better as Sovereignty, in its historical origins, as Jellinek once observed, is "a political concept which later became transformed"[5] with a view to securing a juristic asset to the political power of the State.

It is my contention that political philosophy must get rid of the word, as well as the concept, of Sovereignty:—not because it is an antiquated concept,[6] or by virtue of a sociological-juridical theory of "objective law";[7] and not only because the concept of Sovereignty creates insuperable difficulties and theoretical entanglements in the field of international law; but because, considered in its genuine meaning, and in the perspective of the proper scientific realm to which it belongs—political philosophy—this concept is intrinsically wrong[8] and bound

4. Roland R. Foulke, *A Treatise on International Law* (Philadelphia: John C. Winston Co., 1920): "The word sovereignty is ambiguous. . . . We propose to waste no time in chasing shadows, and will therefore discard the word entirely. The word 'independence' sufficiently indicates every idea embraced in the use of sovereignty necessary to be known in the study of international law" (p. 69).

5. Georg Jellinek, *Recht des modernen Staates: Allgemeine Staatslehre* (Berlin, 1900), p. 394.

6. Cf. Hugo Preuss, *Gemeinde, Staat, und Reich als Gebietskörperschaften* (Berlin, 1889); Charles E. Merriam, *History of the Theory of Sovereignty since Rousseau* (New York: Columbia University Press, 1900).

7. Cf. Léon Duguit, *Law in the Modern State* (New York: Viking Press, 1919). I am in agreement with Duguit as regards the necessity of discarding both the concept of the non-accountability of the State and the concept of State Sovereignty, not as regards the reasons upon which his conclusions are founded.

8. From another philosophic outlook, this is also the position of Harold J. Laski. Cf. his *Studies in the Problem of Sovereignty* (New Haven: Yale University Press, 1917) and *A Grammar of Politics* (New Haven: Yale University Press, 1925).

   Professor MacIver, in his book *The Web of Government*, has made out the case against Sovereignty in a remarkably forceful manner (cf. R. M. MacIver, *The Web of Government* [New York: Macmillan Co., 1947], pp. 48–51, 69–73).

to mislead us if we keep on using it—assuming that it has been too long and too largely accepted to be permissibly rejected, and unaware of the false connotations that are inherent in it.

Is a somewhat pedantic remark, but dealing with accuracy in the use of words, permissible at this point?

Just as the words πόλις or *civitas* are often translated by "state" (though the most appropriate name is "commonwealth" or "body politic," not "state"), so the words *principatus* and *suprema potestas* are often translated by "sovereignty," the words κύριος or *princeps* ("ruler") by "sovereign." [9] This is a misleading translation, which muddles the issue from the start. *Principatus* ("principality") and *suprema potestas* ("supreme power") simply mean "highest ruling authority," not "sovereignty" as has been conceived since the moment when this word made its first appearance in the vocabulary of political theory. Conversely, "sovereignty" was rendered at that moment by *majestas* in Latin and ἄκρα ἐξουσία in Greek, as was well known at the time of Jean Bodin.[10]

II · JEAN BODIN'S SOVEREIGN PRINCE

Jean Bodin is rightly considered the father of the modern theory of Sovereignty. For Bodin, the king did not possess supra-mundane Sovereignty, which has absolutely nothing above itself. God was above the king, and the supreme power of the king over his subjects was itself submitted to "the law of God and nature," [11] to the requirements of the moral order.[12]

---

9. Cf. Aristotle *Politics* iii. 15. 1286b31; iv. 4. 1290a32, etc.; where Aristotle said κύριος, the Oxford translation, under the editorship of W. D. Ross, puts *sovereign*. Thomas Aquinas *Sum. theol.* i–ii. 90. 3, obj. 3; 96. 5, corp., obj. 3, and *ad* 3, etc.; where Aquinas said *princeps,* the translation edited by the English Dominicans puts *sovereign*.

10. Cf. Jean Bodin, *De la république* (Paris: Chez Jacques du Puys, 1583), Book I, chap. 8.

11. *Ibid.,* Book I, chap. 8.

12. Mr. Max Adam Shepard ("Sovereignty at the Crossroads: A Study of Bodin," *Political Science Quarterly,* XLV [1930], 580–603) has insisted that Bodin was at the crossroads between the medieval notion of the Prince—submitted to the law (the human law), not as to its *vis coactiva,*

But the king was Sovereign, the king was possessed of human Sovereignty. Let us, then, listen to Bodin's words:

"Il est icy besoin de former la définition de souveraineté, par ce qu'il n'y a ny jurisconsulte, ny philosophe politique, qui l'ayt définie." [13]

"La souveraineté est *la puissance absolue et perpétuelle d'une République.*" [14]

---

but as to its *vis directiva* (cf. *Sum. theol.* i–ii. 96. 5, *ad* 3)—and the modern ("monist") notion of the Prince, completely free from any law on earth. See also Professor Charles McIlwain's observations on Bodin and Hobbes in his article, "Sovereignty in the Present World," *Measure*, 3d issue, 1950. It is true that, inevitably, Bodin remained to some extent tributary to the Middle Ages and did not get the full distance on the road later traversed by Hobbes and Austin. But if he made the Sovereign bound to respect the *jus gentium* and the constitutional law of monarchy (*leges imperii*), this was because, in his view, when it came to such things as the inviolability of private property, or the precepts of *jus gentium*, or the "laws of the realm" like the Salic Law, expressing the basic agreement in which the power of the Prince originates, human laws and tribunals were *only the expresions or the organs of Natural Law itself*, so that, as a result, their pronouncements were valid even with regard to the Sovereign. This peculiar view of Bodin's (based, moreover, on a wrong idea of Natural Law) was to be discarded by the further theorists of Sovereignty, and in this sense he stopped halfway. Yet the fact remains that Bodin's sovereign was only subject to Natural Law, and to no human law whatsoever as distinct from Natural Law, and that is the core of political absolutism.

On Jean Bodin see Roger Chauviré, *Jean Bodin auteur de la République* (Paris, 1914); A. Ponthieux, "Quelques documents inédits sur Jean Bodin," *Revue du XVIe siècle*, Vol. XV (1928), fasc. 1–2; A. Garosci, *Jean Bodin* (Milan, 1935); Pierre Mesnard, *L'Essor de la philosophie politique au XVIe siècle* (Paris: Boivin, 1936), pp. 473–546, "La 'République' de Jean Bodin," and "Jean Bodin et la critique de la morale d'Aristote," *Revue Thomiste*, Vol. III (1949).

13. Bodin, *op. cit.,* Book I, chap. 8, p. 122. "For so here it behoveth first to define what majestie or Soveraigntie is, which neither lawyer nor politicall philosopher hath yet defined" (The Six Bookes of a Commonweale written by J. Bodin, a famous Lawyer, and a man of great Experience in matters of State; out of the French and Latine Copies, done into English, by Richard Knolles. London, Impensis G. Bishop, 1606, p. 84).

14. *Ibid.,* p. 122. "Majestie or Soveraigntie is the most high, absolute, and perpetuall power over the citisens and subjects in a Commonweale" (English trans., p. 84).

"Ceste puissance est *perpétuelle*," [15] that is, "pour la vie de celuy qui a la puissance" [16] [as opposed to those who "ne sont que dépositaires, et gardes de ceste puissance jusques à ce qu'il plaise au peuple ou au Prince la révoquer." [17]]

"Si le peuple octroye sa puissance à quelcun tant qu'il vivra, en qualité d'officier, ou lieutenant, ou bien pour se descharger seulement de l'exercice de sa puissance: en ce cas il n'est point souverain, ains simple officier, ou lieutenant, ou régent, ou gouverneur, ou gardien, et bail de la puissance d'autruy." [18] But *"Si la puissance absolue luy est donnée purement et simplement, sans qualité de magistrat, ny de commissaire, ny forme de précaire, il est bien certain que cestuy-là est, et se peut dire monarque souverain: car le peuple s'est dessaisi et dépouillé de sa puissance souveraine, pour l'ensaisiner et investir: et à luy, et en luy transporté tout son pouvoir, auctorité, prérogatives, et souveraineté."* [19]

Now what does "puissance *absolue*" mean?—*"Le peuple ou les seigneurs d'une République peuvent donner purement et simplement la puissance souveraine et perpétuelle à quelcun pour disposer des biens, des personnes, et de tout l'estat à son plaisir, et puis le laisser à qui il voudra, et tout ainsi que le propriétaire peut donner son bien purement et simplement,*

15. *Ibid.*, p. 122. "This power ought to be perpetuall" (p. 84).
16. *Ibid.*, p. 126. "For the tearme of the life of him that hath the power" (p. 87).
17. *Ibid.*, p. 122. "Seeing that they are but men put in trust, and keepers of this soveraigne power, untill it shall please the people or the prince that gave it them to recall it" (p. 84).
18. *Ibid.*, p. 127. "If the people shall give all their power unto any one so long as he liveth, by the name of a magistrat, lieutenant, or governour, or onely to discharge themselves of the exercise of their power: in this case he is not to be accounted any soveraigne, but a plaine officer, or lieutenant, regent, governour, or guerdon and keeper of another mans power" (p. 88).
19. *Ibid.*, p. 127. "If such absolute power bee given him purely and simply without the name of a magistrat, governour, or lieutenant, or other forme of deputation, it is certaine that such an one is, and may call himselfe a Soveraigne Monarch: for so the people hath voluntarily disseised and dispoyled it selfe of the soveraigne power, to sease and invest another therein; having on him, and uppon him transported all the power, authoritie, prerogatives, and soveraigneties thereof" (p. 88).

sans autre cause que de sa libéralité, qui est la vraye donation: et qui ne reçoit plus de conditions, estant une fois parfaicte et accomplie." [20]

Thus *"le Monarque est divisé du peuple."* [21]

And "le poinct principal de la majesté souveraine et puissance absolue, gist principalement à donner loy aux subjects en général sans leur consentement." [22]

"Le Prince souverain n'est tenu rendre conte qu'à Dieu." [23]

"Le Prince soverain ne doit serment qu'à Dieu." [24]

"La souveraineté n'est limitée, ny en puissance, ny en charge, ny à certain temps." [25]

"Le Prince est l'image de Dieu." [26]

"Or tout ainsi que ce grand Dieu souverain ne peut faire un Dieu pareil à luy, attendu qu'il est infini, et qu'il ne se peut faire qu'il y ayt deux choses infinies, par démonstration nécessaire: aussi pouvons nous dire que le Prince que nous avons posé comme l'image de Dieu, ne peut faire un subject égal à luy, que sa puissance ne soit anéantie." [27]

20. *Ibid.*, p. 128. "For the people or the lords of a Commonweale, may purely and simply give the soveraigne and perpetuall power to any one, to dispose of the goods and lives, and of all the state at his pleasure: and so afterward to leave it to whom he list: like as the proprietaire or owner may purely and simply give his owne goods, without any other cause to be expressed, than of his owne meere bountie; which is indeed the true donation, which no more receiveth condition, being once accomplished and perfected" (pp. 88–89).
21. *Ibid.*, p. 143. "The monarch is divided from the people" (p. 99).
22. *Ibid.*, p. 142. "So wee see the principall point of soveraigne majestie, and absolute power, to consist principally in giving laws unto the subjects in generall, without their consent" (p. 98).
23. *Ibid.*, p. 125. "Whereas the prince or people themselves, in whome the Soveraigntie resteth, are to give account unto none, but to the immortall God alone" (p. 86).
24. *Ibid.*, p. 143. "A soveraign prince next under God, is not by oath bound unto any" (p. 99).
25. *Ibid.*, p. 124. "So that Soveraigntie is not limited either in power, charge, or time certaine" (p. 85).
26. *Ibid.*, pp. 156, 161. "The prince is the image of God."
27. *Ibid.*, Book I, chap. 10, p. 215. "For as the great soveraigne God, cannot make another God equall unto himself, considering that he is of infinit power and greatnes, and that there cannot bee two infinit things,

III · THE ORIGINAL ERROR

Thus Bodin's position is perfectly clear. Since the people have absolutely deprived and divested themselves of their total power in order to transfer it to the Sovereign, and invest him with it, then the Sovereign is no longer a part of the people and the body politic: he is "divided from the people," he has been made into a whole, a *separate* and transcendent whole, which is his sovereign living Person, and by which the other whole, the immanent whole or the body politic, is ruled from above. When Jean Bodin says that the sovereign Prince is the image of God, this phrase must be understood in its full force, and means that the Sovereign—submitted to God, but accountable only to Him—transcends the political whole just as God transcends the cosmos. Either Sovereignty means nothing, or it means supreme power *separate* and *transcendent*—not at the peak but *above* the peak ("par dessus tous les subjects") [28]— and ruling the entire body politic *from above*. That is why this power is absolute (ab-solute, that is non-bound, separate), and consequently unlimited, in its extension as well as in its duration, and not accountable to anything on earth.

Let us observe at this point that there is no command without some kind of separation. *Segregatus ut imperet,* "separate, in order to command," Anaxagoras said of the νοῦς, the divine Intellect. After all, does not any man, once put in command, begin by separating himself from others in a certain measure, be it by means of a bigger chair or a less accessible office room? Yet it is the kind of separation which is the point at issue. As regards political command, separation is truly and genuinely required only as an *existential* status or condition for the *exercise* of the right to govern. But with Sovereignty separation is

---

as is by naturall demonstrations manifest: so also may wee say, that the prince whom we have set down as the image of God, cannot make a subject equall unto himselfe, but that his owne soveraigntie must thereby be abased" (p. 155).

28. "Car souverain (c'est à dire, celuy qui est par dessus tous les subjects) ne pourra convenir à celuy qui a faict de son subject son compagnon" (*ibid.,* Book I, chap. 10; *ed. cit.,* p. 215).

required as an *essential* quality, one with the very *possession* of that right, which the people have supposedly given up entirely, so that all the essence of power—henceforth monadic, as indivisible as the very person of the Sovereign—resides in the Sovereign alone. No wonder that finally an essence other than common humanity was to be ascribed to the person itself of the Sovereign.

Here we are confronted with the basic wrong of the concept of Sovereignty, and the original error of the theorists of Sovereignty. They knew that the right to self-government is naturally possessed by the people. But for the consideration of this *right* they substituted that of the total *power* of the commonwealth. They knew that the "prince" receives from the people the authority with which he is invested. But they had overlooked and forgotten the concept of *vicariousness* stressed by the mediaeval authors. And they replaced it with the concept of physical transfer and donation.

In other words, they discussed the matter in terms of *goods* (or material *power*) held either in ownership or in trusteeship, instead of discussing it in terms of rights possessed by essence or by participation. If a material good is owned by the one, it cannot be owned by the other, and there can only be a question of transfer of ownership or a donation. But a right can be possessed by the one as belonging to his nature, and by the other as participated in by him. God is possessed by essence of the right to command; the people are possessed of this right both by participation in the divine right, and by essence insofar as it is a human right. The "vicars" of the people or deputies for the people are possessed (really possessed) of this right only by participation in the people's right.[29]

In reality, then, even in the case of monarchy—but not absolute—it should have have been maintained that since the prince is the "vicar of the multitude" or the deputy for the people, his right in this capacity is the very right of the people, in which he has been made a participant by the trust of the people and which still exists in the people, far from having

29. See Jacques Maritain, *Man and the State* (Chicago: The University of Chicago Press, 1951), chap. v., pp. 133–38.

been uprooted from the people in order to be transferred to
him. Thus the prince should have been considered at the peak
(but not above the peak) of the political structure, as a part
representing the whole (and not as a separate whole), or as a
person commissioned to exercise the highest authority in the
body politic, who has *vicariously* possession of this authority
as a maximum *participation* in the right naturally possessed by
the people. Such a prince (whose concept never materialized in
human history, except perhaps, to some extent, in the case of
St. Louis [Louis IX of France]) would have been separate from
the people as to the existential status required by the exercise
of the right to command. But he would not have been divided
from the people as to the possession of this right—on the contrary! since he possessed it in a vicarious manner and by participation. He would have been accountable to the people. He
would have been a king, but not an absolute king; a prince,
but not a sovereign prince.

IV · What Does Sovereignty Mean.
The Hobbesian Mortal God

The concept of Sovereignty took definite form at the moment
when absolute monarchy was budding in Europe. No corresponding notion had been used in the Middle Ages with regard
to political authority. St. Thomas treated of the Prince, not of
the Sovereign. In the feudal times the king was but the Suzerain
of Suzerains, each one of whom was possessed of his own rights
and power. The jurists of the mediaeval kings only prepared in
a more or less remote way the modern notion of Sovereignty.
It is from the time of Jean Bodin on that it forced itself upon
the jurists of the baroque age.

Even leaving aside the theory of the *divine right* of kings,[30]
which was to flourish at the time of Louis XIV, the idea was
that the king as a person possessed a natural and inalienable
right to rule his subjects from above. Once the people had

30. That is, absolute power directly conferred on the king by God, not in-
    directly through the people's transferring the "absolute power of the
    Commonwealth" to him.

agreed upon the fundamental law of the kingdom, and given the king and his descendants power over them, they were deprived of any right to govern themselves, and the natural right to govern the body politic resided henceforth in full only in the person of the king. Thus the king had a right to supreme power which was *natural and inalienable*, inalienable to such a degree that dethroned kings and their descendants kept this right forever, quite independently of any consideration of the will of the subjects.

And since this natural and inalienable right to supreme power resided only in the person of the king, with regard to the body politic but independently of the body politic, the power of the king was supreme not only as the topmost power existing in the highest part of the body politic, but as a monadic and supernal power existing *above* the body politic and *separately* from it. So the king reigned over his subjects from above, and took care of their common good from above; he was a full-dress political image of God (a royal privilege which was to become rather detrimental to God in the sequel). And any restriction on the supernal independence and power of the king could only come from a free and gracious concession granted by the king (though most often, in actual fact, under pressure) to such or such parts of the whole populace beneath.

Such was the idea, and the purpose for which the word Sovereignty was coined.[31] We cannot use the concept of Sovereignty without evoking, even unawares, that original connotation.

What is, therefore, the proper and genuine meaning of the notion of Sovereignty?

Sovereignty means two things:

31. I mean, in the vocabulary of political theory. The word "sovereign" (from Low Latin *superanus,* "Ex optimatum ordine, princeps") was employed long ago in the common language, meaning any official endowed with superior authority, for instance, "superior judge." Du Cange (see *Summus*) quotes an edict of the French King Charles V, made in 1367, which reads: "Voulons et ordonons que se . . . le Bailli ou autre leur souverain. . . ."

First, a right to supreme independence and supreme power which is a *natural* and *inalienable* right.

Second, a right to an independence and a power which in their proper sphere are supreme *absolutely* or *transcendently,* not *comparatively* or as a *topmost part* in the whole. In other terms, it is *separately* from the whole which is ruled by the Sovereign that the independence of the Sovereign with regard to this whole and his power over it are supreme. His independence and power are not only supreme *in relation to* any other part of the political whole, as being at the top or highest part of this whole; they are supreme *absolutely* speaking as being above the whole in question.

Sovereignty is a property which is absolute and indivisible, which cannot be participated in and admits of no degrees, and which belongs to the Sovereign independently of the political whole, as a right of his own.

Such is genuine Sovereignty, that Sovereignty which the absolute kings believed they possessed, and the notion of which was inherited from them by the absolute States, and the full significance of which has been brought to light in the Hegelian State—and, long before Hegel, in the Hobbesian *Mortal God.*

Let us re-read at this point Hobbes' unforgettable page: Whereas the agreement of irrational creatures is natural, he says, "that of men is by Covenant only, which is Artificiall: and therefore it is no wonder if there be somewhat else required (besides Covenant) to make their Agreement constant and lasting; which is a Common Power, to keep them in awe, and to direct their actions to the Common Benefit.

"The only way to erect such a Common Power, as may be able to defend them from the invasion of Forraigners and the injuries of one another and thereby to secure them in such sort, as that by their owne industrie, and by the fruites of the Earth, they may nourish themselves and live contentedly; is, *to conferre all their power and strength upon one Man, or upon one Assembly of men, that may reduce all their Wills, by plurality of voices, unto one Will: which is as much to say, to appoint one Man, or Assembly of men, to beare their Person;* and everyone to owne, and acknowledge himselfe to be Author of what-

soever he that so beareth their Person, shall Act, or cause to
be Acted, in those things which concerne the Common Peace
and Safetie; *and therein to submit their Wills, everyone to his
Will, and their Judgments, to his Judgment.* This is more than
Consent, or Concord; *it is a real Unitie of them all, in one and
the same Person,* made by Covenant of every man with every
man, in such manner, as if every man should say to every man,
'I Authorize and give up my Right of Governing my selfe, to
this Man, or to this Assembly of men, on this condition, that
thou give up thy Right to him, and Authorize all his Actions
in like manner.' This done, the Multitude so united in one
Person, is called a *Common-Wealth,* in Latin *Civitas.* This is
the Generation of the great LEVIATHAN, *or rather (to speak
more reverently) of that* MORTALL GOD, to which we owe under
the *Immortall God,* our peace and defence. For by this Authoritie, given him by every particular man in the Common-
Wealth, *he hath the use of so much Power and Strength
conferred on him, that by terror thereof, he is inabled to forme
the wills of them all,* to Peace at home, and mutuall ayd against
their enemies abroad. *And in him consisteth the Essence of the
Common-Wealth;* which (to define it) is One Person, of whose
Acts a great Multitude, by naturall Covenants one with another, have made themselves every one the Author, to the end
he may use the strength and means of them all, as he shall
think expedient, for their Peace and Common Defence.

   "And he that carryeth this Person, is called SOVERAIGNE, *and
said to have* SOVERAIGNE POWER; *and every one besides, his* SUB-
JECT." [32]

V · NEITHER THE BODY POLITIC NOR
THE STATE IS SOVEREIGN

Now what is the situation in reality, first, with regard to the
body politic, and second, with regard to the State?

   The *body politic* has a right to full autonomy. First, to full
internal autonomy, or with respect to itself; and second, to full

---

32. *Leviathan,* ed. R. A. Waller (Cambridge: At the University Press, 1904),
    Part II, chap. xvii.

external autonomy, or with respect to the other bodies politic. The full *internal* autonomy of the body politic means that it governs itself with comparatively supreme independence (or greater than that of any part of it): so that no one of its parts can, by usurping government, substitute itself for the whole and infringe upon its freedom of action; the full internal autonomy of the body politic means also that it governs itself with comparatively supreme power (or greater than that of any part of it): so that no one of its parts can, by substituting itself for the whole, infringe upon the topmost power enjoyed by the agencies of government through which the whole governs itself.

The full *external* autonomy of the body politic means that it enjoys comparatively supreme independence with regard to the international community, that is, an independence which the international community—as long as it remains merely moral and does not exist as political society, therefore has no political independence of its own—has no right and no power forcibly to make lesser with respect to itself. As a result, each body politic, as long as it does not enter a superior, larger political society, has above itself no power on earth which it should be forced to obey. The full external autonomy of the body politic means also that it can exert externally topmost power in making war on another body politic.

The right of the body politic to such full autonomy derives from its nature as a perfect or self-sufficient society: a nature, be it observed in passing, which present bodies politic are losing, as a matter of fact, to a greater and greater extent, so that they keep their right to full autonomy only as a remnant, and because they are not yet integrated in a larger, really perfect and self-sufficient, political society. In any case, when a body politic decides to beome part of a larger political society, say, a federal political society, it gives up, by the same token, its right to full autonomy, though it keeps, in fact and by right, a limited autonomy, much more limited, obviously, as external autonomy than as internal autonomy.

Now I say that the right of the body politic to full autonomy, which I have just analyzed, is a *natural* right, even an *inalien-*

able right: I mean *in the sense* that nobody may forcibly deprive it of this right; but *not at all in the sense* that the full independence in question is itself inalienable, and that the body politic cannot freely surrender its right to it, if it recognizes that it is no longer a perfect and self-sufficient society, and consents to enter a larger political society. As a result the full autonomy of the body politic implies the *first* element inherent in genuine Sovereignty, namely a *natural* and—in one sense—*inalienable* right to supreme independence and supreme power. But it does not imply the second element. For it is clear that the body politic does not govern itself *separately from itself* and *from above itself.* In other words, its supreme independence and power are only comparatively or relatively supreme (as proper to this given whole with respect to its parts, and also with respect to the unorganized community of the other wholes). So the *second* element inherent in genuine Sovereignty, namely the *absolutely* or *transcendently* supreme character of independence and power, which in genuine Sovereignty are supreme *separately* from, and *above,* the whole ruled by the Sovereign (and which, in the external sphere, make even the possibility of any superior larger political society repugnant in itself to the very essence of the Sovereign)— the second element inherent in genuine Sovereignty is obviously irrelevant to the very concept of the full autonomy of the body politic.

Let us consider now the State. The State is a part and an instrumental agency of the body politic. Therefore it has neither supreme independence with regard to the whole or supreme power over the whole, nor a right of its own to such supreme independence and supreme power. It has supreme independence and power only with regard to the other parts of the body politic, subject to its laws and administration, and it has a right to such comparatively supreme independence and power only as come to it from the body politic, by virtue of the basic structure or constitution which the body politic has determined for itself. And the exercise of this right by the State remains subject to the control of the body politic.

As regards, furthermore, its *external* sphere of activity, it is only as representing the body politic, and under its control, that the State enjoys, with regard to the international community, a right to a supreme independence which (as we have seen apropós of the body politic) is only *comparatively* and *renounceably* supreme,—and can also exercise the topmost power in making war on another State.

As a result, neither the *first* element inherent in genuine Sovereignty, namely a *natural and inalienable* right to supreme independence and supreme power, nor the *second* element inherent in genuine Sovereignty, namely the *absolutely* and *transcendently* supreme character of that independence and power, which in genuine Sovereignty are supreme *separately* from, and *above,* the whole ruled by the Sovereign (and which, in the external sphere, make even the possibility of any superior, larger political society repugnant in itself to the very essence of the Sovereign)—neither the first nor the second element inherent in genuine Sovereignty can by any means be ascribed to the State. The State is not and has never been genuinely sovereign.

VI · Nor Are the People. Rousseau's Sovereign State

To sum up, let us then say that the concept of Sovereignty, taken in its proper and genuine meaning, does not apply to the body politic, except as regards the first of the two elements it implies; and that it does not apply at all to the State.

No doubt it is permissible to use the term Sovereignty in an improper sense, meaning simply either the natural right of the body politic to full autonomy, or the right which the State receives from the body politic to topmost independence and topmost power with regard to the other parts and power agencies of the political society or with regard to the external relations between States. Yet in doing so one runs the risk of becoming involved in the worst confusion, since the word Sovereignty always connotes obscurely its genuine, original meaning. And so one is in danger of forgetting that no human agency has by virtue of its own nature a right to govern men. Any right to power, in political society, is possessed by a man or a human agency in so far as he or it is in the body politic a *part* at the service of the common good, a part which has received this right, within certain fixed bounds, from the people exercising their fundamental right to govern themselves.

As concerns finally the people, the second element inherent in genuine Sovereignty—namely the absolutely and transcendently supreme character of the independence and power, which in genuine Sovereignty are supreme separately from, and above, the whole ruled by the Sovereign—that second element inherent in genuine Sovereignty is obviously not present in the people any more than it is in the body politic. It is therefore better to say of them, as of the body politic, that they have a natural and inalienable right to *full autonomy,* that is, to comparatively supreme independence and power with regard to any part of the whole itself which is composed of them, and in order to have this very whole brought into existence and into activity. As we observed . . . [elsewhere],[33] it would be simply nonsensical to conceive of the people as governing themselves *separately from themselves and from above themselves.*

Yet it is such a nonsensical notion which is at the core of Jean-Jacques Rousseau's *Contrat Social.* The myth of the *Votonté Générale*—which is in no way a simple majority will, but a monadic superior and indivisible Will emanating from the people as one single unit, and which is "always right" [34]—was only a means of having the separate and transcendent power of the absolute king transferred to the people while remaining separate and transcendent, in such a way that by the mystical operation of the General Will the people, becoming one single Sovereign, would possess a separate, absolute, and transcendent

33. Cf. Jacques Maritain, *Man and the State,* p. 25.
34. Jean-Jacques Rousseau, *The Social Contract,* trans. Henry J. Tozer (London: Allen & Unwin, 1920), Book II, chaps. iii and iv. p. 123: "It follows from what precedes that the general will is always right . . ." and p. 126: "Why is the general will always right, and why do all invariably desire the prosperity of each. . . ."

power, a power from above over themselves as a multitude of individuals. As Rousseau put it, *"le pacte social donne au corps politique un* POUVOIR ABSOLU *sur tous ses membres; et c'est ce même pouvoir qui, dirigé par une volonté générale, porte le nom de* SOUVERAINTÉ.[35] *"La souveraineté, n'étant que l'exercice de la volonté générale, ne peut jamais, s'aliéner, et le souverain, qui n'est qu'un être collectif,* NE PEUT ÊTRE REPRÉSENTÉ QUE PAR LUI-MÊME."* [36] *"L'autorité suprême ne peut pas plus se modifier que s'aliéner;* LA LIMITER C'EST LA DÉTRUIRE."* [37] *"La puissance souveraine n'a nul besoin de garant envers ses sujets. . . . Le souverain,* PAR CELA SEUL QU'IL EST, EST TOUJOURS TOUT CE QU'IL DOIT ÊTRE."* [38]

Thus Rousseau, who was not a democrat,[39] injected in nascent modern democracies a notion of Sovereignty which was destructive of democracy, and pointed toward the totalitarian State; because, instead of getting clear of the separate and transcendent power of the absolute kings, he carried, on the contrary, that spurious power of the absolute kings to the point of an unheard-of absolutism, in order to make a present of it to the people. So it is necessary that "each citizen should be in perfect independence of the others, *and excessively dependent on the State. . . . For it is only the power of the State* which makes the freedom of its members." [40] The Legislator,

35. *Ibid.*, Book II, chap. iv, p. 125: ". . . the social pact gives the body politic an absolute power over all its members; and it is this same power which, when directed by the general will, bears, as I said, the name of sovereignty."

36. *Ibid.*, chap. i, p. 119: "I say, then, that sovereignty, being nothing but the exercise of the general will, can never be alienated, and that the sovereign power, which is only a collective being, can be represented by itself alone."

37. *Ibid.*, Book III, chap. xvi, p. 190: ". . . the supreme authority can no more be modified than alienated; to limit it is to destroy it."

38. *Ibid.*, Book I, chap. vii, p. 113: ". . . the sovereign power needs no guarantee toward its subjects. . . . The sovereign, for the simple reason that it is so, is always everything that it ought to be."

39. *Ibid.*, Book III, chap. iv, p. 160: "If there were a nation of gods, it would be governed democratically. So perfect a government is unsuited to men."

40. *Ibid.*, Book II, chap. xii. The original reads: "En sorte que chaque

that superman described in the *Contrat Social,* offers us a pre-
view of our modern totalitarian dictators, whose "great soul
is the true miracle which should prove" their "mission," [41] and
who have to "alter man's constitution in order to strengthen
it." [42] Did not Rousseau think moreover, that the State has
a right of life and death over the citizen? "When the prince
has said to him: it is expedient for the state that you should
die, he must die, since it is only on this condition that he has
safely lived up to that time, and since his life is no longer a
nature's boon only, but a conditional gift of the state." [43]
Finally, as concerns matters of religion, he insisted that "the
philosopher Hobbes is the only one who has clearly seen the
evil and its remedy, and who has dared to suggest to unite in
one single authority the two heads of the eagle, or *to reduce
everything to political unity, without which never state or
government will be rightly constituted.*" [44] Rousseau's State
was but the Hobbesian Leviathan, crowned with the General
Will instead of the crown of those whom the Jacobin vocabulary called "les rois et les tyrans."

But let us come back to our subject-matter. As a result of
the principles set forth by Rousseau, and because the long-ad-
mitted notion of the *transcendently* supreme independence
and power of the king had been simply transferred to the

---

citoyen soit dans une parfaite indépendance de tous les autres, et dans
une excessive dépendance de la cité. . . . Car il n'y a que la force de
l'état qui fasse la liberté de ses membres."
41. *Ibid.,* Book II, chap. vii.—"La grande âme du législateur est le vrai
miracle qui doit prouver sa mission."
42. *Ibid.*—"Celui qui ose entreprendre d'instituer un peuple doit se sentir
en état . . . d'altérer la constitution de l'homme pour la renforcer."
43. *Ibid.,* chap. v.—"Et quand le prince lui a dit: Il est expédient à l'Etat
que tu meures, il doit mourir, puisque ce n'est qu'à cette condition
qu'il a vécu en sûreté jusqu'alors, et que sa vie n'est plus seulement
un bienfait de la nature, mais un don conditionnel de l'Etat."
44. *Ibid.,* Book IV, chap. viii.—"De tous les auteurs chrétiens, le philosophe
Hobbes est le seul qui ait bien vu le mal et le remède, qui ait osé
proposer de réunir les deux têtes de l'aigle, et de tout ramener à
l'unité politique, sans laquelle jamais état ni gouvernement ne sera
jamais bien constitué."

people, thus making all individual wills lose any independence of their own in the indivisible *General Will,* it was held as a self-evident principle, at the time of the French Revolution, that the Sovereignty of the people,—absolute, monadic, transcendent as every Sovereignty,—excluded the possibility of any particular bodies or organizations of citizens enjoying in the State any kind of autonomy. "It is of necessity that no partial society should exist in the state." [45]

Similarly, such a transferring, to the people, of the mythical idea of the inalienable right of the king to *transcendently* supreme power resulted, in the early and mythical, purely Rousseauist stage of democratic (spurious democratic) philosophy, in making the deputies of the people mere instruments deprived of any right to govern:[46] whereas, in truth, they are possessed—vicariously, and by participation, but really—of this right, with the responsibility involved; since, having been put in charge, within certain fixed limits, by the people exercising their right to full autonomy, they have been, to the same extent, vested with authority, by virtue of that very choice of the people, and, first and foremost, by virtue of the order

---

45. *Ibid.,* Book II, chap. iii.—"Il importe donc . . . qu'il n'y ait pas de société partielle dans l'Etat."

46. "La souveraineté ne peut être représentée, par la même raison qu'elle ne peut être aliénée. . . . *Les députés du peuple ne sont donc ni ne peuvent être ses représentants; ils ne sont que ses commissaires;* ils ne peuvent rien conclure définitivement. Toute loi que le peuple en personne n' a pas ratifiée est nulle; ce n'est point une loi. Le peuple anglais pense être libre, il se trompe fort; il ne l'est que durant l'élection des membres du parlement: sitôt qu'ils sont élus, il est esclave, il n'est rien. Dans les courts moments de sa liberté, l'usage qu'il en fait mérite bien qu'il la perde" (*Contrat Social,* Book III, chap. xv). Trans. Tozer, p. 187: "Sovereignty cannot be represented for the same reason that it cannot be alienated. . . . *The deputies of the people, then, are not and cannot be its representatives; they are only its commissioners* and can conclude nothing definitely. Every law which the people in person have not ratified is invalid; it is not a law. The English nation thinks that it is free, but is greatly mistaken, for it is only during the election of members of Parliament; as soon as they are elected, it is enslaved and counts for nothing. The use which it makes of the brief moment of freedom renders the loss of liberty well-deserved."

through which God maintains nature and societies, and through which alone men can be made bound in conscience to obey other men.

There is no need to add that the will of the people is not sovereign in the vicious sense that whatever would please the people would have the force of law. The right of the people to govern themselves proceeds from Natural Law: consequently, the very exercise of their right is subject to Natural Law. If Natural Law is sufficiently valid to give this basic right to the people, it is valid also to impose its unwritten precepts on the exercise of this same right. A law is not made *just* by the sole fact that it expresses the will of the people. An unjust law, even if it expresses the will of the people, is not law.

Here again the vicious dialectic of Sovereignty was at work. For Jean Bodin had indeed submitted the Sovereign to the law of God, but the inner logic of the concept was to make Sovereignty free from every—even heavenly—limitation. From the fact alone that he existed, was not the Sovereign always, as Rousseau put it, all that he ought to be? In actual fact Sovereignty required that no decision made by the Mortal God, or law established by the General Will, could possibly be resisted by the individual conscience in the name of justice. Law did not need to be *just* to have force of law. Sovereignty had a right to be obeyed, whatever it might command. Sovereignty was above moral law. The story came to its end once the Sovereignty of the abstract entity of the State had been substituted for the Sovereignty of the king, and the Sovereignty of the State had been confused with the Sovereignty of the Nation and the Sovereignty of the People. The Sovereignty of the totalitarian State is the master of good and evil as well as of life and death. That is *just* which serves the interest of the Sovereign, that is, of the People, that is, of the State, that is, of the Party.

VII · CONCLUSIONS

It seems to me that the conclusion to be drawn from all the preceding considerations on the concept of Sovereignty is clear. The major texts that I have quoted from such unimpeachable witnesses as Jean Bodin, Thomas Hobbes, and Jean-Jacques Rousseau, should suffice to enlighten us as to the genuine meaning of this concept. In order to think in a consistent manner in political philosophy, we have to discard the concept of Sovereignty, which is but one with the concept of Absolutism.

The question is not a question of words only. Of course we are free to say "Sovereignty" while we are thinking full autonomy or right to decide without appeal—as we are free to say "omnipotence" while we are thinking limited power, or "drum" while we are thinking flute. Yet the result for our own way of thinking and for intelligible intercommunication would appear questionable. Professor Quincy Wright observes with good reason that "the state still seems to exist different from subordinate government agencies and other associations and a term is needed to define it." [47] The point is that the term needed is not Sovereignty.

Sovereignty is a curious example of those concepts which are right in one order of things and wrong in another. It loses its poison when it is transplanted from politics to metaphysics. In the spiritual sphere there is a valid concept of Sovereignty. God, the separate Whole, is Sovereign over the created world. According to the Catholic faith, the Pope, in his capacity of vicar of Christ, is sovereign over the Church. Even, in a merely moral sense, it may be said that the wise man, and first and foremost the spiritual man, have a kind of sovereignty. For they are possessed of an independence which is supreme *from above* (from the Spirit), with regard to the world of passions and the world of the law, to whose coercive force they are not subjected, since their will is of itself and spontaneously in

47. Quincy Wright, *Mandates under the League of Nations* (Chicago: University of Chicago Press, 1930), pp. 281–82.

tune with the law.[48] They are further "separate in order to command," that is, to tell the truth. And the spiritual man "judges all things, yet himself is judged of no man." [49]

But in the political sphere, and with respect to the men or agencies in charge of guiding peoples toward their earthly destinies, there is no valid use of the concept of Sovereignty. Because, in the last analysis, no earthly power is the image of God and deputy for God. God is the very source of the authority with which the people invest those men or agencies, but they are not the vicars of God. They are the vicars of the people; then they cannot be divided from the people by any superior essential property.

Sovereignty means independence and power which are *separately* or *transcendently* supreme and are exercised upon the body politic *from above:* because they are a natural and inalienable right belonging to a whole (originally the person of the sovereign Prince), which is superior to the whole constituted by the body politic or the people, and which, consequently, either is superimposed on them or absorbs them in itself. The quality thus defined does not belong to the State. Ascribed to it, it vitiates the State. Three implications of Sovereignty are especially to be considered in this connection.

First, as regards external Sovereignty: the sovereign State— each individual sovereign State—is by right *above* the community of nations and possessed of absolute independence with regard to this community. As a result, no international law binding the States can be consistently conceived. Furthermore, this absolute independence is inalienable (*unrenounceable*), because by virtue of its notion the sovereign State is a monadic entity which cannot cease to be sovereign without ceasing to be a State. As a result, no day can dawn—as long as the States behave consistently with their so-called Sovereignty—on which they could possibly give up their supreme independence in order to enter a larger political body, or a world society.

Secondly, as regards internal Sovereignty: the sovereign State is possessed of a power which—instead of being *relatively highest,* because in actual fact something must be at the top

48. Cf. Thomas Aquinas *Sum. theol.* i–ii. 96. 5.
49. Paul, I Cor. 2:15.

to decide without appeal—is a power *absolutely supreme,* as is necessary with a monadic whole superimposed on the body politic or absorbing it in itself. And this *absolute* power of the sovereign State over the body politic, or the people, is all the more unquestionable as the State is mistaken for the body politic itself or for the personification of the people themselves; do they not obey only themselves, by obeying the State? As a result, the pluralist idea is not only disregarded, but rejected by necessity of principle. Centralism, not pluralism, is required. It is at the price of a patent self-contradiction that the sovereign States will reluctantly accept the smallest amount of autonomy for particular agencies and associations born out of freedom. Through the inner logic of the notion of Sovereignty, they will tend to totalitarianism.

Thirdly, the sovereign State is possessed of a supreme power which is exercised *without accountability.* How could this notion of the non-accountability of the Sovereign be conceivable if it did not refer to something *separately* and *transcendently* supreme? As Mr. Robert Lansing observed, "the power to do all things without accountability" is coincident with the Sovereignty of God. As to human Sovereignty, it "may be defined as the power to the extent of human capacity to do all things on the earth without accountability." [50] Well, the attribute thus defined is all that could be wished for by the deified Potentates, Despots, and the Emperors of ancient times in their most celestial ambitions. In modern times it has been ascribed to the State on the fictitious ground that the State is the people personified, and that the people can do anything without accountability. Yet the real process has been a transfer of the power without accountability of the personal Sovereign to the so-called juristic personality of the State. Thus was instilled in the latter a principle directly contrary to the principle which makes the people the final judge of the stewardship of their governmental officials; accordingly, the democratic States were involved in serious inconsistency. At all events the State was sovereign; as a result it was to endeavor perseveringly, in accordance with the principle of non-accountability, to escape the people's supervision and control.

50. Robert Lansing, *Notes on Sovereignty,* p. 3.

To the extent to which the sovereign State succeeds in this effort, the non-accountability of the supreme decisions by which the body politic is committed has a clear meaning: it means in actual fact that *the people* will pay for the decisions made by the State in the name of their Sovereignty. As a French common saying puts it, "ce sont toujours les mêmes qui se font tuer," always the same ones are getting killed. The woes of the people settle the accounts of the not-accountable supreme persons or agencies, State, ministries, committees, boards, staffs, rulers, lawgivers, experts, advisers,—not to speak of the *intelligentsia,* writers, theorists, scientific utopians, connoisseurs, professors, and newspapermen.

The *intelligentsia* has not been commissioned by the people: it is not accountable to the people, except morally. (For to teach or write on the assumption that what one puts forth "is of no consequence" is permissible only to insane persons.) But the State is accountable indeed; the State, as well as all governmental agencies and officials, is accountable to the people. Do not the people have a right to supervise and control the State? How could the State be subject to supervision if the power it exercises were a power without accountability?

But if the State is accountable and subject to supervision, how can it be sovereign? What can possibly be the concept of a *Sovereignty liable to supervision, and accountable?* Clearly, the State is not sovereign.

Nor, as we have seen, are the people. Nor do they exercise a power without accountability. Their right to self-government and full autonomy makes them not accountable to any tribunal or particular agency in the body politic. But the power they exercise, either by mass reflexes and extra-legal means, or through the regular channels of a truly democratic society, is in no way a power without accountability. For they are the very ones who always foot the bill. They are sure to account to their own sweat and blood for their mistakes.

The two concepts of Sovereignty and Absolutism have been forged together on the same anvil. They must be scrapped together.

three

THE
ARGUMENT
OF POLITICAL
SCIENCE

Stanley I. Benn

THE USES OF
"SOVEREIGNTY"

I

Jean Bodin defined "sovereignty" as "supreme power over citizens and subjects, unrestrained by law." Since then criticisms of theories in which the term ,has been employed have led to repeated attempts to redefine it and to distinguish different kinds of "supreme power" and examine the relations between them. For Austin the sovereign is "a *determinate* human superior, *not* in a habit of obedience to a like superior, (receiving) *habitual* obedience from the *bulk* of a given society." [1] Applying this notion to the British Constitution Dicey finds it necessary to distinguish "legal sovereignty" and "political sovereignty." [2] Lord Bryce employs a different distinction. "Legal sovereignty," he says, is primarily the concern of the lawyer: "The sovereign authority is to him the person (or body) to whose directions the law attributes legal force." [3] This kind of sovereignty, Bryce says, "is created by and concerned with law, and law only." [4] But it is also possible to detect a "practical sovereign": "The person (or body of persons) who can make his (or their) will prevail whether with the law or against the law. He (or they) is the *de facto* ruler." [5] More

From *Political Studies,* vol. III, no: 2 (June 1955), pp. 109–22. Reprinted by permission of the author and the publisher.

1. J. Austin, *Lectures on Jurisprudence* (5th ed.), p. 221.
2. A. V. Dicey, *Law of the Constitution* (9th ed.), p. 72.
3. Lord Bryce, *Studies in History and Jurisprudence,* vol. ii (1901), p. 51.
4. Ibid., p. 56
5. Ibid., pp. 59–60.

recently Mr. W. J. Rees has attempted an exhaustive analysis of the ways in which "sovereignty" has been used and has tried to establish three possible senses.[6] He begins with "power": "To exercise power . . . is to determine the actions of persons in certain intended ways. There are, however, different species of power, and these may be distinguished according to the means used to determine persons' actions." [7] He distinguishes three such species to each of which corresponds a species of supreme power, or sovereignty.

> "*Legal sovereignty*" is a capacity "to determine the actions of persons in certain intended ways by means of a law . . . where the actions of those who exercise the authority, in those respects in which they do exercise it, are not subject to any exercise by other persons of the kind of authority which they are exercising." [8] "A person or a body of persons may be said to exercise *coercive sovereignty,* or supreme coercive power, if it determines the actions of persons in certain intended ways by means of force or the threat of force, and if the actions of the persons who exercise the power, in those respects in which they do exercise it, are not themselves capable of being similarly determined." [9] "To exercise *political influence* . . . is to determine in certain intended ways the actions, jointly or severally, of the legal and coercive sovereigns, provided always that their actions are determined by some means other than a rule of law or a threat of force . . . . To exercise *sovereignty* in this sense is to exercise political influence, as now defined, to a greater degree than anyone else . . . ." [10]

"Legal sovereignty," it seems, might be attributed to Parliaments or amending organs or constitutions; [11] "coercive sover-

6. W. J. Rees, "The Theory of Sovereignty Restated," in *Mind,* vol. lix (1950).
7. Ibid., p. 511.
8. Ibid., p. 508. (My italics S.I.B.)
9. Ibid., p. 511. (My italics S.I.B.)
10. Ibid., p. 514. (My italics S.I.B.)
11. Ibid., pp. 516–17. It is not clear from this passage that Mr. Rees would ascribe legal sovereignty to a constitution. Such an ascription has been made by other writers, however (e.g. by Sir Ernest Barker in *Principles of Social and Political Theory,* p. 61, and Lord Lindsay in *The Modern Democratic State,* pp. 222–9), and I propose to examine the implications of this usage.

eignty" to armies or similar organized forces or a socially coercive power such as existed under the frank-pledge system; [12] "influential sovereignty" to a ruling class, the majority of the electorate, a priesthood, or some other such group." [13]

I propose in this paper to isolate and examine these and other usages, to try to discover in what kinds of study, if any, each is likely to be useful; and to determine whether they possess any common element that would justify the use of the one word "sovereignty" to cover them all.

II · LEGAL SOVEREIGNTY

It has often been said that a "legal sovereign" is necessary in every state if legal issues are to be settled with certainty and finality.[14] From one point of view, this necessity derives from the nature of a judicial decision understood as one determin-

12. W. J. Rees, op. cit., p. 509.
13. Ibid., p. 513.
14. E.g. Sir Ernest Barker, op. cit., p. 59: "There *must* exist in the State, as a legal association, a power of final legal adjustment of all legal issues which arise in its ambit." W. J. Rees, op. cit., p. 501: "Laws can only be effectively administered if there exists some final legal authority beyond which there is no further legal appeal. In the absence of such a final legal authority no legal issue could ever be certainly decided, and government would become impossible." J. W. Salmond: *Jurisprudence* (10th ed. by Glanville Williams), App. I, p. 490: "It seems clear that every political society involves the presence of supreme power . . . . For otherwise all power would be subordinate, and this supposition involves the absurdity of a series of superiors and inferiors *ad infinitum*." But contrast John Chipman Gray, *The Nature and Sources of the Law*, p. 79 (quoted by W. Friedmann, *Legal Theory*, 2nd ed., p. 147): "The real rulers of a political society are undiscoverable. They are the persons who dominate over the wills of their fellows. In every political society we find the machinery of government. . . . We have to postulate one ideal entity to which to attach this machinery, but why insist on interposing another entity, that of a sovereign? Nothing seems gained by it, and to introduce it is to place at the threshold of Jurisprudence a very difficult, a purely academic, and an irrelevant question." Gray seems to argue (*a*) that the influential sovereign is undiscoverable; (*b*) that the jurist is needlessly multiplying the entities by postulating a legal sovereign. But (*b*) is not a necessary inference from (*a*).

ing a dispute within the framework of established rules (as distinct from one made according to subjective criteria). The judge called upon to settle a dispute sees law as a system of rules to guide his decision; and such a system needs criteria of validity determining which rules belong to it; it needs a supreme norm, providing directly or indirectly the criteria of validity of all other norms, and not itself open to challenge.[15]

Where a written constitution exists, it is approximately true to say that the constitution itself provides such a supreme norm; and in this sense one may speak of the "legal sovereignty of the constitution." An amendable written constitution will provide criteria for identifying valid amendment. But even so the constitution may not be altogether identified with the supreme norm; for there may be rules for its interpretation which judges accept as binding but which are not prescribed in the constitution. Effectively, therefore, it is the traditional judicial interpretation of the constitution that is the supreme norm.

The absence of a written document does not vastly alter the situation. The supreme norm in English law is provided in

15. Cf. H. Kelsen, *General Theory of Law and State* (1945), p. 124: "The legal order . . . is therefore not a system of norms coördinated to each other, standing, so to speak, side by side on the same level, but a hierarchy of different levels of norms. The unity of these norms is constituted by the fact that the creation of one norm—the lower one —is determined by another—the higher—the creation of which is determined by a still higher norm, and that this *regressus* is terminated by a highest, the basic norm which, being the supreme reason of validity of the whole legal order, constitutes its unity." And Salmond, op. cit., sec. 50: "It is requisite that the law should postulate one or more first causes whose operation is ultimate, and whose authority is underived. In other words, there must be found in every legal system certain ultimate principles from which all others are derived, but which are themselves self-existent. . . . Whence comes the rule that Acts of Parliament have the force of law? This is legally ultimate; its source is historical only, not legal . . . . No Statute lays it down. It is certainly recognised by many precedents, but no precedent can confer authority upon precedent. It must first possess authority before it can confer it. If we enquire as to the number of these ultimate principles, the answer is that a legal system is free to recognise any number of them, but it is not bound to recognise more than one."

part by the maxim "Parliament is sovereign." But this leaves open the question "What is an Act of Parliament?" A judge must be able to refer to a criterion superior in status to an Act, which will establish which rules are Acts. (In a recent article [16] Mr. Geoffrey Marshall has drawn attention to the way in which the interpretation of Parliamentary sovereignty is changing. The critical question, in his view, is: "What is Parliament?" This seems to me to put the problem the wrong way. A judge requires not a definition of the organ Parliament, but a criterion by which to recognize a norm of the type "Act of Parliament." For judicial decisions are reached in the light of norms, not of organs. Mr. Marshall seems to argue that there is a difference in principle between the view typified by Lord Campbell's dictum that the Parliament roll provides conclusive evidence of a statute's validity [17] and the rule in *Harris* v. *Dönges* which implies that a rule issuing from Parliament by a procedure other than legally prescribed is not an Act.[18] But the difference is not that Parliament is held, in the one view, to be above the law, and, in the other, to be subject to law; it lies in the stringency of the criteria which, in the view of the court, a rule must satisfy in order to be deemed an Act of Parliament.)

An Act of Parliament, therefore, is subordinate to the supreme constitutional norm. It is, however, a rule of a special type in that its binding force cannot be challenged on the grounds that it is in *substantial* conflict with any superior norm. (In this respect it differs from an Act of Congress or

16. G. Marshall, "What is Parliament? The Changing Concept of Parliamentary Sovereignty," in *Political Studies,* vol. ii, No. 3 (1954), pp. 193–209.

17. In *Edinburgh and Dalkeith Rly Co.* v. *Wauchope* (1942): "All that a Court of Justice can do is to look to the Parliamentary roll: if from that it should appear that a bill has passed both Houses and received the Royal assent, no Court of Justice can inquire into the mode in which it was introduced into Parliament, nor into what was done previous to its introduction, of what passed in Parliament during its progress in its various stages through both Houses."

18. See G. Marshall, op. cit., for a full discussion of this and other relevant cases.

a statutory instrument.) In view of this peculiarity, it might be useful to ascribe to Acts of Parliament *immediate* supremacy as decisive rules in questions of substance, while the norm from which their validity derives might be termed *ultimately* supreme. This is a reinterpretation of a distinction made by Sir Ernest Barker, who ascribes ultimate sovereignty to the constitution and immediate sovereignty to a supreme legislative organ; but it avoids the awkward asymmetry of his ascription: [19] the word "sovereignty" can scarcely be precisely and unambiguously defined and yet fit with equal comfort both an organ and a norm.[20]

The interpretation of "legal sovereignty" I have offered has, I believe, the advantage that while meeting the judicial need for an ultimate point of reference, it avoids the criticisms directed against the command theory with which the notion of sovereignty has traditionally been associated. Whether law is command is irrelevant. For the judge is interested in the "source" of a law only if by "source" is meant the higher norm from which its validity derives; its legislative origin is a fact to be assessed according to established legal criteria. Further, "legal sovereignty," as I conceive it, need not imply that law is "effective," i.e. generally observed in an actual community. A student might apply ancient legal principles to hypothetical cases; in so doing he would be acting in a way closely parallel to a judge or an English bench, and would find the same necessity for a supreme norm. The same would apply to the student of Utopian or Erewhonian law. Again, "sanction" is non-essential to "sovereignty" in this sense, and the difficulties which arise in applying some legal theories of sovereignty to constitutional and administrative law thus do not arise here.[21]

19. Sir Ernest Barker, op. cit., bk. ii, sec. 5. Sir Ernest recognizes the asymmetry, but considers it "inherent in the nature of the case" (p. 63).
20. Ibid., loc. cit.; and W. J. Rees, op. cit., pp. 516–17.
21. Cf. L. Duguit, *Law in the Modern State*, p. 31: "In those great state services which increase every day . . . the state . . . intervenes in a manner that has to be regulated and ordered by a system of public law. But this system can no longer be based on the theory of sovereignty. It is applied to acts where no trace of power to command is to be found. Of necessity a new system is being built, attached indeed

This notion of the "supreme norm" is essential to any study of the rules governing decisions within a normative order. It is of primary importance for the practising lawyer, and for the jurist. It is also of significance to the administrator, and to the student of administration interested in the legal sources and limitations of administrative discretion rather than in the motives which determine the exercise of discretion.

In historical or sociological studies and those concerned with moral questions the notion of a supreme norm is at most only indirectly relevant. If we ask such questions as "How do laws develop?," "What governs the content of law in this (or any) community?," "What is the role of law in this (or any) society?," [22] we shall need a way of distinguishing law from other modes of social control, but the judicial criterion of validity will not necessarily be an element in such a principle of differentiation. Of course, any description of the life of a community must, to be complete, include an account of its judicial system, and so of the assumptions made by the men whose business it is to reach decisions within this normative order; but the supreme norm will figure in a sociologist's account as a feature of the conceptual apparatus employed by lawyers, not as part of his own.

Similarly, in asking the moral question "What ought laws to be like?" we need to distinguish laws from, say, conventional moral rules. But the principle of differentiation must now be related to those aspects of law which constitute it a distinct problem (e.g. the coercive sanction, or the presumption that most people will obey it), and the judicial criterion of validity will not necessarily figure as part of it.

The questions of political science are both normative and descriptive. If the political scientist is concerned with the state

by close bonds to the old, but founded on an entirely new theory. Modern institutions . . . take their origin not from the theory of sovereignty, but from the notion of public service." (Quoted in H. E. Cohen, *Recent Theories of Sovereignty*, p. 40.) This notion is in no way incompatible with the view of sovereignty I am suggesting.

22. Cf. R. Wollheim's distinction between questions about law which are in Jurisprudence, and those which are not, in "The Nature of Law," in *Political Studies*, vol. ii (1954), pp. 139–40.

as a normative order, the idea of the supreme norm will have the same relevance for him as it has for the lawyer; but if his questions concern men's actual political behaviour, his view of law will be much more that of the sociologist.

III · LEGISLATIVE SOVEREIGNTY

The approach to "legal sovereignty" that I have suggested derives from reflection upon the activities of a judge, for whom the law appears, at any particular moment, as a body of given rules to guide his judgement. For the political scientist, however, law appears in the process of creation; he is concerned with law-making and law-makers; [23] he is interested in "legislative organs," and not merely in "legal norms." I propose accordingly to inquire now whether there is a place in the political scientist's vocabulary for "supreme legislative organ," and what it might mean to attribute "supremacy" in this way. To distinguish the supremacy of a norm from that of a legislative organ, I propose to use "legal sovereignty" for the former and "legislative sovereignty" for the latter.

A political scientist might significantly classify legislative organs in a legal order into superior and inferior (or subordinate), and he might arrange them hierarchically as a sort of reflection of the judge's hierarchy of norms. The judge will deem an Act of Parliament superior in status to a statutory instrument; the political scientist will deem Parliament superior in competence to a minister acting as legislator. But does it follow that the necessity which leads the judge to postulate a supreme norm is paralleled by a similar necessity leading the political scientist to postulate a supreme legislative organ? Such an organ would be omnicompetent, that is, competent to legislate on all matters without the possibility that any of its rules might be invalidated by reason of conflict with

23. Cf. Kelsen, op. cit., p. 39: "If we adopt a static point of view, that is, if we consider the legal order only in its completed form or in a state of rest, then we notice only the norms by which the legal acts are determined. If, on the other hand, we adopt a dynamic outlook, if we consider the process through which the legal order is created and executed, then we see only the law-creating and law-executing acts."

some other rule not of its own making.[24] It might reasonably, therefore, be called "legislative sovereign." But such a sovereign is not logically necessary to a legal order. A constitution might allocate fields of legislative competence between co-ordinate organs, or place certain matters beyond the competence of any organ (e.g. by a Bill of Rights); and in respect of such limitations the constitution might be unamendable. (This qualification is important, since the competence to amend the constitution in these respects would be, on an ultimate analysis, omnicompetence.) In such a case, there would be no omnicompetent organ. On the other hand, one might speak of one organ with supreme competence *in a particular field* or of several such organs; and that would mean that though the rules of such an organ might be invalidated by reason of conflict with the constitution they could not be invalidated through conflict with the rules of any other *organ*. But one cannot say *a priori* that every legal order *must* possess one or more "supreme legislative organs" even in this sense. A constitution that is unamendable (at least in respect of its allocation of fields of competence) might constitute two (or more) organs co-ordinate in the same field, so that a rule enacted by either might set aside a rule of the other. A judge operating such an order would require only some general prescription to show which of conflicting rules enacted by different organs he should deem binding; and this could be met by the principle that in case of conflict a later rule should repeal an earlier. This might be highly inconvenient if the co-ordinate organs were operated by men of different opinions, and competition developed for the latest place. But this could be avoided without making one organ supreme in each field, if, for example, co-ordinate organs were operated by members of one highly disciplined political party, or by men who reached decisions by mutual agreement before legislating. The judge need not then be faced with conflicts any oftener than he is in England.

There is thus neither logical nor practical necessity for a

24. Except for a rule of another organ to which this one had expressly delegated a limited competence to make rules, in a given field, of equal status to its own (e.g. by a "Henry VIII" clause).

legislative sovereign in every state, though there may be states
in which such organs are discoverable. But it should be stressed
that to ascribe "sovereignty" to a legislative organ in either
of the senses just considered is to attribute to it not "power,"
in the sense of ability "to determine the actions of persons
in certain intended ways," [25] but legal capacity or "competence"; it is to say no more than that a judge will set an organ's
rules in a particular kind of relation to the rules of other
organs. It is, indeed, a statement about the formal structure
of a legal order. It does not presuppose any actual ability
possessed by the men acting through an organ to determine
the action of other persons in intended ways. It does not even
require that the action of the judge himself should be so determined; for the person occupying judicial office may disregard the law. Law is normative: it prescribes how a person
must act to function as a judge within the legal order; it does
not predict that he *will* so act.

Yet it is true that law-making is one way of "determining the
actions of persons in certain intended ways." A sociologist seeking to explain behaviour in a community would need to take
its statutes into account, since the knowledge that a particular
rule is a statute may condition the behaviour of those subject
to it. Consequently, legislators can often be regarded as determining the actions of persons in intended ways. But there is
no warrant for automatically transferring "supremacy" as applied to competence to any power deriving from such competence. It is not, for instance, necessarily true that the men
who operate the organ termed "supreme" receive more obedience than those operating a "subordinate" organ. The amend-

---

25. "Power" suffers from a systematic ambiguity. When we refer to "the
    powers of Local Authorities," "Parliament's power to legislate on any
    subject whatsoever," or "legislative powers of Ministers," we mean
    "competence" or "entitlement"—i.e. that they are "empowered" to act
    in this or that way. This is a quite different sense from that implied
    by Mr. Rees's definition: "to determine the actions of persons in cer-
    tain intended ways." The "power" possessed by a Local Authority
    to organize concerts is clearly not power in this second sense. Neither
    is it a species of a "power" genus. Mr. Rees's argument suffers from
    his failure to make this distinction. *Vide* op. cit., p. 511.

ing organ of the U.S.A.—Congress together with three-fourths of the States—is omnicompetent (or very nearly so), yet the Eighteenth Amendment was much less effective than most Acts of Congress.[26] "Supremacy," then, is relevant, when applied to legislative organs, only when a legislative act is considered as a directive to a judge: in all other contexts it is out of place.

IV · The Sovereignty of the State in Its International Aspect

There remains to be considered, before leaving the juristic field, the sense of "sovereignty" as applied in international relations.

It has often been argued that state "sovereignty" is incompatible with international law. The term implies that the state is a self-sufficient legal order; and this must mean that a judge operating that order need seek no further than its own supreme norm. The traditional problem then arising is put by Kelsen in the following terms:

> That the State is sovereign means that the national legal order is an order above which there is no higher order. The only order that could be assumed to be superior to that of the national legal order is the international legal order. The question whether the

26. This is not to suggest that "supreme legislative power" is necessarily meaningless. It could conceivably be used in historical and sociological studies. To attribute it to A might mean (1) that all the laws he made were invariably effective and could not be overturned (which would be the "power" equivalent to "supreme competence"); (2) that they were more generally effective than any one else's (though the use of "superior" rather than "supreme" might accord better with common usage); or (3) that his laws were usually effective, and his conduct was not determined by laws made by others. Examples of (1) probably cannot be found; (2) would be useful only if the effectiveness of laws depended on their sources, which seems improbable; (3) might be true of a few autocrats, but must be unusual. A fourth apparent possibility, viz. that in consequence of A's possessing supreme legislative competence his laws are more likely to be effective, *ceteris paribus*, than rules liable to invalidation, is really only another way of saying that the legal order is effective. None of these senses seems important and I shall not consider them further.

State is sovereign or not thus coincides with the question whether or not international law is an order superior to national law.[27]

A pluralistic position, he argues, is inadmissible: two legal orders with conflicting norms cannot be simultaneously valid for the same territory.[28] The choice lies, therefore, between the primacy of international law, with non-"sovereign" national legal orders deriving validity from it, and the primacy of national law endowing international law with validity to the extent that it recognizes it. But the consequence of the second view is "state solipsism," [29] for now only one State can be held to be sovereign: other legal orders exist for it only as derivatives of itself, either directly or indirectly through its recognition of international law. Kelsen adds:

> It is, however, logically possible that different theorists interpret the world of law by proceeding from the sovereignty of different States. Each theorist may presuppose the sovereignty of his own State, that is to say, he may accept the hypothesis of the primacy of his own national legal order. Then he has to consider the international law which establishes the relations to the legal orders of the other States and these national legal orders as parts of the legal order of his own State, conceived of as a universal legal order. This means that the picture of the world of law would vary according to what State is made the basis of the interpretation. Within each of these systems, erected on the hypothesis of the primacy of national law, one State only is sovereign, but in no two of them would this be the same State.[30]

Kelsen appears to regard this solution as irrefutable but unsatisfactory. I believe, however, that otherwise stated it can throw light on the place of "sovereignty" in international law, and of international law within the structure of "sovereign" national orders.

Within the English legal framework an English judge will take cognizance of international law as a part of English law to the extent that its rules do not conflict with other rules of English law; the national laws of other states will equally

27. Kelsen, op. cit., p. 384.
28. Ibid., p. 363.
29. Ibid., p. 387.
30. Ibid., p. 386.

be subject to the criteria of validity of the English legal order, and in so far as they are recognized by a judge will become parts of that order. In this sense, then, it is true that for the English judge, the only sovereign order is his own. But *mutatis mutandis* the same is true of a French or any other national judge. Each can operate only within his own order, and for him it is self-sufficient. This is again true of the international lawyer. His order is a self-sufficient order embracing national orders as subordinate parts. A given rule may well be valid in one of these orders (national or international) and invalid in another. But there is not here, as Kelsen supposes, any contradiction, and if it involves "State solipsism," this need cause no embarrassment. Kelsen's argument, that "two norms which by their significance contradict and hence logically exclude one another, cannot be simultaneously valid," misses the point. He requires that there shall be only one *objectively valid* legal order. But to ascribe "self-sufficiency" to an order rules out the ascription to it of "validity," which for Kelsen is meaningful only *within* an order. Accordingly, many such systems can logically exist, side by side, and none can claim greater legal validity than another.

It follows, as a corollary to this analysis, that if the international lawyer refers to "sovereign orders," or the national lawyer to "*other* sovereign states," then the sense of the word "sovereign" as here used must be different from that in which either applies the term to his own order, as self-sufficient. He is now using it of a particular type of partial order, analogous to other partial orders, like "corporations," recognized by various legal orders. The precise definition of "a sovereign state" in any given legal order is a question of particular not of general jurisprudence and cannot be settled by reflection upon the nature of legal systems in general.

V · SOVEREIGNTY AS "SUPREME COERCIVE POWER"

"Sovereignty" as "supreme coercive power" is not, I believe, relevant to or meaningful in a normative study of political institutions.

If we begin by defining the state as a coercive order, that

is, as an order maintained by the exercise or threat of physical force, then coercive power is, by definition, necessary to it. If we define it in some other way, then, in Mr. Rees's phrase, coercive power is "causally necessary" to it, if it is to be capable of surviving violent opposition. In either case, the coercive power attributed is a mode of operation, or an institutional framework, within which action is undertaken by whatever men happen to occupy the appropriate offices or to fit the constitutional categories which the order provides.

For instance, to say that in a particular state the coercive power is exercised by the Army is to say that this mode of state action is the proper function of any group which satisfies a set of legal or conventional conditions constituting it the coercive organ of the state, and which acts according to the procedures proper to such an organ (e.g. under orders from the Minister for War or the Commander-in-Chief). In this context only one coercive power is possible in a state: for the term must refer either to a mode of action within the single normative order, or to the organs whose mode of action it is. If several organs employ this mode, they all operate within the same order, and so jointly constitute its coercive power. The state's coercive power may therefore in a sense be divided, but so long as we think of the state as an order there is no point in saying of one or other organ, or of a group of organs, that it is supreme. For "supremacy" implies the possibility of conflict, and a conflict of coercive organs is incompatible with the conception of the state as an order. Thus if conflict does arise between groups qualified to act as coercive organs, then at least one group must be acting otherwise than as a state organ. For example, an army in rebellion against the established Government is not acting as a state organ. (Of course, in any territory at any moment there may well be more than one actual coercive organization: in 1932, besides the coercive forces of the German Republic there existed the Brown Shirts. But the Brown Shirts were not part of the state order.)

One further point—the distinction drawn by Mr. Rees between political orders in which coercive sovereignty is exercised by an institutionally coercive power and those in which it is exercised by a socially coercive power [31] is misleading in two ways. To reserve the term "institutional" for coercive power exercised by professional armies, &c., obscures the fact that where all, or nearly all, the members of a community collectively constitute the coercive organ, their function *is* "institutional." Secondly, inasmuch as Mr. Rees has in mind the classification of political orders, the attribution of "supremacy" to coercive organs is redundant, and nothing is lost by abandoning the term.

In historical and sociological studies, "supreme coercive power" may well be meaningfully used. A statement like: "By 1649, the New Model Army had emerged as the supreme coercive power in England" is not concerned with institutional relations in the English constitutional order, but with power relations between groups of men in a particular territory. In such studies we may well compare the coercive power of one group with that of another. For the historian, Brown Shirts and Communists are as much factors of the 1932 German situation as were the armed forces of the Republic, and he might declare one of them "supreme," in the sense that, had armed conflict developed, it could have defeated its rivals. It is doubtful, however, whether the term is helpful in describing any but the simplest situations. In peaceful conditions we could say that coercive sovereignty is exercised by the coercive organs of the state; and after a civil war we could attribute it to a victorious army that remained united. But it would rather mislead to try to apply it, for example, to Sicily in the days of the Mafia or France in the days of the Maquis.[32] In any case, even if the seat of coercive sovereignty can be located, the possibilities of inquiry opened up are limited. It will give us no way of understanding the importance in the determination of policy of those controlling the coercive organs of the state. Taken collectively, the German army, navy, air force, Gestapo, and S.S. may have constituted the coercive sovereign in Hitler's Germany; but to understand the part played by those controlling these organs in shaping political events we

31. W. J. Rees, op. cit., pp. 509–10, and Section I above.
32. Cf. Lord Bryce, op. cit., p. 63.

have to consider them separately, not collectively, and to examine their mutual relations and rivalries and the power each exercised at any given moment. To lump in problems of this sort is to obscure rather than to illumine.

VI · SOVEREIGNTY AS "THE STRONGEST POLITICAL INFLUENCE"

The first question here concerns the type of discussion to which "influence" may be relevant. I drew a distinction earlier [33] between words of two logical types—"competence" and "power" (as ability to determine the actions of persons in intended ways). "Influence" is a word of the same type as "power." To establish A's *competence* we examine his status in a normative order; to establish his *influence* we must observe how men behave in relation to him, whether for instance they act on his suggestions or consult his wishes. "Influence," and consequently "the strongest political influence," have thus no place in a normative study. It is only in historical or sociological studies that they can be meaningfully employed. It is of course true that a man's status in a normative order may be a source of influence; but the extent of that influence, and, indeed, its very existence, cannot be established by normative study.

Is the search for "an influential sovereign" likely to be fruitful in historical and sociological studies? We must distinguish, first, two senses of "influence": as in (1) "Climate influences vegetation" and (2) "Rasputin's influence over Nicholas II." In (1) no more than "effect" is implied: there is no suggestion of intention; in (2) the effect produced is one intended. When we speak of "the strongest political influence" we are presumably thinking of some group which can shape governmental policy to its own purposes. We are using "influence" therefore in sense (2).

Now we should not say that a group was the "influential sovereign" merely because it had occasionally shaped government policy as it intended. That would multiply sovereigns endlessly

33. Section III above.

and deprive the term of all points. As Mr. Rees has pointed out, "sovereignty" resembles dispositional words in that it implies recurrent capacity to determine policy in intended ways under understood conditions.[34] In seeking an influential sovereign, therefore, we should be seeking a stable dominant influence over a fairly wide range of political issues.

In states of one type a single group (e.g. a ruling class), able decisively to influence policy whenever it operated, could be regarded as such an influence. The value of this approach, however, would depend on the range of common interests from which the group's identity derived and which therefore constituted its field of operation. In states of another type Governments are sensitive to pressures from diverse interests, and political decisions are thus the outcome of an interplay of influences rather than expressions of a single dominant influence. If we seek an influential sovereign here, then, we are likely to be seriously misled; terms like "lobby" and "pressure group" will be much more appropriate analytical concepts.

Sometimes influence is attributed to "the electorate" or "the majority" as one might attribute it to "the bankers" or a "ruling class." This is a mistake. Groups such as "the bankers" or "the ruling class" derive identity from common interest and homogeneity of intention; "the electorate" denotes a state organ. All that electors have in common is the right to vote. Severally, or in groups, they may exercise influence deriving from electoral competence; but there is not therefore one super-influence of the electorate as such. An election is a procedure in which influences are pitted against one other; what emerges is a result, or an "effect," not a new influence. We cannot say of the electorate that it influences policy as it intends; it has no single intention, only a multitude of intentions given different weights by the electoral process. It is no more accurate to assign influential sovereignty to "the majority" (as Mr. Rees seems to do).[35] In any election a certain aggregate of interests is more numerous than another, and this arithmetical relation, corresponding to a recognized legal procedure, is a source of influ-

34. W. J. Rees, op. cit., pp. 514–15.
35. Ibid., pp. 512–13.

ence for the groups concerned. But the aggregates at the next election will be differently constituted; in five elections there will be five majorities; and we should not treat them as though they were one group, *the* majority, exercising a stable dominant influence. Consequently, the inference to be drawn from "The majority (or the electorate) is sovereign" is not that Government is sensitive to a specified influence but that it is sensitive to *all* influences.

Finally, "influential sovereignty" might be applied to an organization, like a Church or a Communist party, which has a policy on all, or most, matters, and is able to make it effective. But here again the policy is not the intention of a group identifiable by common interest, but the result of an interplay of influences within the organization. The internal politics of influential organizations need to be interpreted in terms of pressure groups just as much as do the politics of states. To attribute sovereignty to the Communist party is not to provide an explanation of the changes in Soviet policy since 1917: it is the struggle for power within the party that is the point of interest for the student of Soviet history.

The concept "influential sovereignty" has the disadvantage, then, that it may direct attention to the wrong questions, or conceal the need for inquiry beyond the point where the influential sovereign has been identified.

VII

In this paper I have identified six senses in which "sovereignty" might be meaningfully employed:

(a) to express the supremacy of a norm in a legal hierarchy, as viewed by a lawyer, or by a student concerned with the legal limits of discretion;

(b) in a study of constitutions as normative orders, to refer either to the omnicompetence, or to the supreme competence within its field, of a legislative organ;

(c) to express the self-sufficiency of a legal order from the point of view of a lawyer operating within it;

(d) to refer to a particular kind of partial order, the definition of which may vary from one legal order to another (its utility in this sense being limited to particular jurisprudence);

(e) to express the ability of bodies such as armed forces to defeat all probable rivals;

(f) to express the ability of a sectional interest decisively to influence policy.

The first four senses are relevant to normative studies and cannot be directly utilized in historical or sociological studies without confusion. Each of them is a useful concept in its own field, but they seem to have little in common. The first two share the idea of "supremacy" but in slightly different senses of that word; the third is an expression of totality, rather than supremacy; the fourth implies neither notion. The fifth and sixth senses, unlike the first four, do simply ability to determine other people's conduct; and it is in these senses alone that sovereignty implies supreme power. These two senses may be relevant to historical or sociological studies, and are not relevant to normative studies; their usefulness where they are relevant is limited, for they can be seriously misleading.

In the light of this analysis it would appear to be a mistake to treat "sovereignty" as denoting a genus of which the species can be distinguished by suitable adjectives, and there would seem to be a strong case for giving up so Protean a word.

Kenneth C. Cole

THE THEORY OF THE STATE AS A SOVEREIGN JURISTIC PERSON

The casual student of Western political history encounters sovereignty in a number of guises. In the stage of absolute monarchy, it was a personal endowment of princes; in the stage of democracy, it seems to be a collective endowment of the "nation" or the "people." In the latter period, moreover, a definition of law as the command of a sovereign becomes increasingly popular.

These various contexts for sovereignty will already have suggested the protean possibilities of the general conception, but the student will have had little difficulty in sensing its generally anticonstitutional influence. Even popular sovereignty, which sounds the least dangerous, has had to be offset by opposing institutions in accounting for the relatively high constitutional morality of the democratic system.

From *The American Political Science Review*, vol. XLII, no. 1 (February 1948), pp. 16–31. Reprinted by permission of the author and the publisher.

The writer is deeply indebted to Professor Edward S. Corwin for many suggestions in pursuing a line of inquiry of which the present article is a relatively small part. Documentation in a field as heavily fought over as "sovereignty" is likely to be both superfluous and embarrassing in a short article. One can hardly help regurgitating much that has already been adequately compiled, but he can hardly hope to credit all contributions to his own thinking. There is, however, one short but beautifully penetrating discussion to which acknowledgment must be made at all costs. That is the well known Sabine and Shepard Introduction to Krabbe's *The Modern Idea of the State* (New York, 1927).

While, therefore, it is not surprising to find sovereignty again (and in a still different guise) when we examine the leading conceptions of American public law, one well may marvel to find it accorded a key position among them. For, strange to say, the sovereignty of the *state* is widely accepted as the cornerstone of a legal edifice which the lawyers themselves appear to have laid. Absolutism of some sort seems to have been accepted by those one would expect to find least disposed to concede it. But sovereignty in the hands of the lawyers is absolute in form only. They have succeeded in concocting a doctrine which appears to concede everything to the politically mighty of the earth without clearly conceding much of anything to anyone.

In accomplishing this minor miracle, some confusion has been inevitable. In fact, the entire argument seems designed to deny in the conclusion what has been stated in the premise without appearing to do so. We start with a profound obeisance to a supreme will which is supposed to account for all of the law, but apparently we do not have to stay on our knees, because the wielder of this absolute power turns out itself to be in some sense the creature of law, and hence no more awesome to the initiated than the genii to Aladdin with his marvellous lamp.

If we have thus made the juristic theory sound a little like something out of the *Arabian Nights,* it is certainly not because we wish to minimize it as a mere exercise in dialectics undertaken as an exhibition of professional virtuosity. Far from it. The initial idolization of the state was to some extent forced upon the lawyers by the pressure of historical events which made it seem discreet to concede the full lawmaking potential of some political will. Moreover, despite the legally grotesque character of the concession, sovereignty has managed to acquire a certain respectability among middle-of-the-road jurists, due in large part to the far-fetched alternatives proposed by its most articulate opponents. Obviously, these are circumstances which must be inquired into more closely.

The first and clearest necessity which the critical events of the sixteenth century pointed to was that of shifting to a particularist system of maintaining order. During the Middle Ages, there had been an attempt to establish a universal order under the aegis of the Christian faith and upon the foundation of a common European tradition reaching back to the twin classical models of Greece and Rome. This order had never worked to insure the sort of peace required for development of the economic arts of trade and commerce. Sporadic violence was chronic in the entire system. When, finally, the schism within the religious community occurred, it became evident that the old order was doomed. The only alternative was to accept the dismembered parts as self-sufficient units within which to rehabilitate strong government.

The principle of sovereignty was the great ideological weapon used by the nation-states in accomplishing it. Of course there were other weapons as well. Nationalism in particular was a sentiment much played upon in the formation of these states. So was personal loyalty to certain royal houses. But sovereignty, the more abstract expression of particularism in political affairs, proved much stronger in the long run. Sovereignty, as exemplified in the various indepenent governments, came deliberately to create nationalism instead of building upon it; and personal loyalty to rulers gave way to loyalty to the state as an impersonal entity maintaining the entire social structure by which the individual enjoyed the good things of life.

There is a sense, therefore, in which sovereignty may be said to have provided a shelter necessary for the preservation of Western civilization after the religious wars. On the other hand, however, we must emphasize that the kind of "sovereignty" called for on this account does not by any means measure up to the pretensions of the sovereignty which actually came to be claimed by the nation-states. What each sovereign could reasonably claim as a prerequisite for effective local government was a finality of decision on all issues arising within his realm. This was because the responsibility for maintaining order could not be discharged without insulating the system of law enforcement within the state from all outside control. Hence the device of forbidding appeals from national courts to any foreign or international tribunals may be justified on this basis.

But insulation of the nation-state in the matter of law *en-*

forcement is a very different thing from insulation as respects law itself. The maintenance of order on a particularist basis requires that local interpretation of general law be final; it does not require a denial of the existence of a general law. If we want an explanation for this last increment of national isolation, we must look to a somewhat different aspect of nation-state building.

This process involved the use of force against other states even more prominently than it involved the use of force internally. There have been no hermit states in the modern world. Commercial contacts between states have always been maintained, and were even greatly intensified as the state system became fixed in its present pattern. The lack of a common superior has accordingly meant that war had to be contemplated as the principal business of states, and a prime factor in determining their internal organization.

War, in turn, demands mobility on the part of the successful contestant. It must be able to command the instant services of all within its borders, and it must—especially as affects international relations—be in a position to adopt and change its policies without being hampered by the necessity of justifying these changes in terms of any general or universal law. Hence a definition of law which credits some determinate political agency with absolute and exclusive law-making authority is the ideal solution of the problem for the nation-state viewed as a war-making association.

This was not, however, the only historical pressure to which the lawyers were subjected on behalf of sovereignty. Quite apart from the growth of nationalistic particularism, other events have pointed in the same general direction. Thus the rate of social change since the Industrial Revolution has been tremendously increased. Established judicial techniques of law-declaring proved inadequate to keep the law abreast of the times. "Legislation" had to be relied upon to an ever-increasing extent, and this fact encouraged a construction of law in terms of the active policy-making will which is so prominent a feature of this method.[1]

1. The writer here records his obligation to Dean Pound for a particularly stimulating lecture.

To be sure, it was not really necessary to renounce the old-fashioned conception of law in order to achieve sufficient flexibility for the purpose in hand. The legislative function *might* have been construed simply as a sphere of relatively wide rule-making discretion under a constitutional law anchored (however broadly) in precedent. But it was easier to swim with the tide of the other events already mentioned. So there was a tendency to resolve the problem of legal change by parting with the anchor instead of "playing out more rope": sovereignty was uncritically accepted as a demonstration that the fact of power automatically generates law in each disparate manifestation of will. In short, the troublesome old problem of a legal definition of authority can be side-stepped by turning to an authoritarian definition of law.   .

Nothing is clearer in the aftermath of this bit of legerdemain than that the Banquo's ghost of traditional law cannot be so easily laid. Yet, in accounting for the extraordinary vogue of sovereignty, it is well to bear in mind that the necessity for more and more government played an important part. Since sufficient elbow-room was not afforded government by historical judicial procedures for assuring continuity of principle, it was argued that continuity itself was outmoded. The modern state leviathan was thus given a socially plausible excuse to ignore traditional conceptions of legality by the economic dynamism of the eighteenth and nineteenth centuries.

Yet it is entirely unlikely that sovereignty could have achieved the standing of a thoroughly respectable doctrine in the schools of legal and political philosophy without something more than the pressure of historical events. And the fact is that it did become a respectable doctrine—due largely, as was said above, to the mistakes of its most prominent opponents. The latter, in attacking sovereignty on behalf of a variety of interests, have usually either overlooked the truly vulnerable aspect of the doctrine or proposed palpably unacceptable alternatives. More important, they have often added many to the ranks of the defenders who should never have been there.

The ultra-conservative "right-wing" attack on sovereignty has been peculiarly inept considering the practicality of the modern age. The members of this group have persisted in identifying law with rules which are abstractly right or just. This is substantially the old natural law position—almost bound to represent a lost cause in the face of modern empiricism which definitely discourages reliance upon the ideal in the definition of anything as "fact." Over against such an approach, the defender of sovereignty has accordingly had a ridiculously easy victory. He merely insists that he is distinguishing "what is" from what "ought to be" when he employs a postulated sovereign will as the mark of the former in matters of law.

Of course natural law is not the only (or even the proper) recourse for those conservatives who want to take account of the affinity between law and morals. The institutionalization of law may be recognized, not in a body of rules guaranteed to be right in themselves, but in certain characteristic procedures providing an appropriate setting for the determination of just rules. This is the line proper for moderate conservatives or traditionalists in jurisprudence; but it is a line much more distinctly traced in the practices and attitudes of lawyers than in their theory. Indeed, in the matter of theory, the traditionalists have been notoriously weak—another reason, incidentally, why sovereignty has been enabled to gain a "foothold" in their thinking.

So much, then, for the manner in which the conservatives have handled (or mishandled) the issue of sovereignty. The various left-wing attacks on the doctrine are more interesting. They all accept the empirical hypothesis with a vengeance, since their basic criticism of sovereignty is precisely that it does not sufficiently exclude the ideal in the definition of law.

The prevailing socialist view of the state rejects sovereignty as a spurious attempt to identify law with a national or universal will, whereas (it holds) both law and the state are merely instruments of the exploiting class. Thus, while the socialists recognize the arbitrariness of sovereignty clearly enough, they see no way of reclaiming law from this arbitrariness short of the millennium of the classless society. In the meantime, the best that they can suggest is the substitution of one kind of arbitrariness for another. The dictatorship of the proletariat

is to take the place of the *bourgeois* legal order,[2] and, as between the avowed arbitrariness of dictatorship and the (at least
disguised) arbitrariness of sovereignty, who can blame the con-
stitutionalist for choosing the latter?

The so-called pluralists cannot be characterized as readily as
the socialists because they do not constitute a sect. In the main,
however, their attack on sovereignty has been in behalf of
corporate groups within the state which are regarded as ful-
filling social functions coördinate with those served by the
latter. They deny, accordingly, that the existence of churches
and trade unions (to mention only two prominent examples of
such associations) is contingent on the will of the state as the
theory of sovereignty seems to require.

There is much to be said for the pluralist point of view. The
state institution or association is certainly not entitled to claim
any such moral superiority over other groups as is assumed by
the idealist philosophers, for example. But the pluralists have
not generally distinguished between reducing the state to the
level of other associations in the community and reducing the
law of the state to the level of a competing system along with
the "laws" of other groups. Hence, in eliminating sovereignty
they leave us with no legal basis for coördinating the activities
of all groups—a situation which undermines the basis for maintaining ordered relationships within our present national communities.[3]

Here again, the ineptitude of the attack on sovereignty has
brought many to its defense who would not otherwise have
taken the field. The answer to pluralism is monism; and all
monism has to stand for to constitute an effective answer is the
necessity for some integrating, unifying principle in the legal
community—some judicial organ entitled to determine the competence of all other organs. Monists, therefore, while frequently
classified as defenders of state sovereignty, may actually be
defending it only as the symbol for order, logic, symmetry in

2. Rudolph Schlesinger, *Soviet Legal Theory* (New York, 1945), pp. 32.
   33, mentions the confusion in Soviet jurisprudence on this point.
3. Cf. Paul Ward, *Sovereignty* (London, 1928), pp. 82–124. The author,
   however, goes on to discuss Duguit as a pluralist, which is a common
   error.

legal arrangement—a far cry from the arbitrariness of decision which recognition of will as the symbol for law invites.

Sovereignty has been attacked also from still a different angle by jurists employing the sociological approach. The sociological approach to law represents an attempt to define the legal order as essentially non-normative, i.e., as a system of scientifically verifiable conclusions derived from an objective survey of social needs or "interests." Sovereignty, of course, stands most conspicuously in the way of any such construction of law because the sovereign is supposed to create law "out of thin air," as it were, by the unilateral imposition of his supreme will on the subordinate wills of his subjects.

Now the sociological approach has the great merit of disclosing the vicious subjectivity of any theory of law which looks to the content of determinate wills for its basic rules. Its equally great defect, however, lies in the assumption that the only way to get away from this bad subjectivity is to turn to the physical sciences as the appropriate model for juristic science. Thus the sociological jurist wants the judge to derive his rules for human conduct from observation of the facts in the same way that the laboratory technician formulates scientific laws. All of which means that the kind of objectivity appropriate to the physical sciences is being assigned to the moral sciences—under the illusion, no doubt, that the legal order can be turned into an extensive project of "social engineering."

Unfortunately for such "scientists," it has not been difficult to demonstrate that this optimism is simply naïve. Legal rules are not like scientific conclusions, nor are judges properly social engineers. Somehow choices, oughts, values, are registered in the law, and if these are not in the facts which the judge takes as his materials for decision, he must put them in himself. The sociological jurist may deplore any recognition of this element as metaphysical, but the metaphysic he refuses admission at the front door is always surreptitiously introduced at the back door.[4] This inevitably puts the orthodox defender of sovereignty in a relatively favorable position: he can at least say

4. This is the point, if not the exact language, of Harold Laski in his introduction to Leon Duguit, *Law in the Modern State* (New York, 1919), p. xxvii.

that he does not mask the realities of the situation behind a façade of science. So law as the command of the sovereign has not suffered unduly at the hands of the sociologist.

Then there is another, and more sophisticated, application of scientific method to the problem of law which must be considered. The legal realists do not make the mistake of identifying the legal order with scientific principles of social engineering. They err in the opposite direction by reducing the legal order to the positively conditioned behavior of judges. This position derives by degrees from one aspect of Austin's emphasis upon enforceability as the test of law. His principal thesis, no doubt, is that the over-all enforceability of the rules prescribed by a given political superior confers a title to authority upon him which lawyers must use in assigning a uniform validity to *all* his commands. But he also defines legal obligation in terms of the actual or factual liability of the individual subject of law to some sanction in the event of disobedience. This opens up the possibility of defining law as what happens instead of what ought to happen according to formal rules. Law has now become a reflex of an environment which includes such things as the state of the judicial digestion as well as (and perhaps even more prominently than) the verbalizations of the law books. In this view, of course, sovereignty becomes a completely empty proposition, because no generalizations (least of all those in which legislative commands are couched) can be rationally responsible for the law.

On the other hand, it would be hard to imagine a more striking example of "throwing the baby out with the bath," since there is really no law left when the realists finish insulating it from the sovereign.[5] Only a mass of disconnected judgments, variously induced in a multitude of magistrates by processes which only psychoanalysts can trace, remains of an edifice which even the advocates of sovereignty left with a kind of integrity based on the assumption that the content of the sovereign will could have some universal meaning for the judges.

5. Benjamin Cardozo makes this point very neatly in *The Nature of the Judicial Process* (New Haven, 1921), p. 126. See also Felix Cohen, *Ethical Systems and Legal Ideals* (Camden, 1933), pp. 230–249, for a good technical appraisal.

Considering the futility of these various attacks on sovereignty, it can be understood why most lawyers have felt committed to the doctrine even though uncomfortably aware of some of its anomalies. They were aware, for example, that the doctrine in the hands of John Austin had two outstanding defects. In the first place, it could not be applied universally because a single organ of government was not everywhere in a position to remake the law at will. In the second place, they felt that the definition of law as commands, imposed by some flesh and blood individual or group of individuals upon everyone else, was far too crude an expression of the part played by coercion in the legal order.

So the juristic theory of the state [6] proposed to remedy these defects by vesting sovereignty in the whole state instead of in a single organ of government, and by construing the state as an abstract impersonal entity entirely distinct from any flesh and blood individuals who might from time to time act for it. The state, in short, is a purely juristic person capable of acting only through agents or representatives.

Now it will be obvious at once that this conception has only formal significance as applied to countries like Britain where the supreme legal authority of one organ of government *is* recognized. Of course, we may say, if we like, that Parliament is only an agent of the sovereign British state instead of being (as Austin maintained) itself sovereign. But if we assume (as the juristic theory has to assume) that this agent is entitled to invoke the name of the state for anything it does, the distinction is without substantial difference. As much arbitrariness would be implicit in the state's sovereignty as in any other kind of sovereignty.

We turn, therefore, to the application of the juristic theory to those situations where legal authority is not concentrated in any one organ or agency. Here the theory postulates that the conditions of agency are determined by "the law" instead of by

6. The indebtedness of W. W. Willoughby to Laband and Jellinek is nowhere more clearly expressed than by Willoughby himself. But since the latter's application of the theory to American public law instances its most prominent "working," what follows turns directly on *The Fundamental Concepts of Public Law* (New York, 1924).

the agent. In other words, it is not simply the fact that a designated agent has acted in the name of the state which warrants
us in assuming that the will of the state is being expressed. He
must have acted in accordance with certain rules which set real
limits or bounds to his authority. And the question, therefore,
becomes: Whence comes this highly important law?

The sovereign, of course, cannot be relied upon for much
help at this point. Strictly speaking, we cannot even identify
the sovereign until we have the rules in question, because it is
only the kind of acts which are specified in the rules that can
be attributed to him. And it would be even more incongruous
to credit the (as yet unidentified, and in any event, completely
abstract) sovereign with the capacity to make and unmake
agents and their powers after the fashion of a flesh and blood
ruler.

The juristic theory (sad to say) never does get around the first
objection. But it makes a valiant effort to answer the second
by recourse to the analogy of the corporation. The corporation,
as an institution of private law, is usually described as a juristic
person whose title to existence is conferred upon it by the state
in the form of a charter setting forth the purposes for which it
was created, the method of designating its officers or agents, and
the extent of their various powers. Only if agents are selected
in the manner prescribed by the charter, and only if they
act within the powers assigned to them, are their acts recognized by the courts as expressing the will of the corporation.

When the state is regarded as a corporation, to be sure, its
charter must be regarded as either a spontaneous crystallization
of the naked power relations in the community or an equally
spontaneous manifestation of the Divine Spirit. But, however
vague and fanciful its explanation for the genesis of the state
as corporation, the theory does avoid the even more fanciful
notion that the abstract will of the corporation can alter the
course of its own existence. It simply holds that the charter em-
braces the whole life potentiality of the state as of the corporation. No change is possible in any fundamental sense because
the terms of the charter are conclusive as to both the method

and content of whatever deviation from the initial course is legally possible.

In commenting on this "state as corporation" version of sovereignty, we must first note that the possibility of its fruitful application is opened up only where and when written constitutions like our own have been adopted. But where this has been done, the theory undoubtedly has a certain plausibility. The constitution becomes the charter of the state-corporation which fixes the basic conditions for the exercise of all legal power. The courts enforce its provisions, applying the corporation doctrine of *ultra vires,* with the result that they need recognize no act as official in the slightest degree if either the title of the actor, or the nature of the particular act, fails to coincide with a judicial reading of constitutional provisions. A remarkable degree of judicial control may thus be attained while paying at least lip service to the principle of sovereignty.

We may not infer that this has been accomplished—even in times of relative social stability—without considerable strain on the dialectics of constitutional law. But these (for our present purposes minor) defects may be put to one side in order to concentrate on the main issue. At the moment, we are concerned to emphasize again that the theory is totally incapable of accounting for fundamental legal change. And this is the more distressing because, as a theory of sovereignty, it is supposed to supply us with some definite authority capable of moving the law whither its will listeth.

When the question is on amendment of the constitution, therefore, advocates of the theory are bound to flounder most painfully. They intensely dislike to confess that no existing agency, organ, or procedure under the constitution can be legally capable of breaking its bonds. On the other hand, it is equally evident that no one can do anything (even quasi-officially) in a legal order which is regarded as a mere projection of a supreme will other than what that will has decreed in its first and last testament.

Naturally, this dilemma is purely academic so long as the constitution *happens* to provide for a process of amendment, which *happens* to be unqualified in scope, and which process *happens* to remain tolerably satisfactory to the politically self-conscious elements in the community. But all these circumstances must occur if the theory is to prove viable. When they do not, constitutional exegesis is without guide posts.

As a matter of *fact,* most of the expositors of a constitutional theory based on the juristic-person idea have been disposed to indulge the sovereignty implications of their hypothesis at the expense of its apparatus of corporate personality. Instead of continuing to view the state as corporation, they look for the state as creator of the corporation. In other words, "state" must now be translated into concrete terms. It becomes a synonym for the "people," or the individual authors of the constitution, or, perhaps, the political organ of which the authors of the document were members when the constitution was put in force.

The first of these possibilities is probably the least satisfactory from the standpoint of the lawyer. Nothing whatever can be made out of a popular will as a dynamic contributor to law without assuming very elaborate rules of organization. The "people" are certainly less able to constitute anything, without first being constituted by something, than any other collective entity we can think of. So the fact that the framers of the document may have presumed to speak in the name of the people is of precious little significance in designating a sovereign.

Let us turn, then, to the authors of the constitution themselves. Are they to be regarded as sovereign? Presumably not (at least for purposes of amending the document), for they can hardly avoid the vicissitudes of old age and death. Metaphorical references to the "Fathers" of the constitution are quite clearly irrelevant for law at this point.

On the whole, therefore, the most attractive stop-gap candidate for sovereignty of those mentioned above is the third, i.e., the *organ* originally employed to draft the constitution. This combines the idea of authorship of the authoritative document with continuing existence as an institution. And when, as in the United States, the actual framing of constitutions has frequently been entrusted to assemblages called constitutional conventions, the idea has a peculiar attractiveness. We therefore often do find some significant conclusions drawn from such a premise. For example, it is sometimes asserted that a constitutional convention, once assembled, is in fact sovereign and may thereupon amend the existing constitution out of all recognition. Its predecessor made the constitution by legislative act, and, since no sovereign will may bind itself, an entirely new dispensation may be forthcoming in this fashion.

But a constitutional convention is not really a very convincing candidate for sovereignty either. It assembles only on special call by some other organ of government. Moreover, both the agency which convokes conventions and the conventions themselves have pretty generally regarded the finished product as subject to popular ratification. Accordingly, the attribution of sovereignty to a constitutional convention in our public law is really much more equivocal than the attribution of sovereignty to Parliament in the law of England. Indeed, refugees from the juristic theory should have known better than to try Austin's formula on the American situation, for the complexities of that situation furnished one of the principal inducements to abandon Austin in favor of the juristic theory.

As illustrated in American legal literature, therefore, this last-minute scramble to locate some sovereign will capable of amending the constitution without regard to its terms has not been particularly edifying. Nor have less ambitious efforts to graft provisos upon the written word of the documentary sovereign been any more convincing. A great deal of learning has been wasted, for example, on the question whether the will of the sovereign may be made consistent with the use of a process of amendment which he did not specify, or the use of a different one than he specified, or even the use of a specified process to do something expressly excluded in the grant of the amending power.

Actually, of course, it is simply fatuous to try to make the hypostasized will of a sovereign incorporate a license to overreach that will in any respect. It is far better to recognize frankly that there is no will to which we can appeal at this point. The question is really whether the living custom of the constitution, as ingested by the common law, is consistent with as much variation upon the methods laid down in the document as is proposed. Constitutional change involves a *process* which gains nothing by being referred to the will of anyone. And this conclusion—which we have come to after having run the juristic theory to the ground as it were—suggests some parting observations on the pretensions of all theories of sovereignty.

Stripped to its bare essentials, the exercise of power must always be considered from the standpoint of law as the exercise of a right by some entity defined by law. If this entity is a single human being, the rules defining his legal personality are very simple. It suffices usually to name him, whereupon the extent of his rights becomes the practical measure of the relative importance of law and will in the exercise of power. It is conceivable, moreover, that the authority given him by law may be unlimited—even to the point of determining his own successor, and without any special stipulations as to how his will is to be evidenced. This would amount to a practical abdication of law in favor of will and explains why the latter should, under such extreme circumstances, be accepted as a substitute for the former.

But it does not explain why, under conditions far removed from personal absolutism, lawyers should ever have accepted will as a substitute for law—as in the various modern theories of sovereignty. Why should they, in fact, have conceded that Austin's definition of law derived any support from democratic conditions—even where, as in England, one organ of government is of paramount importance?

One answer to this is fairly clear. Decisions of such far-reaching effect as were ever made by the most nearly absolute monarch are now frequently reached in and through an organ of government like the British Parliament. It is a convenient figure of speech to say that such an organ is exercising legally absolute authority. Ergo, the law is simply recognizing a different legal person (and will) as supreme than it did in the case of unlimited monarchy.

It would seem, however, that lawyers should have no excuse for regarding this as more than a metaphor. For (except where the influence of the juristic theory has been felt) the law is careful *not* to assign legal personality to the collective entities called parliaments or congresses. Technically speaking, therefore, they do not exercise any legal authority whatever. Legal authority is being exercised in very small increments by a large number of natural persons as they collaborate in a legally defined process of reaching decisions which the courts accept as conclusive. From this point of view, accordingly, the supremacy of an organ of government which has no separate legal personality should never be translated into the supremacy of any will.

But it is at this point that Austin manages to confuse the issue. He assumed for his sovereign an essentially non-legal personality. Any sociological entity which could be identified as exerting effective force or power in the community could also be treated as supreme for law. The sovereign is above the law, not in the law. He has neither legal rights nor legal duties. Hence no legal personality need be assigned him.

The technical fallacy in this conceptualization is easy to point out: Austin's sovereign is as much in need of accepted marks of identification for law as any of his subjects. He does not make himself intelligible *to* the law from above, as it were, any more automatically than they make themselves intelligible *in* the law from below. Rules of law must be equally presupposed in both cases identifying the actors in the legal drama. The fact that no specific legal personality is assigned an entity must mean that it can have no capacity to determine any legal relations.

Austin's insistence, then, that the sovereign needs no legal personality in the same sense in which the subject needs a legal personality is the entering wedge for a specious defense of the modern doctrine of sovereignty. Once given this point, the advocate can use many cases in which the law recognizes the finality of a defined process of decision as evidence that will is its foundation as well under democratic conditions as under autocratic conditions. Certainly no such inference should be drawn. The Austinian manipulation of legal personality is thoroughly corrupt, and we must not allow it to obscure

the fact that law, in the shape of a complex of highly significant procedural rules, always bulks sufficiently large in the
democratic *milieu* to distinguish this situation radically from
personal dictatorship. Sovereignty is progressively more and
more absurd as the rules which must be presupposed in order
to identify the sovereign become more complex.

There are, to be sure, various other ways of encouraging
arbitrariness in government than the conceptualizations of
the Austinians and the neo-Austinians. Indeed, these conceptualizations do not operate uniformly to this end, nor are
they necessarily more effective than certain others. It is clear,
for example, that the neo-Austinian device of the juristic
theory (to which most of the foregoing discussion has been
devoted) may even operate "in reverse," as it were, by clamp-
ing a much more rigid vise on political experimentation than
the method of the common law. Yet there is an unpredictable
explosiveness inherent in even the caged sovereign will of the
state which makes it a highly dubious medium for the legal
institution—even if it would not have suited Hitler.

Austin's unglossed teaching comes considerably closer to
the specifications for dictatorship, yet it is significant that
apologists for the Third Reich were not satisfied with the
postulate of a factually dominant will. They drew heavily on
the mystic general will of Rousseau—minus the mechanics of
the electoral process—to endow the Leader with a title to
absolute power.

Again, it is far from clear that the will symbolism for law
(however formulated) is the only constitutionally vicious influence to be guarded against. Those modern positivists who
have turned to the model of the natural sciences for their
construction of law are in the vanguard of a movement which
is palpably enervating from the standpoint of constitutional
ethics. And the Vienna School, intent on establishing a *tertium
quid* for law which will emancipate it from both the physical
and the moral sciences, is scarcely less enervating, although
this is not the place to pursue that argument farther.

When all is said and done, however, it is the will symbolism
in one or other of its orthodox sovereignty versions which

still requires our most vigilant housekeeping attention. This is the reason for concentrating on the concrete organ and the abstract state as candidates for that mythical political god-head in which power becomes *de jure* without benefit of law. And we ought to note in closing, no doubt, the ultimate dependence of all imperative theories of law upon the metaphysics of revealed religion—a model, however, which the secular institution should be under no obligation to follow. Certainly it need not follow for want of a substitute symbolism. "Reason" is universal by definition, and if we want to emphasize the transcendent quality of the values in the legal order, reason is a far safer symbol than will—no matter how mystic a personality is invoked as its *träger*. And if we want to emphasize those values realized in the satisfaction of mundane "wants" or "interests," we have only to rescue "custom" from the close embrace of the positivists in order to convey a sense of the gradual absorption of these values into the corpus of the law without in any way suggesting a deterministic bias. And if we want to emphasize both of these features of the legal order, there is always Coke's "artificial reason of the law," which does not suffer unduly by comparison with more "enlightened" formulae of modern legal science.

four

THE
BEHAVIORALIST
APPROACH

Karl W. Deutsch

THE CONCENTRATION OF DECISIONS: SOVEREIGNTY AND VULNERABILITY IN POLITICAL SYSTEMS

Any major decision system is likely to include a considerable number of feedback processes and of the corresponding loop patterns of communication channels. Each of these feedback loops may contain one or several critical stages or *decision points,* at which either the behavior of the feedback can be changed or at which the behavior of one feedback loop produces a critical change in the behavior of another. Points at which feedbacks of stored information from memory facilities interact with feedback processes based on current outside information are decision points of this kind.

The set of important decision points in a system may show a lower or higher degree of concentration, and perhaps of hierarchy. If all important decisions are concentrated at one point, and if decisions made at that point tend to govern or override all decisions made elsewhere in the system, the performance of the system may resemble the situation of concentrated sovereignty, familiar from the absolute monarchies of seventeenth- and eighteenth-century Europe.

The concentration of decisions in such a system corresponds to some extent to the concentration of symbols of legitimacy, and the imputation of responsibility to the individual princes, ministers, or rulers. If the political system follows a series of decisions that leads to disaster, the actions or omissions of these few persons tend to be viewed as its causes.

An even more essential characteristic of sovereignty is the absence of any recognized input channel of controlling or over-riding information from outside the system. In the theory of sovereignty no outside organizations, as well as no outside preferences or values, may be permitted to interfere with the working out of the internal decision probabilities of the system.

Finally, the concentration of all overriding decisions at a single point implies that no autonomous subsystem is permitted to function within the larger political organization, at least not with any degree of autonomy sufficient to modify or override the decisions made at the top.

Although these principles of organization were practiced by the absolute monarchies of Europe from the days of Machiavelli to those of Frederick of Prussia, they have been inherited to a large extent by the modern unitary state. To be sure, in such states the concentrated sovereignty inherited from absolute monarchs may be distributed among a small number of high-level institutions according to some pattern of constitutional arrangements. In practice, however, most of the important decisions still appear to be highly concentrated. A few dozen ministers, officials, and judges and, perhaps, a few hundred legislators seem to be holding among them the entire concentrated power of the state. According to widespread belief, this small circle of decision-makers is, or ought to be, impervious to all outside influences, particularly to influences from abroad, as well as highly resistant to special regional or sectional pressures.

The decisions of such a political system are believed to be "ultimate" or "final," in the sense that there is no further instrumentality for modifying or changing them after they have reached a particular stage, point or institution in the system. Each of these points or institutions functions in the manner of a court of last resort for the class of decisions entrusted to it, and is held to have the power of *"ultimacy"* or *finality* in respect to them. Even though this power of ultimacy is no longer concentrated in the hands of a single person, as it was in the days of absolute monarchy, it is still concentrated in what looks like a small and easily identifiable region, and it is believed to inhere in the state as a whole.

Despite its seeming plausibility, this scheme may represent a highly imperfect description of the actual state of affairs. Studies of domestic politics may show that the actual workings of the decision-making process are far more impersonal; that the resulting decisions may often be unpredicted and may even seem unpredictable; and that all attempts to allocate responsibility for major decisions to particular individuals may end up in a maze of alibis, in which each decision-maker may sincerely believe and plausibly show that he did only what he had to do in the circumstances of the time. In the field of political decisions concerning war and peace, both the debate about the guilt for World War I and the war-crimes trials after World War II have demonstrated the degree of complexity and impersonality to be found in present-day political decisions systems.

Overestimating the concentration of decisions at a single point is apt to lead to an overestimation of the importance of particular offices or persons. If only Minister X could be converted or assassinated, if only the "right man" could be put into Ministry Y—so runs the argument—then soon all would be well, or at least the worst could be prevented. Usually such notions prove to be mistaken, both because the social setting may produce new officeholders very similar to the former incumbent and because the actual range of discretion permitted to each particular office or decision-maker may prove much smaller than imagined.

The same consideration may well apply to the problem of estimating the vulnerability of governments to the destruction of crucial points or institutions in the decision system by aerial bombardment, or to infiltration by adherents of a particular ideology or agents of a foreign power. The higher the actual degree of concentration of decisions, the greater the actual degree of vulnerability is apt to be; and the greater the imagined degree of such concentration, the greater may be the fear of infiltration or destruction.

Realistic estimates of the actual situation can be made only on the basis of a careful mapping out of the distribution and configuration of decision points, the extent of their mutual support and control, and the presence or absence of reserve facilities for taking over the functions of decision points and partial decision systems that have been temporarily incapacitated or destroyed. A not wholly dissimilar problem has long existed in a field seemingly far removed from politics. Problems of damage control in battleships has involved precisely such questions as to how a ship is to continue in operation after its captain has been lost or its bridge destroyed or its steering assembly incapacitated. A study of the "damage-control characteristics" of a given political system might well prove worth undertaking in our atomic age.

The naïve assumption of concentrated sovereignty may even be more misleading in international politics. The emphasis on sovereignty may tend to divert attention from the very real limits that constrain the decisions of even the most powerful nations. No state is omnipotent or disposes of unlimited resources, nor can any government expect unlimited sacrifices from its population. If we are to analyze the actual working of political autonomy under these conditions, it may be useful to distinguish three categories:

1. *Limit probabilities,* that is, the probability that the behavior of the government, or state, will run into a physical, social, economic, or military limit, such as overwhelming resistance, external force, or inner difficulties.

2. *Limit signals,* that is, signals, data, or information announcing the approaching or the presence of such a physical or social limit. Such limit signals must be received by the decision system, interpreted, and applied to the control of its further behavior in a more or less efficient manner.

3. *Limit images,* that is, images of such physical or social limits, of their configurations, and of the probability of meet-

ing them under particular conditions. To be effective, such images would have to be stored in the memory facilities of the system, as well as recalled and fed back into the control of its behavior. Such limit images may, of course, be elaborate or crude, precise or vague, realistic or misleading; and they may or may not be used effectively by the system.

Effective behavior on the part of any autonomous organization requires the organization to remain within its limits of action or survival, and thus to satisfy its limit probabilities through the use of limit signals and limit images. Sovereign states face the same task in this respect as do other autonomous organizations, but they face it with an added difficulty. While their behavior is subject to limits and limit probabilities, and while they usually receive some limit signals, *sovereign states as a rule exclude limit images.* They teach their citizens, as well as many of their lawmakers and officials, to reject as unreal, or at least as illegitimate, all constraints or limits upon their own decisions or upon the behavior of their country. In addition to the absence of institutionalized limit images, sovereign states may also be endangered by the low status, both in terms of prestige and of treatment in communication, of such limit signals as they actually may receive. Facilities for the reception, treatment, and use of limit signals may be extremely deficient, and may leave the government in danger of running sometimes head on into some actual limit to its power . . .

five

THE
JURISTIC
POSITION

Hans Kelsen

SOVEREIGNTY AND
INTERNATIONAL LAW

The term "sovereignty," while denoting one of the most important concepts of the theory of national and international law, has a variety of meanings, a fact that causes regrettable confusion in this theory. The most current of these meanings is, according to the etymological origin of the term that derives from the Latin *superanus,* that of a special quality of the state, the quality of being a supreme power or supreme order of human behavior. There are, however, authors who, in spite of their assertion that sovereignty is an essential quality of the state, admit that even the "sovereign" states are bound by the norms of morals in general, or the Christian moral order in particular, and hence that they are subjected to this order. To be sovereign seems to be incompatible with being subject to a normative order; thus to maintain the idea of the state as a supreme authority this term is understood to mean only a supreme *legal* authority, so that "sovereignty" of the state means only that the state is not subject to a legal order superior to its own legal order, *i.e.,* the national law.

Yet, this concept of state sovereignty becomes problematical if international law as a legal order obligating and authorizing the state is taken into consideration. That international law imposes obligations or confers rights upon the state, does not mean, as it is sometimes assumed, that international law obligates or authorizes a being that is not human, but a kind

From *The Georgetown Law Journal,* vol. 48, no. 4 (Summer 1960), pp. 627–40. Reprinted by permission of the author and the publisher.

of superman or a superhuman organism. There does not exist such a superman or superhuman organism in society, wherein the individual human being alone is real. What we call society or community is either the factual coexistence of individuals or a normative order of their mutual behavior. Only human beings can be obligated or authorized to behave in a certain way; only the behavior of human beings can be the content of legal obligations and legal rights. International law obligates and authorizes the state to behave in a certain way by obligating and authorizing human beings in their capacity as organs of the state to behave in this way. That these individuals as organs of the state fulfill the obligations imposed by international law and that they exercise the rights conferred by international law, that their behavior is regarded as the behavior of the state, that it is attributed to the state, means only that such behavior is referred to the personified legal order that determines the individuals who have to fulfill the obligations imposed by international law and to exercise the rights conferred by international law. This is the legal order which is usually designated as the "law of the state" in language that differentiates between the state and its law.

This law is a coercive order which is limited in its validity to a certain space and which is relatively centralized. As such it differs from the international legal order, which is not limited in its territorial validity and which is relatively decentralized. That international law obligates and authorizes the state to behave in a certain way means that international law leaves it to the national legal order to determine the individuals who by their behavior will have to fulfill the obligations imposed by international law and to exercise the rights conferred by international law, that international law delegates the determination of these individuals to the national legal order.

The state as a social order is identical with the law called "its" law—it is a specific legal order. Whereas the state as a person, as a subject of international law, is the personification of this legal order. The idea of the state as a superman or as a superhuman organization is the hypostatization of this personification. Sovereignty in the sense of supreme authority

can be nothing else but the quality of a legal order. Therefore, the problem of the sovereignty of the state is the problem
of the sovereignty of the national legal order in its relation to
the international legal order.

I · THEORIES OF THE RELATION

In reference to this relation, two theories exist that are
diametrically opposed, one dualistic (or pluralistic if one considers the multitude of the states or national legal orders), and
the other monistic. According to the first, international law
and national law, *i.e.,* the particular national legal orders, are
different systems of norms independent of each other in their
validity; but according to this theory they are simultaneously
valid, so that it would be possible to judge a certain human
behavior both from the point of view of international and national law and not from the point of view of only the one *or*
the other. The monistic theory holds that international law
and national law form a unity. This unity may be achieved
epistemologically in two ways: either international law is conceived of as superior to national law, meaning that the validity
of the latter derives from the former; or, conversely, national
law is conceived of as superior to international law, whose
validity is based on national law. We speak in one case of the
primacy of international law, in the other of the *primacy of
national law.*

If we recognize that obligation and authorization of the
state by international law means that the international legal
order delegates to the national legal order the power to determine the individuals whose behavior forms the content of the
obligations and rights established by international law, then
the dualistic construction of the relation between international
and national law collapses. For reasons of the logic of norms
it is not possible to assume the simultaneous validity of two
systems of norms regulating human behavior, if these systems
are valid independently from each other and therefore may
conflict with each other, the one prescribing that a certain
action ought to be performed and the other that this action
ought not to be performed. Two norms, one of which prescribes

that *A* ought to be, and the other that *A* ought not to be, cannot be assumed as simultaneously valid, just as two judgments, the one of which asserts that *A* is, whereas the other declares that *A* is not, cannot be true together.

The logical principle of contradiction, it is true, does not, or at least not directly, apply to norms, because norms are neither true nor false; but it does apply to statements describing norms (which statements necessarily are *ought* statements) in the same way as to *is* statements describing facts. The possibility that there is a scientific description, without contradictions, of the relation between international and national law can be proved; and that means that there are no conflicts between international and national law which would necessitate a dualistic construction, thereby excluding the assumption of their simultaneous validity. It can also be shown that positive international law contains in its principle of efficacy a norm that determines the reason and the sphere of validity of the national legal order, so that the assumption of an epistemological unity of international and national law is possible.

II · The Monistic Construction

The problem of sovereignty is, therefore, to be solved exclusively on the basis of the monistic construction of the relation of international and national law, *i.e.*, either by the primacy of international law or by the primacy of national law. It is to be noted, however, that the difference between these two monistic constructions refers only to the reason of validity of international and national law and not to their contents. As to its contents, international law is identical in either case. Seen from the viewpoint of legal theory, both constructions are equally possible. Their difference is, as we shall see later, the difference between two systems of reference.

The Primacy of National Law

Starting from a national law as a valid normative order, *i.e.*, a system of norms prescribing that men ought to behave in a certain way, one is faced with the question, how is the validity of international law to be founded from this starting point? This is possible only by assuming that international law is valid for a state if it is recognized by this state as valid for its organs. But it can be recognized only with the content it has in the moment of recognition. Since it is assumed that not only an express but also a tacit recognition of international law is possible, *i.e.*, recognition through factual obedience to and application of the norms of international law by the state in question, it follows that, on the basis of this theory of recognition, international law may be and actually is regarded as valid for all states. This opinion is prevailing in the Anglo-American jurisprudence. It is expressed in modern state constitutions which contain provisions to the effect that the law-applying organs are bound by the norms of general international law and of particular international law as created by treaties of the state in question. Thus, international law becomes part of the national legal order, and the reason of the validity of international law is placed in this national legal order, wherefrom the relation between them is construed. In this way the primacy of national over international law is established. It is this primacy of national law which in the traditional theory is presented as sovereignty of the state.

"Sovereignty" in this sense is not an apperceptible or otherwise objectively recognizable quality of a real thing; it is a *presupposition,* viz., the presupposed assumption of a system of norms as a supreme normative order whose validity is not to be derived from a superior order. Whether the state is sovereign cannot be answered through an inquiry into its natural or social reality. The sovereignty of the state, as seen from the viewpoint of a theory of law, is not a certain amount or degree of real power. Even states which in comparison with the so-called "great powers" do not have any significant power are regarded as equally sovereign as these great powers. The question whether a state is sovereign is only the question of whether one *presupposes* a national legal order as a supreme order. And this is the case if one regards international law as valid for the state only if it is recognized by the state, if one regards the "will" of the state as the reason for the validity of international law.

The Primacy of International Law

If, on the other hand, one starts from international law as a valid normative order, one is faced with the problem, how to found the validity of national law from this starting point. In this case the reason for the validity of the national legal order must be sought in international law. This is possible, because, as pointed out, the principle of efficacy, a norm of positive international law, determines both the reason for and the sphere of the validity of national law. This norm of international law determining the reason for the validity of the national legal order is usually presented in the statement that according to international law the government of a community existent within a certain firmly circumscribed space, if it exercises effective control over the members of this community and is independent of other governments of analogous communities, is to be regarded as the legitimate government, and the community under this government as a state in the sense of international law.

It does not matter whether the government exercises its effective control on the basis of a previously established and still valid constitution, or on the basis of a constitution that has been established by this government in a revolutionary way. Expressed in legal terms: A norm of general international law authorizes an individual or a group of individuals to establish and apply on the basis of an effective constitution a normative coercive order; it thereby legitimates this coercive order as a legal order valid within the territorial and temporal sphere of its factual efficacy and the community constituted by this legal order as a state in the sense of international law. If the efficacy of the national legal order is regarded as the condition of its validity and if this condition is stipulated in a norm of international law, then the reason of the validity of the national legal order can be seen in this norm of international law. This international law, then, can be conceived of as a universal legal order, superior to and comprising, as partial legal orders, all national legal orders—a universal legal order through which the coexistence in space and the succession in time of the national legal orders become legally possible. This is the meaning of the primacy of international law.

If this construction of the relation between international and national law is accepted, one cannot speak of sovereignty of the state in the original and proper sense of this term. The "sovereign," *i.e.,* the supreme order, is the international and not the subordinated national legal order. The term "sovereign states," if used in this construction, acquires a meaning utterly different from its original and proper sense. It expresses that the national legal order is subject only to the international and to no other national legal order, or, as it is formulated in a personificative language, that the state is legally independent of other states. The so-called "sovereignty" of the state would thus be nothing else but the name for the direct dependency of the national on the international legal order. It is therefore recommendable not to use the misleading term "sovereignty of the state" when one assumes the primacy of international law. In this case it is, moreover, not permissible to speak of a "relative" sovereignty of the states, as some writers do, because this formula implies a contradiction in terms.

III · The Concept of Sovereignty

The term "sovereignty of the state" in the original sense of the term is properly used only if the primacy of national law is assumed. Yet it remains more than questionable whether the writers who prefer this construction of the relation between international and national law would be willing to accept its consequences, because it follows from this construction that only the sovereignty of *one* state could be presupposed and the sovereignty of this state would exclude the sovereignty of all other states.

Those who accept the primacy of national law do so not to save the sovereignty of one state only, but the sovereignty of all states; they presuppose the principle of *sovereign equality* of all members of the international community. This principle, however, cannot be maintained on the basis of the primacy of national law. This construction of the relation between national and international law, it is true, may start from *any* state, but always only from *one* state; and only the state which is the starting point of the construction can be presupposed as sovereign. The relation of this state to the other states is established by international law which, as a consequence of the primacy of national law, is to be conceived of as part of this national law of the state that is the starting point. According to international law, other communities are "states" in their relation to this state only if recognized as such by the state which is the starting point, *i.e.,* only if in the opinion of the competent organ of this state they fulfill the conditions prescribed by international law. If international law is part of the national law of the recognizing state, the reason of the legal existence of the other states, *i.e.,* the reason of the validity of the other national legal orders, lies in the law of the recognizing state, *i.e.,* in the national legal order on the basis of which the recognition takes place. As a consequence of the primacy of national law the other states must be regarded as subordinated to this national legal order which includes international law as part of it. Hence, they cannot be presupposed as sovereign. Only the recognizing state, which is the starting point of the construction, or, more exactly formulated, only the national legal order on the basis of which the recognition takes place can be supposed to be sovereign, for only this national law is not subordinated to international law, it being conceived of as a part of this national law.

If, however, international law is conceived of as part of national law, it is necessary to distingiush between national law in a narrower and national law in a wider sense of this term. National law in the narrower sense is the national legal order comprising the norms of the state constitution and the norms created in accordance with this constitution by custom, legislation, judicial and administrative acts. National law in the wider sense is the national legal order comprising the norms of the national law in the narrower sense and in addition the norms of international law (created by state custom and treaties) recognized on the basis of the national law in the narrower sense. The relationship between these two parts of the national law in the wider sense must be interpreted as a relationship of super- and sub-ordination, the international law being superior to the national law in the narrower sense. This relationship is expressed in a figure of speech by saying that the state which recognizes international law as binding subjects itself to international law. The national law in the narrower sense is subordinated to the international law which is part of the national law in the wider sense, and hence the national law in the narrower sense is not sovereign; just as the national law of the other, the recognized, states is not sovereign because subordinated to the international law that is part of the national law of the recognizing state.

After a state has recognized international law (and this recognition of international law must not be confused with the recognition of a community as a state) and thus has incorporated international law into its own law, *i.e.*, the national law in the wider sense, the national law in the narrower sense has the reason of its validity in the international law to which it is subordinated within the framework of the national law in the wider sense; just as the national law of the other states has the reason of its validity in this international law. However, with respect to the national law in the wider sense of which the international law is a part and which is the starting point of the construction of the primacy of national law, international law is not the supreme reason of its validity, for this international law, valid only because recognized, has the reason of its validity in the "will" of the recognizing state, that is to say, in its national law in the wider sense of the term. What is called primacy of national over international law is the relationship between the national law in the wider sense and international law which is part of it. Only the national law in the wider sense, and not the national law in the narrower sense, is sovereign. And this sovereignty means nothing more than that the international law is presupposed to be superior to the national law in the narrower, but not to the national law in the wider sense whose part it is. When in traditional jurisprudence the "state" is characterized as "sovereign," it is only—or in the first place—the national legal order in the narrower sense, or the community constituted by this legal order, which is meant. But "state sovereignty" in this sense must mean that the state is subject only to international law. Since, however, only the national legal order in the wider sense, comprising international law as a part of it, can be presupposed as sovereign in the proper sense of this term, it is recommendable to speak of "primacy of national law" instead of "state sovereignty" when this construction of the relationship between national and international law is chosen.

IV · Misapplication of the Concept of Sovereignty

As already mentioned, the content of international law is not influenced by the choice of either construction of the relation between international and national law or by the presupposition or nonpresupposition of the sovereignty of the state. The content of the national law also remains unaffected by the construction of its relation to international law and by the presupposition or nonpresupposition of the sovereignty of the state. It is therefore a misuse of either one or both constructions or—what amounts to the same thing—of the concept of sovereignty, if, as is done frequently, decisions are deduced from this concept that can only be based on the content of positive international or of positive national law. This happens, for instance, if adherents of the primacy of international law, who do not regard sovereignty as an essential quality of a state, deduce from the assumption that the state is subject to international law the principle that in case of a conflict between international and national law the international law prevails over the national law and the national law is to be regarded as null.

In this respect we have first to note that a norm of national

law—and that means a valid norm, because if invalid it is not
a norm—cannot be null; it can be only annullable. Further
that it can only be annulled on account of its conflict with
international law if international or national law provides
a procedure leading to its annulment. But there is no such
procedure provided by general international law. The assumption of its superiority over national law cannot make
up for the lack of such a norm. Positive international law stipulates only a sanction as a reaction against the establishment
of a norm of national law which is in conflict with international law; and this sanction is, as it is usually formulated,
directed against the state, the legal order of which contains
the norm in question. This means that the norm remains
valid from the point of view of not only the national but also
of the international law, but the state exposes itself to a sanction of international law. There is no logical contradiction
in this description of the situation because the law prescribes
a certain behavior only in that it stipulates that a sanction
ought to be executed in case of a contrary behavior. Thus,
two norms, one of which provides a sanction as reaction against
a certain behavior, and the other a sanction as reaction against
the contrary behavior, can be valid and be applied together.
This can be demonstrated in the case of a norm of international
law which provides as reaction against a certain behavior
the specific sanctions of international law—war or reprisals,
and in the case of a national law which provides as reaction
against the contrary behavior the specific sanctions of national
law—punishment or execution. It may be, for example, that
two states, *A* and *B,* by an international treaty assume the obligation not to nationalize a citizen of the other state without
the consent of the latter, but that a statute of state *A* obligates
an organ to nationalize a person who fulfills certain conditions without regard to the consent of the state of which this
person is a citizen, even if he is a citizen of state *B*. If the
organ of state *A* in violation of the obligation imposed upon
it by its national law refuses to nationalize a citizen of state
B who fulfills all the conditions required by the statute of
state *A,* it exposes itself to a sanction of its national law. But

state *A* exposes itself to a sanction of international law if its organ in violation of the treaty fulfills its obligation under national law and naturalizes the person concerned without the consent of state *B*. The statute of state *A* remains valid; it is not annulled by the treaty; nor is the treaty annulled by the statute.

From the viewpoint of legal policy such a situation is most undesirable. It is therefore recommendable to establish institutions of international or of national law which make it possible to annul the norm of national law that is in conflict with international law. Yet, where this possibility does not exist, the norm of national law remains valid alongside the norm of international law. In this case there exists a teleological conflict, but not a logical contradiction between international and national law. There is no need to assume either nullity or annullability of the norm that conflicts with international law in order to maintain the epistemological unity of national and international law in the sense of the primacy of international law.

From the superiority of international law over the state it is sometimes deduced that the sovereignty of the state can be considerably restricted, and that thus an effective legal world organization may be possible. In the political ideology of pacifism the primacy of international law plays a decisive part because it excludes the sovereignty of the state. However, the sovereignty of the state which is excluded by the primacy of international law is something different from the sovereignty of the state which is restricted by international law. The meaning of the former is supreme legal authority; the meaning of the latter is freedom of action of the state, *i.e.,* unlimited competence of the national legal order. This competence can be limited by international law whether this law is supposed superior to, or part of, the national legal order. Whether we assume the one or the other construction of the relation between international and national law, a legal world organization is possible in both cases.

Even more exposed to misuse is the primacy of national law, which is based upon the assumption of the sovereignty of the state. This assumption leads to the view that international law is valid only because it is recognized by the state, thus being part of the legal order of the state. This view then leads to the false conclusion that the state is not necessarily bound by the treaties it has concluded and that it is incompatible with its nature as a sovereign power to subject itself to an international tribunal with compulsory jurisdiction, or to be bound by a majority decision of a collegiate organ, even if this tribunal or the collegiate organ and its procedures are established by a treaty to which the state is a party.

Equally decisive as the role that the primacy of international law plays in the pacifistic ideology is the role that the primacy of national law, the sovereignty of the state, plays in the ideology of imperialism. In both cases the ambiguity of the concept of sovereignty is involved, but if the state has recognized international law, which therefore is valid for this state, then its international obligations and rights are exactly the same as those established by an international law conceived of as superior to national law, and the norm of international law according to which states have to respect the treaties concluded by them, whatever content the treaties may have, is valid. That it is valid within the framework of a national legal order makes no difference. According to international law, no content can be excluded from the norms established by treaty by arguing that this content is incompatible with the nature or with the sovereignty of the state which concludes the treaty.

The idea that the sovereignty of the state, *i.e.*, the state as a supreme power, is not in conflict with international law because international law is valid for the state only if recognized by this state, and hence is not superior to the state, is quite compatible with the fact that a state, in recognizing international law by virtue of its sovereignty, and thus making it a part of its own law, restricts its sovereignty, that is to say, restricts its freedom of action or competence by accepting the obligations established by general international law and by the treaties concluded by itself.

How far this sovereignty of the state can be restricted by

international law recognized by the state can be answered only by examining the content of international law; the answer cannot be deduced from the concept of sovereignty. Yet, the positive international law does not limit the restriction of state sovereignty in its meaning of freedom of action or competence. It is quite possible to establish, by a treaty under international law, an international organization centralized to such a degree that it assumes the character of a state, which implies that the contracting states which become members of this organization lose their own character as states. The question how far the government of a state through treaties under international law shall or may restrict the freedom of action of its state is a question of politics. The answer to this question cannot be deduced either from the primacy of international or from the primacy of national law.

V · LIMITATIONS OF THE SCIENCE OF LAW

The antagonism between the two monistic constructions of the relation between international and national law, *i.e.*, the two ways of establishing epistemologically the unity of all valid law, shows a striking parallel to the antagonism between a subjectivistic and an objectivistic world view. The subjectivistic view starts from one's own sovereign *ego* in order to comprehend the external world. Therefore, it cannot conceive it as an external world; it must conceive it as an internal world, as idea and will of the *ego*. Likewise the construction known as primacy of national law starts from one's own sovereign state in order to comprehend the external world of law, *i.e.*, the international legal order and the other national legal orders. Therefore, it can conceive them only as internal law, as part of the legal order which is the starting point of this view. The subjectivistic egocentric interpretation of the world leads to solipsism, the opinion that only the *ego* exists as a sovereign being and that everything else exists only in and through the *ego,* so that the claim of others to be sovereign *egos* cannot be honored. Likewise, the assumption of the primacy of national law leads to the idea that only this national law, *i.e.,* the state which is the starting point of this view, one's own state, can be sovereign because this sovereignty excludes the sovereignty of all other states. In this sense the primacy of national law may be characterized as state subjectivism, even as state solipsism.

On the other hand, the objectivistic world view starts from the real external world in order to comprehend the *ego,* not only the *ego* of the one who entertains this view, but everyone's *ego,* with the intention to conceive this *ego* not as a sovereign being, not as the center of the world, but only as an integral part of the world. In analogy to this view, the primacy of international law starts from the external world of law, from international law as a valid legal order, in order to comprehend the legal existence of the individual states. In doing so it cannot consider them as sovereign authorities, but only as partial legal orders within the framework of a total, the international legal order.

The antagonism of the two world views in no way affects the scientific cognition of the world. The world as the object of this cognition remains the same and the natural laws that describe the world remain unchanged regardless of whether this world is conceived of as the internal world of the *ego* or the *ego* as being within the world. In the same way the antagonism of the two legal constructions remains without any influence upon the contents of the law, be it the international or the national law. Their norms remain unchanged whether international law is considered to be valid within national law, or national law to be valid within international law.

The antagonism between the two legal constructions may be compared also with the contrast between the geocentric cosmic system of Ptolemy and the heliocentric cosmic system of Copernicus. Just as in one of the two legal constructions it is one's own state that is the center of the legal world, thus in the cosmic system of Ptolemy it is our earth that stays in the center around which the sun turns. And just as in the other construction the international law forms the center of the legal world, so in the cosmic system of Copernicus the sun is the center around which the earth turns. Yet this contrast of the two cosmic systems is only a contrast of two different systems of reference. The famous physicist Max Planck interprets this contrast as follows: "If we accept for instance a system of reference [Bezugssystem] firmly connected with our earth, we must say that the sun moves in the sky; but if we transfer the system of reference to a fixed star, the sun rests immovably. In the antagonism of these two formulations there is neither contradiction nor obscurity; there are only two different ways of viewing the object. According to the theory of relativity, that at present may be regarded as an established part of the science of physics, both systems of reference and both ways of viewing the object that corresponds to them are equally correct and legitimate; it is on principle impossible to decide between them through measurement or calculation without arbitrariness." [1] The same applies to the constructions of the relation between international and national law. Their difference is based upon the difference of two systems of reference. One of them is firmly connected with the legal order of one's own state or national legal order; the other is firmly connected with the international legal order. Both systems are equally correct and equally legitimate. To decide between them on the basis and with the specific means of the science of law is impossible.

The science of law can only describe both systems and ascertain that one of the two systems of reference has to be accepted in order to determine the relation between international and national law. The decision for one or the other of the systems is outside the science of law. This decision may be determined by political considerations rather than scientific. One who appreciates the idea of the sovereignty of his own state, because he identifies himself with his state in his enhanced self-consciousness, will prefer the primacy of national law to the primacy of international law. On the other hand, one who cherishes the idea of a legal world organization will prefer the primacy of international law. This does not mean, as mentioned before, that the hypothesis of the primacy of national

1. Max Planck, *Vorträge und Erinnerungen* 311 (1949).

law is less favorable to the ideal of a world organization than the primacy of international law. Yet, it seems to justify a policy of declining any essential restriction of the freedom of action of the state. Such a justification is based on a fallacy for which the ambiguity of the concept of sovereignty is responsible. Yet, this fallacy is an iron part of the political ideology of imperialism that operates with the dogma of the sovereignty of the state. This applies, *mutatis mutandis,* to the preference of the primacy of international law. This construction is not less favorable to the political ideal of state sovereignty, in the sense of freedom of action of the state, than the construction of the primacy of national law. But it seems that the primacy of international law justifies more effectively an essential restriction of the freedom of action of the state than the primacy of national law. This too is a fallacy, but, as a matter of fact, this fallacy plays a decisive part in the political ideology of pacifism.

A true science of law exhibits these fallacies; it deprives them of the semblance of logical proofs, which as such could not be refuted; it reduces them to the role of political arguments to which counter-arguments of the same kind may be opposed. In doing so it frees the way to political development of either without postulating or justifying the one or the other. As a science it remains totally indifferent towards both.

K. W. B. Middleton

SOVEREIGNTY IN
THEORY AND PRACTICE

It is customary to apologise for choosing such a well-known
theme as that of sovereignty to discuss. But excuses would
only be called for if general agreement had by now been
reached on the subject, or alternatively if it had lost its importance. It is very clear that neither supposition is true of
the conception of sovereignty. As an eminent international
lawyer has recently said, "Sovereignty has become the central
problem in the study both of the nature of the modern State
and of the theory of international law." [1] It is therefore not
superfluous to inquire once again what the term really means,
or at least whether any consistent and useful meaning can be
attached to it. It has been so much encrusted with superstition
and prejudice in the course of the last 400 years that some
people would discard it altogether. Thus Sir Ivor Jennings
prefers to talk of the "supremacy" rather than the "sovereignty" of Parliament, because the former word is not "associated with politico-theological dogmas." But the difficulties
cannot be avoided by using a synonym, and attempts to show
that the conception of sovereignty is itself otiose or worthless
can hardly be called very successful. One thing is certain, that
sovereignty is an unpopular idea nowadays, and writers on
international affairs in particular may be counted on to speak
of it severely. The argument of the following pages is that

From *Juridical Review*, vol. LXIV, no. 2 (1952), pp. 135–62. Reprinted by
permission of the publisher.
  1. J. L. Brierly, *The Law of Nations*, 4th ed. (1949), p. 7.

sovereignty can be given a definite meaning, and that, both within the State and in a society of States, it is an indispensable conception.

There are two essential points in the argument. The first is that, while it belongs to the field of politics, sovereignty is properly, and can only be, a legal conception. That is to say, it is a matter of political authority and not of political power. The point is not new, but it is necessary to make it at the start because confusion between *de jure* and *de facto* supremacy has done, and still does, more to obscure thought on the subject than anything else. Probably it results in part from the fact that the word "power" is used in a double sense, sometimes to denote the physical and moral force at the disposal of a government to make its will obeyed, and sometimes to denote the right of a government to exercise that force, as when it is said that a Minister has or has not the power under an Act of Parliament to make a certain Order.[2] Any discussion of sovereignty that does not distinguish between "power" in the former and "power" in the latter sense is just a waste of time. Everybody, of course, is free to use words as he pleases, so long as he uses them consistently in one sense or another. Sovereignty may be taken to mean supreme power (or force) and not supreme authority. The trouble with those who, like Hobbes and Austin, write of sovereignty as if it were equivalent to supreme power is that they fail to identify it completely with *de facto* supremacy. They maintain that authority is a creation of power, that right rests on might, but it is a theory of authority which they are asserting all the same, not a theory of power. A true theory of power would seek to explain not political obligation but political obedience, and questions of law would be irrelevant to it except in so far as they may be a psychological factor influencing human behaviour.

2. There is a similar ambiguity in the Latin word *"potestas,"* which, as McIlwain points out in his *Constitutionalism and the Changing World*, pp. 26 *et seq.*, may mean either *auctoritas* or *potentia.* He has no doubt that it was the former meaning that Bodin had in view in his famous definition of sovereignty as *summa in cives ac subditos legibus-que soluta potestas.*

The distinction between political authority and political power is necessary because in any political community the person or persons who are invested with the right to exercise power may be, and often are, different from those who in fact mainly exercise it. It is trite constitutional doctrine in this country that Parliament is sovereign, but we all know that the country is not ruled by Parliament. On the other hand, there is a close and subtle connection between authority and power. As Bryce remarked, they tend to coalesce, since in time *de facto* supremacy ripens into *de jure* supremacy, while the latter also attracts to itself the former.[3] It is as inconceivable, in a constitutional State, that the *de jure* government should have no actual power at all as that the *de facto* government should have no legal authority at all. The contrast between the paramount authority of Parliament and its inferiority in actual power, which is so impressive a feature of the British system of government, is less obvious even in some other parliamentary countries. In France, for example, the National Assembly has a much larger share of real power. It is, however, perhaps safe to say that political and legal supremacy nearly always fail to some extent to coincide exactly.

The practical difficulty of accepting the doctrine of the absolute legislative supremacy of Parliament led Dicey to distinguish between the legal and the political sovereign. "But the word 'sovereignty' is sometimes employed in a political rather than in a strictly legal sense. That body is politically sovereign or supreme in a State the will of which is ultimately obeyed by the citizens of the State. In this sense of the word the electors of Great Britain may be said to be, together with the Crown and Lords, or, perhaps, in strict accuracy independently of the King and the Peers, the body in which sovereign power is vested." [4] It would surely be more appropriate, if different kinds of sovereignty are to be classified, to make a three-fold division into (1) practical sovereignty, which belongs in this country to the Government,

3. James Bryce, *Studies in History and Jurisprudence,* vol. II, pp. 64–65.
4. *Law of the Constitution,* 9th ed., p. 73.

or the Cabinet; (2) legal sovereignty, which is possessed by
Parliament; and (3) ultimate political sovereignty, which resides in the electorate. But, on the assumption that sovereignty
means supreme authority and not supreme power, any classification of different sorts of sovereignty is altogether inaccurate
and inept. Indeed, Dicey's cautious choice of language indicates that he employs the term "political sovereign" in a
loose sense. There can only be one kind of sovereign, the legal
ruler, if the word "sovereignty" is to have precise significance,
and the fact that he may in practice be subject to the will
of another person does not make that person a sovereign.
The much-quoted saying of Gray that the real rulers of a
society are undiscoverable is an exaggeration, but political
supremacy is difficult to define and locate, and if it means
that in every State there is necessarily some person or persons whose will prevails in the end it would seem often to
be non-existent. If we try to pin it down we arrive at some
surprising consequences. Most absolute monarchs have allowed themselves to be dominated by a minister or a mistress.
But it would be odd to speak of Louis XV as the legal sovereign of France and Madame de Pompadour as the political
sovereign. No doubt the verdict of the British electorate, as
expressed by the result of a general election, will always be
accepted by the citizens as final. That is not at all the same
thing as to say that ultimately they obey the will of the electorate. Can the electorate be said to have a will, because every
three or four years the electors in 600 constituencies have the
right to choose between two or three candidates put forward
by opposing political parties? It is frequently the case that
the party with a majority in Parliament obtained the votes
of a minority of the electorate, and even of the electors who
actually voted. Do the citizens then obey the will of the
electorate? In any event, does it make sense to say that the
citizens, who are the electors, obey their own will?

Dicey's distinction between the legal and the political sov-
ereign is, moreover, unhappy because it tends to imply that
Parliamentary sovereignty is nothing but a legal conception.
This is a complaint that may be made more fairly against

other writers, perhaps, than against Dicey himself. If Parliament is the legal sovereign and the electors the political sovereign, says Sir Ivor Jennings, then "legal sovereignty is not sovereignty at all. It is not supreme power. It is a legal concept, a form of expression which lawyers use to express the relations between Parliament and the Courts." [5] Again, according to Professor E. C. S. Wade, legal sovereignty is "merely a lawyer's rule which is accepted and acted upon because it suits political conditions in a State that the unrestricted power of law-making should rest in Parliament alone." [6]

Is the sovereignty of Parliament really a mere lawyer's rule? No doubt it is normally the case that, as Jennings says, the Government governs, "and the function of Parliament is first to register its decisions, secondly to serve as an outlet for individual and collective grievances, and thirdly to warn a Government when it is becoming unpopular." [7] But this is only half the truth. In a sense Parliament may be compared to an absolute monarch who has given his whole confidence to a powerful minister, a Wolsey or a Richelieu. The minister governs the country, but he does so on sufferance. His power, and his head, depend on the goodwill of the monarch, and he may lose them both at any time. However blunt of speech, he would scarcely be so bold as to tell his master that the royal supremacy was a lawyer's rule. Parliament is, of course, supreme in a rather different fashion from an absolute monarch. Yet it has a much more than merely nominal power to assert its legal authority. Although the Government as a rule controls Parliament, it is at the same time the creature of Parliament and can be overthrown just as suddenly and completely as a favourite who has lost his master's confidence. Only occasionally do heads roll, like those of Asquith in 1916, or Chamberlain in 1940, or the Labour ministers in 1931. But the latent power of life and death which Parliament possesses is something that must always be reckoned with, and its legal authority has therefore in practice a political significance far beyond the modest part which Jennings assigns to it.

5. *The Law and the Constitution*, 3rd ed. (1943), pp. 139–140.
6. Dicey, *Law of the Constitution*, 9th ed. (1948), introduction, p. xli.
7. *Op. cit.*, p. 169.

There are various reasons why Parliament usually behaves with such docility. One of them, and it is a salient difference from the position of some other legislatures, is that, while it can always throw out the Government, the Government can also throw it out at any time. This in turn depends on a more fundamental reason, namely that Parliament as such does not exist. The word "Parliament" is merely a convenient way of describing the Queen in her legislative capacity, the House of Lords and the House of Commons. If we say that Parliament can do anything but turn a man into a woman, we are asserting in hyperbolical form that the three parts of the legislature, acting together, have supreme and complete political authority. But if we speak of Parliament as if it were a single body, possessing a collective will and capable of making collective decisions, we speak quite nonsensically. How can it be a single body when the three parts of the legislature function independently of one another, have no common organs and never even meet except on ceremonial occasions? A sovereign consisting of the "tripartite body" of the Queen, the Lords and the House of Commons, to use Austin's expression, is strictly a chimera. And a sovereign made up of the Queen, the Lords and the electors (a notion which he thought more accurate) is an even greater monstrosity.

If it is borne in mind that Parliament only exists in name, it is easier to see how it can be dominated by the Government. The House of Commons, were it the sole sovereign, would be a more formidable body than as one of three authorities which share sovereignty. By using the legal powers of the two Houses to supplant the monarch as head of the executive, and by using the legal powers of the monarch, in particular the royal prerogative of dissolution, to keep the two Houses in check, the Government, or rather the Cabinet, has come to be *de facto* ruler of the country, between general elections and on condition that it commands the support of a majority of the House of Commons. Parliament of course could do away with the prerogative of dissolution. But the House of Commons could not, nor could the two Houses together.

Whether it is a question of political authority, or political power, the person or persons possessing it are creatures of flesh and blood, a Queen, a House of Lords and a House of Commons, not a "Crown" and a "Parliament." If it is a numerous body, the members are so organised as to be capable of acting in a corporate capacity. When he defined a sovereign as "a determinate human superior," receiving habitual obedience from the bulk of a given society and not in the habit of obedience to a like superior, Austin recognised that it must always be possible to point to an organised group of persons where the sovereign is not an individual. His tripartite monster was an attempt to square his definition of sovereignty with the accepted doctrine of Parliamentary supremacy. It has often been pointed out that no sovereign in the Austinian sense can be discovered in a federal State. But if he had analysed the idea of Parliamentary supremacy he would have seen that Parliament cannot be "a determinate human superior," because it is incapable of corporate action, and therefore that his belief in the indivisibility of sovereignty could not be justified. Indeed, unless sovereignty is concentrated in a single person, it must be divided, for an organised body is not really itself capable of possessing sovereignty. It is a contrivance which a number of persons invent when they wish to act effectively together. They, and they alone, are the "determinate human superiors."

The second essential point then which the present argument is concerned to make is that sovereignty can only be vested in an individual or jointly in a number of individuals. An abstraction like Parliament cannot be sovereign, any more than an abstraction can issue, or obey, an order. Sovereignty is a legal conception, but it has to do with human beings, not with phantoms. Since absolute monarchs are not to be found nowadays, at any rate in civilised States, it is no use looking for a single sovereign. All that can be discovered is certain persons who, individually or in groups, have a share of sovereignty. Sovereignty has been put into commission. But it is not the less a reality because of that.

The idea of a division of sovereignty has often presented difficulty because at first sight there seems to be something illogical in two persons, or two independent bodies, sharing supreme authority in the same State. Neither being then supreme over the other, is it not necessary that there should be some third person or persons with the ultimate right to determine the limits of their respective jurisdictions, to keep them within their limits, and to alter the limits when required? Now it is arguable that government is likely to be more efficient where supreme authority is concentrated rather than diffused. But a division of supreme authority, or of supreme power, has nothing anomalous about it. It implies, no doubt, agreement between the persons who share in it, but there is no need for outside intervention. In practice there are always certain rules, whether legal rules or conventional rules, for keeping the joint sovereigns in their place and thus for ensuring that government does not break down through their failure to agree. They are therefore, it may be said, subject to those rules. But this is merely a verbal objection. The fact that the exercise of authority is subject to rules, whether rules of law or of another kind, does not prevent the persons who possess that authority from being sovereign. Subjection to a rule has little in common, except verbally, with subjection to another human being. The former means that sovereignty is limited, the latter would mean that it is controlled.[8] The test of sovereignty is not freedom from legal limitation, but freedom from legal subjection to the will of, and thus legal control by, some other person or persons. This is a corollary of the proposition that sovereignty can only be vested in an individual or an organised body. If there is nobody of flesh and blood to whom the ruler in a State is legally subordinate, then of necessity he must be a sovereign ruler.

It may be conceded that the word "sovereignty" is here used in a different sense from that sometimes given to it. A ruler who is subject to law, although not subordinate to any

8. Bracton's maxim, *Rex non debet esse sub homine, sed sub Deo et lege,* "seems to indicate that the medieval king was an autocrat, was absolute in the sense of having no superior, but was anything but despotic, in that his *jura regalia* left off where the rights of his subjects began. He was in fact limited but not controlled." McIlwain, *op. cit.,* p. 24.

other person, whether within the State or outside the State, is not sovereign, if by "sovereign" is meant one who possesses unlimited and illimitable authority. The question is, whether authority of that description ever really exists, or whether it is not a fiction invented to serve as a justification for political institutions. It is a human instinct to insist on finding a basis for political authority. Men are not content to see it hanging in the air. A myth is needed, and is supplied by Queen, Lords and Commons, or the people as a whole, conceived of as an ideal entity possessing ultimate authority beyond the reach not only of any human rival but of any man-made law as well. The classic expression of the myth was in the French constitution of 1791, which declared that "sovereignty is one and indivisible, inalienable and imprescriptible. It belongs to the nation." The myth still persists, although the eloquent phrases of 1791 are somewhat toned down in the constitution of the Fourth French Republic. In fact, however, supreme authority belongs exclusively, or almost exclusively, to the French parliament, under the Fourth as under the Third Republic, and the so-called sovereignty of the nation is scarcely more than a political principle, secured, no doubt, through certain rules of constitutional law, by which legislative authority is derived from the people and exercised on behalf of the people.

In this country the actual process of legislation differs considerably from the theory, according to which laws are made by two independent legislative bodies, subject to a royal veto. Nor does the theory correspond with the myth, which presents the picture of the Queen seated on her throne enacting laws with the advice and consent of the Peers and of delegates of the people gathered around her. The existence of the myth, however, goes some way to explain how parliamentary sovereignty has come to be accepted as the equivalent of parliamentary omnipotence. What does parliamentary sovereignty signify, not in myth, but in reality? It signifies (1) that the three constituent parts of Parliament, acting together, are entitled to make rules which will invariably be regarded as binding by British courts of law, and will be preferred to rules emanating from any other source whatever; and (2) that the constituent parts of Parliament have the exclusive right to determine by agreement between themselves what their mutual relations shall be and how their authority shall be exercised. These two propositions are established beyond dispute, and, of course, are far from being of interest only to lawyers. But they do not add up to the conclusion that Parliament is omnipotent, even in law. Apart from the fact that Parliament could not legally do certain things, *e.g.*, deny justice to an alien, because they would be contrary to international law, Parliament cannot in any sense be legally omnipotent unless it becomes something more than a name, because both propositions postulate agreement between the three parts of Parliament. It may be said that this is merely technically true, since the royal assent is a formality and the authority of the House of Lords has been reduced to a shadow. Yet in certain circumstances a technical point may come to have vast practical importance.

Let us suppose that the House of Commons obtained the royal assent to a Bill abolishing the House of Lords, and then induced or compelled the Queen to acquiesce in another measure providing that any Bill which had been passed by the House of Commons should be deemed to have received the royal assent. The consequence would be that the House of Commons would in fact become Parliament, and would be fully sovereign. There would be nothing in law to prevent it prolonging its own existence indefinitely, or doing anything else it pleased, contrary perhaps to the will of a clear majority of the electorate. Such a situation is unlikely to arise in the absence of a political conflict serious enough to bring the country to the verge of civil war. In that event the exercise of the Queen's right of vetoing legislation might conceivably become as decisive as was the equally technical point of the King's right to pack the House of Lords by a wholesale creation of new peers in the constitutional conflicts of 1832 and 1911. The maintenance of constitutional government probably in the last resort depends more than is generally realised on technicalities that appear to be accidental survivals from the past.

Joint sovereignty implies divided sovereignty, and that

implies limited sovereignty. Sovereignty in a constitutional State must, perhaps, be limited in some way. Unlimited sovereignty and limited government do not go together. On the other hand, it does not seem to make any fundamental difference how precisely sovereignty is limited, whether by dividing up sovereign authority or by imposing restrictions on its exercise. Every country, or almost every country, except our own possesses a formal constitution, whose provisions enjoy a higher status than those of an ordinary legislative act, and cannot be altered by the legislature, at least by the normal process of legislation. Does it, however, follow that, for example, the Belgian and Irish legislatures are essentially inferior in status to the British, because certain laws cannot be enacted without a special procedure, involving an appeal to the electorate? No doubt the flexibility of the British constitution is a great convenience. But to assert, as Dicey does, that a legislature which lacks this advantage, that is to say the legislature of nearly every other country in the world, is a non-sovereign law-making body is to carry veneration for the Mother of Parliaments to an extravagant length. Where, then, in the case of these lesser breeds, is sovereignty to be located? The answer, apparently, is that sovereignty belongs to that body of persons which has the right to amend the constitution. Thus, following Austin, he suggests that "the legal sovereignty of the United States resides in the States' governments as forming one aggregate body represented by three-fourths of the several States at any time belonging to the Union." [9] Yet, if Parliament is merely a name, such a sovereign is deficient even in that degree of reality. Not only do the governments of the States not form an aggregate body in any way whatever, but it would be illegal for them to attempt, without the consent of Congress, to do so under the constitution of the United States.[10] There are other strange consequences of Dicey's theory. For example, the constitution of the Third French Republic could be amended by a simple majority of the two Chambers sitting together as a National

9. *The Law of the Constitution*, 9th ed., pp. 148–149.
10. Article I, § 10.

Assembly. Were the two Chambers then sovereign or non-sovereign, according to whether they sat separately or together?

There is, perhaps, one instance where a determinate body of persons entitled to make constitutional amendments can be identified, namely where provision is made for amendments to be submitted to the electorate of a country by way of referendum. Here the electorate may possibly be said to be in a proper sense sovereign, since it votes as a whole for or against a particular measure, or series of measures, assuming quite a different part from that which it plays when voting for parliamentary representation in separate constituencies. But this is plainly a very slight foundation on which to construct a theory of the location of sovereignty under a formal constitution. In the case of Belgium, the constitution can only be altered after a proposed amendment has been put before the electorate in a general election and subsequently approved by a two-thirds majority in each house of the legislature, while proposed amendments to the Irish constitution must be submitted directly to the people of the Republic for their approval after being accepted by the legislature. Does it result from this difference of procedure that in Ireland the electorate is sovereign and in Belgium it is not? The most that can be maintained is that, where a referendum is provided for, some small share of sovereignty belongs to the electors, for the circumstances in which they can exercise the right of amending the constitution are restricted, and, in any event, the right is itself perhaps not of major importance. It does not follow, because the constitution is superior in status to an ordinary legislative act, that the power of altering it must be of greater consequence than the power of making ordinary laws.

In practice, formal constitutions, even when they can easily be altered, are not often altered, and then usually in matters of detail. The oldest of existing constitutions, that of the United States, is in all essentials the same as when it issued from the Convention of Philadelphia in 1787. Or rather, it is the same on paper, since the meaning of many of its articles is utterly different from the meaning originally attached to them, not because of formal amendment but partly through judicial interpretation, partly by the growth of usages and conventions, partly owing to the fact that identical words mean different things to different generations of men. However much the meaning of its articles may have changed, the authority of the Constitution is as great, or greater, now than ever it was. It is none the less true that the Senate and the House of Representatives are sovereign bodies. An Act of Congress, provided it keeps within the ambit of Congressional jurisdiction, is just as binding on all American courts of law as an Act of Parliament on British courts, being "the supreme law of the land" equally with the provisions of the Constitution.[11]

By its ultimate right to interpret the Constitution, the Supreme Court has a certain power of control over Federal as well as State legislation. But this power amounts to something quite different from a general censorship of legislative activity. The Supreme Court can pronounce a Federal statute *ultra vires,* but only in the course of determining a particular issue brought before it and subject to a presumption in favour of the validity of the statute. In strict accuracy, the court does not declare the statute to be unconstitutional but merely refuses to apply it on the ground that it is not a law at all. Although the process of interpretation may enable the court to declare within elastic limits what the Constitution means, the fact remains that it must apply the existing law, and that where express powers are granted to Congress by the Constitution its right to exercise them cannot be disputed. Besides, it is a fundamental principle accepted by the court that Congress has a wide range of implied powers in addition to powers expressly bestowed on it. In short, nobody can tell Congress directly what it must not do, far less what it must do, and it is in marginal cases alone, where there is legitimate doubt how far the constitutional sphere of action of Congress extends, that the Supreme Court can intervene decisively, if its intervention is sought by litigants but not otherwise. The court has generally been slow to condemn Federal legislation,

11. Article VI.

and on the whole has done much more to augment than to diminish Federal authority. Since it is itself a part, though an independent part, of the Federal Government, that is not altogether surprising.

Whether or not there is a body of judges, as in the United States, entitled to pronounce upon the constitutional validity of legislation, it would be a mistake to lay too much stress on either the existence or the contents of a formal constitution. It will almost always operate quite differently from the intention of its founders, and more and more as time goes on, since future generations will not let themselves be imprisoned within a political formula designed to suit the needs of their ancestors. Out of filial respect, or because of practical difficulties, they may refrain from altering its provisions, but they will not usually find it hard to circumvent them if they desire. A constitution, however farseeing those who framed it, cannot provide for everything. It will consist of a number of general, and therefore necessarily vague, rules, together with a few matters of detail, principally relating to the organisation and powers of the different branches of government and the relations between them. Its provisions, even if detailed, are addressed, not to the citizens but to those exercising governmental functions. For example, the 18th Amendment to the United States Constitution declared that "After one year from the ratification of this article, the manufacture, sale or transportation of intoxicating liquors within, the importation thereof into, or the exportation thereof from, the United States and all territory subject to the jurisdiction thereof, for beverage purposes, is hereby prohibited." It was not, however, by means of this provision, although its terms could hardly be more specific, that Prohibition was enforced, but by legislation, namely the Volstead Act, passed by Congress in virtue of the Amendment. From the point of view of the citizens (and, after all, government exists for them, not vice versa), what is important is not, at least primarily, how far the legislature has the right to make rules which bind them, but what the rules say and what consequences follow if they are not obeyed. An individual citizen of the United States may take the risk of disregarding a Federal statute if he pleases, on the chance that it may turn out to be unconstitutional, just as a citizen of this country may choose to disobey a Ministerial Regulation, in the expectation that it will be held to be *ultra vires*. But few persons think it wise to take chances of this kind unless, which rarely occurs, the statute or regulation is obviously bad. So far as the ordinary citizen is concerned, an order addressed to him by an authority clothed with a right prima facie to issue that order is one which he will almost invariably regard as obligatory, however much he may dislike it.

If sovereignty cannot be located in the persons who have the right to amend a constitution—except perhaps in certain cases and then to a minor extent, or in a court of law entitled to expound a constitution, or in a constitution itself, which is merely a scrap of paper, or, presumably, in the ghosts of the founding fathers—the question where it is to be discovered still remains to be answered. There seem to be two possible answers. One is that the whole conception of sovereignty is unsound and unnecessary. It is a dogma which owes its origin to a particular set of historical circumstances and which, since these circumstances have ceased to exist, no longer serves any purpose. To inquire where in any State sovereignty is to be found is therefore useless.

If the theory of sovereignty means that to every political community there must be some person or persons possessing unlimited authority, then it is true that sovereignty is an untenable idea. But nobody has ever really conceived of sovereignty as implying freedom from every obligation whatever. Even Hobbes' sovereign is limited, for his authority only lasts so long as he is able to govern effectively, and resistance to him is legitimate if he cannot. He is therefore under an obligation to his subjects to maintain himself in power. Similarly, those who asserted the divine right of Kings, in its most extreme form, while they maintained that subjects must obey the commands of the King even if they were flatly against the laws of God, did not deny that the King was bound by the laws of God. Unlimited legal supremacy is, indeed, a self-contradictory notion, for any ruler who claims to possess legal authority admits by doing so that there is some legal justification for his rule, and accordingly that there must be some limit to what he is entitled to do. To argue the contrary involves the strange conclusion that law can confer on a man the right to act as if law did not exist.

Sovereignty, therefore, is not inconsistent with control by law, human or divine. What it is inconsistent with is control by, or rather legal subordination to, any human being. In this sense there does not seem to be insuperable difficulty in locating it in any existing State, although sometimes, as in the case of the United States and Switzerland, it may be divided up in a complicated fashion. That it is a necessary conception is scarcely open to argument, if consideration is given to what is involved in a political theory which dispensed with it. Unless there is a hierarchy of authorities in a community, each one entitled to issue orders of a certain description, or within a certain sphere, and itself subject to the will of a higher authority, anarchy is bound to prevail. And ultimately it must always be possible to arrive at an authority which is not subject to the will of any other person or persons, whose decision therefore is final. It is not, however, essential that there should be a single person or body of persons invested with the right to make every ultimate decision. Thus the United States Congress (which is itself an authority consisting of two separate and co-ordinate bodies) has an exclusive right to determine customs duties on imported goods,[12] while the legislatures of the States have the sole right to pass divorce laws.[13] In some instances, for example, direct taxation and excises, Congress and the State legislatures have concurrent rights.[14] This, of course, implies mutual restraint and for practical reasons is only conceivable within narrow limits. It would not be possible to give Congress and the State legislatures concurrent rights to regulate the value of the currency or to declare war. But the House of Representatives and the Senate have con-

12. Article I, §§ 8 and 10.
13. 10th Amendment.
14. Article I, § 8, 10th Amendment, 16th Amendment.

current rights in these respects and in almost every other
as well.

II

Let it be assumed that the theory of sovereignty put forward
above is valid, that it enables a clear and consistent, and also
useful, meaning to be attached to that inflated term. The
next step is to show that the theory is applicable within a
society of States in the same way or within a single State. It
is first necessary to distinguish between several different senses
in which the word "State," like the word "sovereignty," is
ordinarily used. In particular, when we speak of the "State"
as opposed to the individual, we mean by "State" something
quite distinct from what we mean when we say that a "State"
is bound by the rules of international law. Looked at from
the inside, the State is, as it were, transparent. We can identify
a cabinet, a legislature, government departments and a judiciary. But these are only organs of the State, and if they are
combined together they still do not constitute the State. The
State is an institution, and as such is an abstraction. It has,
indeed, a certain reality and is more than a mere name, like
Parliament, although the exact manner in which it can be
said to exist is a question that may be left to metaphysicians.
For the purposes of legal or political science, all that matters
is that, perhaps because of the mutability of human affairs
and the brief duration of human lives, men find it essential
to establish institutions, and, when they arrive at some measure of civilization, to create the political institution known
as the State.

Looked at from the outside, on the other hand, the State
is opaque. There is nothing abstract about it. It is nearly,
though not quite, identical with the nation, that is to say
it is a large collection of human beings organised politically
and differing from a crowd or a tribe in degree rather than
in kind. When two States are at war, it is not a question of
two institutions dropping bombs on each other. They would
do no harm if they could, since an institution is immune
from any mortal weapon. Nor is it a question of two govern-

ments fighting a duel. The governments may be the ring-
leaders; but it is the people who are the contestants.

Consequently, while the State as institution cannot be sovereign, the State as political community can be. In the first
case it is an abstraction, no less incapable of possessing supreme authority than of performing governmental functions,
but serving as a vehicle within which authority and power
are exercised. In the second case, the State itself may be sovereign in the same way as any other body of persons, since
it consists of a determinate number of individuals, occupying
a particular territory and acting through agents for whose
behaviour it may be made responsible by other States. The
difference is that between an organisation and the persons
organised. There is a corresponding difference in legal terminology. If a citizen of this country wishes to obtain a legal
remedy against the State he can sue the "Crown," which is
the name given to the State as institution. But when the State
is regarded as a member of the United Nations, that is as a
unit in the society of States, it is called "the United Kingdom."
It is essential, in order to avoid confusion of thought, to keep
in mind these two meanings of the word "State," and, when
dealing with the State in relation to other States, to use the
word only in its concrete sense. No doubt, to speak of "State
sovereignty," referring to the State as institution, is not meaningless, any more than the term "popular sovereignty." Popular sovereignty may be mythical in a proper sense, but it is
by no means devoid of political significance. So, too, if by
"State sovereignty" is meant the supremacy of the State as
institution over other institutions, then the term is certainly
significant. Both "State" and "sovereignty," however, have
here a meaning wholly distinct from that which they bear
when "State sovereignty" is used as equivalent to "national
sovereignty."

The sovereignty of a State as community, or nation, has
a positive and a negative aspect.[15] Positively, a sovereign State

15. The distinction generally made is between internal and external sov-
     ereignty. But positive and negative sovereignty seems to be a more accu-
     rate classification, since it is the nature of the authority, not the place
     where it is exercised, that matters.

has paramount authority over its own territory, including the
air space above and waters round its territory, and over its
individual citizens and any subject communities. Negatively,
a sovereign State is independent, that is to say it is free from
the control of any external authority. It does not appear that
the concept of sovereignty, as applied to a society of States,
can mean anything either less or more than this.

Political reality, of course, need not coincide with the theory,
which is purely legal. A State which is independent in law
may have little appreciable independence in fact. The divorce
between power and right is notoriously wider in the sphere
of international affairs than almost anywhere else. It might
therefore be imagined that the theory of national sovereignty,
being just a principle explaining how States behave, when
they behave in a legal manner, would be a somewhat uncon-
troversial, if not academic, question. But, on the contrary,
it is a principle which arouses the fiercest animosity, and is
often said to be incompatible with peace and international
order. That can hardly be unless it is regarded as something
other than a merely legal principle, by lawyers as well as
laymen. And so quite plainly it is. "For the practical purposes
of the international lawyer," Brierly writes, "sovereignty is
not a metaphysical concept, nor is it part of the essence of
statehood; it is merely a term which designates an aggregate
of particular and very extensive claims that States habitually
make for themselves in their relations with other States." [16]
Like other statements to a similar effect, this is puzzling,
in that it seems to carry the implication that, because a right
may be abused, there is something wrong with the law which
recognises the right. The fact, however, that the right, let
us say, to sue for breach of contract may be liable to abuse,

16. *The Law of Nations*, 4th ed., p. 48. Elsewhere he says of sovereignty
    that it stands for "the power of modern States, the power of their gov-
    ernments to decide and to act without consulting others and without
    concern for anything but their own interests as they themselves conceive
    those interests" ((1949) lxi *Juridical Review*, p. 5). Clearly Dr. Brierly is
    using the word "power" wholly or partly in the sense of force, and not
    purely of legal right.

where a wealthy corporation enters into contractual relations with a poor man, is not considered a reason for arguing that breach of contract should not be actionable, although it may be a reason for laying down certain rules intended to prevent abuse. So, too, the fact that States may frequently abuse the rights which flow from their sovereignty is surely not a good reason for condemning those rights in themselves. It is no doubt desirable that there exercise should be restrained in some way, that a State should not be free to fix the level of its armaments, or regulate its economic life, without regard to the effect upon other States. But claims of this kind, although made in virtue of sovereignty, are not inherent in sovereignty, and could be limited without detracting from it. The doctrine of sovereignty, in its proper sense, is the reflection in legal terms of a factual situation. A legal theory, like a theory of natural science, may be said to be sound or unsound, adequate or inadequate, but moral indignation against it is misplaced. If the theory of sovereignty, or the theory of evolution, have evoked strong emotions, that is only because human beings instinctively resent uncomfortable truths. But when he asserts that men are descended from monkeys, the biologist is only making a statement of fact, not saying that he approves of it; and the legal, or political, scientist, when he puts forward a theory based on the ascertained fact that States behave in a certain way, need not suppose it to be a good or a bad thing that they should behave like that.

While States remain actually and also in law independent of one another, international law cannot dispense with the concept of sovereignty. Indeed, its very existence presupposes the sovereignty of States. A large part, or even most, of its rules are designed to protect their sovereignty from invasion, like the exclusion of matters within the domestic jurisdiction of a State, or the rule that a State is not bound by the provisions of a treaty to which it has not consented. The Covenant of the League of Nations was impliedly and the Charter of the United Nations [17] is expressly based on the principle of the

17. Article 2 (1). The reference to the sovereignty of the members is not otiose, since the Charter contains what is at least in principle a very

sovereignty of the member States. It is accordingly erroneous to think that there is necessarily any opposition between the doctrine of national sovereignty and international law, or international order in so far as it is a product of law. This is only true, it may be objected, because international law is weak and its rules vague and incomplete. Let it be supposed, however, that international law were strong, that its rules were precise and comprehensive, and that States, if they did break its rules, invariably submitted to the decision of an international tribunal. Yet they would still continue to be sovereign States as much as before.

Of course, if national sovereignty means that States are invested with an absolute and unlimited authority above all rules of law, then there is no possibility of reconciling the sovereignty of States with a belief in the obligatory nature of international law. Writers who have attempted this feat have found themselves in a dilemma from which there can be no escape. Either States are subject to international law, in which case they are not supreme in an absolute sense, or else they are free to disregard international law if they think fit, in which case it is not law at all. Most of them, at all events until recently, have fallen back on the latter alternative. Yet it is one which is completely contradicted by the facts of international intercourse. States often act, no doubt, with small or no regard to the rules of the international law, but they never openly admit that they are entitled to do as they please. This is not explained by calling it hypocrisy. The reason is, as has been pointed out above, that a State which asserted that it was not bound by any rule of law could not claim in the same breath that its subjects were legally bound to obey it. It would follow also, if sovereignty meant absolute authority above all law, that a State which entered into a treaty with another State could never claim that the

---

important exception to the general rule in the power given to the Security Council to make decisions binding on all members for the limited purpose of maintaining or restoring peace (Articles 25 and 39). Thus the five permanent members of the Security Council are alone, by reason of their veto, sovereign in the fullest sense.

terms of the treaty were binding on the other State without denying the sovereignty of the latter. But that, again, is obviously a conclusion contrary to the practice of States.

To say that a State surrenders its sovereignty, or any particle of it, by the mere fact of entering into an obligation that imposes a limitation on the exercise of its sovereign rights, is like saying that a man necessarily becomes the servant of another by contracting with him. In other words, freedom of action is one thing and sovereignty is an entirely different thing. A State can surrender part of its sovereignty, or even all of it, by treaty, just as a man can enter into a contract of service with another man. But even an onerous and one-sided treaty obligation may be consistent with the maintenance of full sovereignty by the State upon which the obligation is imposed. Thus in the case of the *Wimbledon* [18] it was argued before The Hague Court that the obligation laid on Germany by the Treaty of Versailles to keep the Kiel Canal open to the vessels of all nations at peace with Germany should not be interpreted literally, because such an interpretation would deprive her of an essential attribute of her sovereignty. But the court declined "to see in the conclusion of any treaty by which a State undertakes to perform or refrain from performing a particular act an abandonment of its sovereignty. No doubt any convention creating an obligation of this kind places a restriction upon the exercise of the sovereign rights of the State, in the sense that it requires them to be exercised in a particular way. But the right of entering into international engagements is an attribute of State sovereignty."

It is clear, therefore, that there is a fundamental distinction between a limitation on the exercise of sovereignty, on the one hand, and a surrender of sovereignty, on the other hand. It seems equally clear that a State only surrenders its sovereignty when it becomes subordinate to another State or States, or to some body of persons capable of asuming authority over it. The mistake of mixing up subjection to law with subjection to a human superior perhaps arises from the common habit of identifying a figure of speech with a

18. P.C.I.J., Series A. No. 1 (1923), at p. 25.

reality. When we say that a State is subject to another State we mean that the latter is entitled to control the actions of the former. But, when we say that a State is subject to a general rule of law or a particular treaty obligation, we mean only that it is bound to conduct itself in accordance with that law or obligation. No question of control by any external authority is involved. Men are not governed, except metaphorically, by law.

The advantage of the theory here maintained, as applied to States in the sense of political communities, is that it seems to enable an adequate definition to be given of national sovereignty, free from ambiguous political implications. Nobody can tell with any approach to precision whether a particular nation or State, Holland or Czechoslovakia, for example, is politically independent or not. A Russian would no doubt declare that the latter was and the former was not. An American or an Englishman would be of the opposite opinion. But neither side would deny, or at least could consistently deny, that Holland and Czechoslovakia are both sovereign States, that they are in law independent. A sufficiently clear distinction can be drawn between a State that is sovereign and one that is not, and between one that is fully sovereign and one that is in some degree only partially sovereign. The test is whether it is free, not *de facto* but *de jure,* from external control and, if not, to what extent it is controlled externally. So long as it possesses some degree of independence in law and paramount authority somewhere, a State must have a share of sovereignty. If it is fully independent in law, however weak politically, and is completely paramount over its own territory and citizens, however limited the territory and scanty the number of citizens, it is fully sovereign. Consequently, a State can be deprived of its sovereignty in whole or in part in two ways only, namely by losing its legal independence, wholly or partly, or by suffering its paramount authority to be superseded in whole or in part. In either case its sovereign rights are not affected unless it becomes subordinate in some way to a human superior. For instance, a State will suffer a total loss of sovereignty if another State acquires a right to veto any measure passed by its legislature; and a partial loss if it allows another State to exercise certain governmental functions within its territory, to the exclusion of its own paramount authority.

It is to be noted that a loss of paramountcy, or positive sovereignty, to another State involves control by that State as well as a loss of negative sovereignty. This is best illustrated in a federal union, which consists of a large political community embracing a number of smaller communities, in such a way that both the larger unit and the smaller units possess sovereign rights, and the individual citizens of the union owe obedience simultaneously to the federal and to the regional governments. Thus in the United States, the Union, or rather its organ the Federal Government, controls the States directly and also indirectly. Its direct control of the States is exercised in virtue of provisions in the Constitution which, for instance, prohibit the States from doing certain things, such as imposing duties on imports or exports, without the consent of Congress.[19] But far more effective is its indirect control of the States, by means of constitutional powers that derogate from their positive sovereignty. That is to say, by possessing direct authority over individual citizens the Federal Government deprives the States of a part, and the most important though not the largest part, of their paramount authority within their own territories. What matters is, not so much that the States cannot regulate imports of goods into their territory, but that the Federal Government can and does. Through this and its other powers the Federal Government dominates the economic life of the States, and indeed prevents them from pursuing, except to a very minor extent, policies of their own choosing in any field open to federal intervention.

Just as the obligatory force of international law is not inconsistent with the sovereignty of States, so they do not lose their sovereignty by being subject to any other abstraction, such as a majority of their own number. If several States join together to form a league, or confederation, either on a universal scale like the League of Nations, or on a regional

19. Article I, § 10 of the United States Constitution.

scale like the American Confederation of 1781–1788, or the German Confederation of 1815–1867, with permanent organs to ensure co-operation between them but without a central body empowered to make decisions binding on the members, then the members retain their full sovereignty, and it is of no essential consequence that certain questions may be decided by a majority vote. A collection of States cannot surrender their sovereignty to themselves, whether their collective decisions require unanimity or not. Suppose that Tom, Dick and Harry agree to go for a walk. If Tom and Harry tell Dick to lead the way, they undertake, as far as their walk is concerned, to submit themselves to the superior authority of Dick. He is sovereign. But if they decide that in case of doubt arising which road to take the opinion of the majority shall prevail, they do not submit themselves to anybody's authority. All three are sovereign. They merely lay down in advance a procedure to be adopted in case of a deadlock of opinion. It is otherwise where States agree to form a union, whether of the kind known as a federal union or of some other kind. If the word "union" is to mean anything it must imply a surrender of sovereignty and therefore the transfer of sovereign rights to an authority distinct from the constituent States. Thus in 1789 a new sovereign State, the United States of America, appeared on the international stage. Instead of 13 United States and a Congress which was merely, as John Adams said, a diplomatic assembly, there came into existence a United States in the singular and a Federal Government having a separate will and exercising authority over them, but not so as to take away their sovereignty altogether.[20]

Supreme authority must exist somewhere within a State, or else conflicts of jurisdiction will lead to anarchy. In the same way it must be discoverable within a society of States, if it is to be a society in any sense at all, and not a jungle. But there is in fact no supra-national authority recognised

20. Since the States are within the Union, it is for them an institution and not a community. Thus it is Congress which possesses sovereignty from their point of view. On the other hand, Congress, being external to them, exercises authority over the States, not over the State legislatures.

by States as superior to them. Sovereignty therefore belongs to them as members of the society individually. It may be true that they often abuse their sovereign rights, and that international order is certain to be precarious unless the rule of law can be established in the international sphere. Yet the problem is not merely, or primarily, a legal one. International law limits the exercise of their sovereign rights to some extent at present. If it is developed further it may be capable of doing so more effectively. Otherwise there is no hope except in setting up a supra-national authority which will curtail their sovereignty. That, however, is mainly a political problem, which must be solved by political means, for to deprive them of supremacy *de jure* while leaving them supreme *de facto* is not sufficient and, indeed, would make international law still weaker than it is instead of strengthening it. If the practical consequence of reforming the law were, not to reform the behaviour of States but to cause them to disregard it more readily, there would be a loss rather than a gain. The doctrine of national sovereignty cannot fairly be blamed for the bad behaviour of States. On the contrary, it serves the purpose of restraining them from worse behaviour, since governments, even if they are not honest enough to uphold the rights of other nations equally with those of their own, are at least able to see that the maintenance of certain rules regulating the behaviour of States generally is in the interest of every nation. But the doctrine of national sovereignty cannot be discredited without destroying the basis of a large part of these rules, so long as States are *de facto* supreme and free from external control.

Of course, when people say, as they so often do, that States must give up part of their sovereignty if they are to preserve themselves from perpetual conflict, it is really *de facto* supremacy that is uppermost in their minds. And it is easy to excuse them, at least if they are laymen, for failing to distinguish *de facto* from *de jure* supremacy, since while the distinction is essential for the purpose of exact reasoning, the two forms of supremacy are in practice often difficult to keep separate. The legal independence of a State may be com-

patible with complete political dependence. But such an extreme case seldom, if ever, occurs. Normally however much
one State is dominated by another there will always be some
residue of self-determination left to it, if only because the
dominant State is unwilling to allow its supremacy to appear
too blatant. It is a great mistake to think that legal supremacy
is equivalent to nominal supremacy or generally that, because
legal right does not always correspond with power, it is therefore unimportant. There are many things one cannot do, although one has the right to do them. But at the least it is a
substantial advantage to have the law on one's side.

Accordingly, while the problems involved in a surrender
by States of their sovereignty are mainly, they are not by any
means solely, political. Let it be assumed that a number of
associated States have decided to establish a union, because
they find that a mere alliance or league between them is insufficient to achieve their objects. They must first of all be
willing to give up, not on paper but in actual fact, part of
their independence in favour of some supra-national body endowed with effective powers. Unless they are prepared for
that, it is meaningless to talk of a surrender of sovereignty.
If, however, the decision is made, the next step is to draw up
a constitution which will settle in precise terms the legal basis
and structure of their union. It is hardly conceivable that
they will be content with anything else, for they run the risk
either that some of the members will interpret their obligations so narrowly that the union becomes a mere name, or,
on the other hand, that they have given up not a part but the
whole of their independence. No doubt, in the last resort a
union, like every other combination of States, must be dependent on the good faith of its members. But all experience
proves that it is unwise to place reliance on good faith alone.

The question of sovereignty is plainly the principal issue
in the constitution of any union of States, as the debates at
Philadelphia in 1787 and the subsequent history of the United
States up to the Civil War show. Everything depends on where
ultimate authority rests, how far the central government is
given a right to control the member States, and what juris-

diction is left to them. It is often, however, taken for granted that the particular form of union, namely federal union, which has been adopted by the Americans and the Swiss and others, is the only possible form of union between States. This is, perhaps, an erroneous opinion. In any event, it is likely that federal union, in the American or Swiss sense, is a constitutional arrangement that can be successful only in certain conditions. To attempt to apply it to an association of large modern States would be a very dubious undertaking. The problem whether a union of a different kind, which left a more important share of sovereignty to the member States, would be practicable is one that still awaits an answer.

Georg Schwarzenberger

THE FORMS
OF SOVEREIGNTY

An Essay in Comparative Jurisprudence

"Is it the word we wish to throw out, or the concept, or the implications of the concept or the word?"

Ch. E. Merriam, *Systematic Politics* (1945)

The place of sovereignty in present-day world society is somewhat enigmatic. It is a fashionable and, at a first glance, persuasive proposition to argue that, on the international level, independence is increasingly giving way to interdependence. In this atmosphere, sovereignty tends to be viewed with somewhat critical eyes. It is thought to be greatly overrated,[1] to suffer from regrettable ambiguities [2] and to show a reprehensible propensity to ideological abuse.[3]

From *Current Legal Problems,* vol. 10 (1957), pp. 264–95. Reprinted with corrections and additional notes by permission of the author and the publisher.

1. *Cf.* Ph. Jessup, *A Modern Law of Nations,* 1948, pp. 12 *et seq.,* and 36 *et seq.,* or E. Sauer, *Souveränität und Solidarität,* 1954, p. 93 *et seq.*

   For an animated discussion of earlier attacks on the concept of sovereignty in international law, *cf.* G. W. Keeton, *National Sovereignty and International Order,* 1939, p. 145 *et seq.*
2. See A. Ross, *A Textbook of International Law,* 1947, p. 33 *et seq.,* or E. Ruck, *Grundsätze im Völkerrecht,* 1947, p. 26.
3. H. Kelsen, *Reine Rechtslehre,* 1934, p. 153, or Ross, *l.c.* above, note 2, pp. 45–6.

Ample evidence of centripetal trends in international society exists. Centrifugal tendencies are not, however, inconspicuous. The call for closer international integration is matched only by the clamour for national self-determination. The cry for a world police force is paralleled only by the growing popularity of neutrality and neutralism, and so the tale of illustrations and counter-illustrations might be inconclusively continued. Thus, the intriguing galaxy of more "modern" concepts and alternatives to the "antiquated" notion of sovereignty [4]—such as active and peaceful co-existence, international solidarity or social interdependence—appears to attain at the most a change in emphasis from one to another aspect of a complex situation. Moreover, none of these alternative terms either excels by greater precision or is less likely than sovereignty to be turned to ideological uses.[5]

I · THE PROBLEM

In this slightly bewildering situation, the task-in-chief appears to provide criteria of some general validity for the detached assessment of the contradictory trends and counter-trends in international law and organisation which are symbolised by the antithesis of independence and interdependence. In order to achieve this object, it is advisable to proceed in a manner

4. To judge by recent studies of high quality, a swing of the pendulum away from the treatment of the topic on the basis of implied liberal-reformist assumptions is noticeable. *Cf.* Ch. Rousseau, *L'indépendence de l'Etat dans l'ordre international,* Hague Academy of International Law, Vol. 73 (1948), p. 173 *et seq.;* Ch. de Visscher, *Théories et Réalités en Droit International Public* (2nd ed.), p. 132 *et seq.;* D. W. Gunst, *Der Begriff der Souveränität im modernen Völkerrecht,* 1953; T. Suontousta, *La Souveraineté des Etats,* 1955, and Professor Rousseau's outspoken Preface to G. Day, *Les Affaires de la Tunisie et du Maroc devant les Nations Unies,* 1953, p. 8.

5. From this angle, the discussion on *Sovereignty and International Co-operation* at the Lucerne Conference (1952) of the International Law Association (*Report,* p. 19 *et seq.*) and Judge Alvarez's *jurisprudence constante,* initiated with his Ind. Op. on *Membership of the United Nations* (*I.C.J. Reports 1947–1948,* p. 69), are both entertaining and instructive.

which avoids rigorously even the suspicion of arbitrary or subconscious selectiveness, whether in favour of "reactionary" or "progressive" conclusions.

It will contribute to this end if, in the first place, an effort is made to reduce the problem to its proper proportions. The over-estimation of the issue is probably due in part to still widespread misconceptions of a methodological character. If it were correct to deduce any legal rules from the principle of sovereignty—or any other legal principle—for other than purely didactic purposes, it would be a matter of signal importance to know whether sovereignty was still a fundamental principle of international law or whether it ought to be exchanged for any other legal principle which had now become the "fertile mother" of new rules of international law. If, however, together with all other principles of international law, sovereignty is recognised for what it is, that is to say, a mere abstraction from actually operative rules,[6] then much of the struggle between the giants in the realm of conceptualism turns out to be mere shadow-fighting. So long as the rules governing the principle of sovereignty are not effectively limited by others underlying whatever the advocated alternative principles may be, the reality of *lex lata* is but little affected.

At the same time, the issue of Sovereignty Evanescent or Triumphant is a real problem. Whether the term is employed to depict realities in the fields of theology, law or political science, it signifies one of two things: supremacy over others (omnipotence) or freedom from control by others (independence).

In law, supremacy and freedom tend to be expressed in terms of jurisdiction and discretion. The significance of this change in terminology depends on the answers to two questions, the one legal, and the other sociological. The former is concerned with the scope of effective limitation of the rules underlying sovereignty in favour of those governing other legal principles. The latter raises wider issues. It involves an evaluation of the real significance of any such limitations in

6. See further Hague Academy of International Law, Vol. 87 (1955), p. 200 *et seq.*, and 9 *Current Legal Problems* (1956), pp. 243–4.

the wider social nexus of a legal system. Thus, to understand the function of sovereignty in mid-twentieth century international law, it is necessary to treat the problem of sovereignty in a manner which avoids excluding *a priori* any potentially relevant facet, whether legal or non-legal.

II · THE FORMS OF SOVEREIGNTY

If the history of ideas teaches any lesson, it is surely that supremacy and freedom are perennial problems. Whether we speak of these issues in terms of sovereignty or call them by any other name, they will always be with us. All that has changed and is continuously changing are the manifestations or forms which, at any particular time or in any particular environment, the phenomenon of sovereignty takes.

This reflection will act as a safeguard against undue concern with any attempt to cope with the problem of sovereignty on a purely verbal basis. It will also explain a hesitation to jettison lightly a concept which, since the days of Thomas Aquinas,[7] has well served generations of theologians, lawyers and political scientists.

At the same time, awareness of the multifarious aspects of the phenomenon of sovereignty will induce open-mindedness towards criticism of the ambiguity of the term *sovereignty*.[8] This can be met, however, by a technique which, in the field of philosophy, Leibniz and Christian Wolff evolved,[9] and which became subsequently known as phenomenology and,

7. On sovereignty in the political thought of ancient India, see Kautilya's *Arthaśātra* (transl. Shamastry), 1929, p. 287 *et seq.*, and on synonyms in Greek philosophy and Roman law, Bodin, *Method for the Easy Comprehension of History* (1583—transl. Reynolds), p. 172. See also E. N. van Kleffens, *Sovereignty in International Law*, Hague Academy of International Law, Vol. 82 (1953), p. 5 *et seq.*

8. See above, p. 160.

9. The distinction drawn by Leibniz between *phenomena realia* and *imaginaria* is as topical as it ever was (*Opera Philosophica, De Modo Distinguendi Phaenomena Realia ab Imaginaria*, Vol. I, 1840, pp. 443–5). For an early definition of *phenomenon*, *cf.* Wolff, *Cosmologia Generalis*, 1731, § 225, p. 173: "*Phaenomenon dicitur, quicquid sensui obvium confuse percipitur.*" *Cf.* also J. Stone, *Legal Controls of International Conflict*, 1954, pp. xlix–1.

in the natural sciences and philology, as morphology. At its simplest, it amounts to the articulate elaboration of all or, at least, all relevant forms of the phenomenon under review. So long as the phenomenon remains amorphous, it may prove impossible or difficult to understand its character and implications. Once the various sides of the problem are separated, the phenomenon as a whole becomes easier to comprehend.[10]

In law, the application of this technique appears indicated when limitation of the analysis to the legal segments of a phenomenon would tend to obscure rather than elucidate its character, yet, at the same time, both its legal and non-legal forms can be clearly distinguished. Even if the phenomenon is predominantly or purely legal, this method may recommend itself. In particular, this applies if a legal phenomenon is common to a number of legal systems, but its manifestations differ because of, for instance, the community environment of municipal law and the society environment of international law. Thus, the phenomenological treatment is the congenial method in the fields of comparative law and comparative jurisprudence. In the case of the phenomenon of sovereignty, both reasons apply and explain the choice of treatment of this topic. It may, it is hoped, convince some that, if duly refashioned, the concept of sovereignty is still an eminently serviceable means of understanding the legal and political realities which we desire to explore. Thus, it is but fitting at Austin's College to offer this paper to his shades as a modest, but appreciative tribute.

The phenomenon of sovereignty is the same from whichever angle it is explored. Some of its manifestations may, however, be more relevant for one branch of knowledge than another. The inductively verifiable raw material, as well as the doctrinal treatment of the topic, suggests that six forms of sovereignty are most likely to assist in exploring the meaning and function of sovereignty in international law and or-

10. For attempts to apply this technique to the principle of universality of international institutions, *cf.* the present writer's *The League of Nations and World Order*, 1936, and *Power Politics*, 1951, p. 430 *et seq.*

ganisation. They may be grouped in three pairs, that is to say, positive and negative sovereignty, political and legal sovereignty, and, finally, absolute and relative sovereignty.

It may be helpful to set out in a table these six forms of sovereignty, together with the criteria which have determined these classifications:

CRITERIA	FORMS OF SOVEREIGNTY *	
Contents of Sovereignty:	Positive	Negative
Field of Manifestation of Sovereignty:	Political	Legal
Scope for Manifestation of Sovereignty:	Absolute	Relative

(a) *Positive and Negative Sovereignty.* Sovereignty as understood in theology and the constitutional theory of the unitary State [11] means omnipotence. In both these contexts, the original semantic meaning of this term makes good sense. In speaking of the sovereignty of God, theologians seek to describe divine supremacy and plenitude of power. In this formulation, the emphasis lies on the positive aspect of the phenomenon of sovereignty, that is to say, the complete subjection of man to God. As a matter of course, a negative statement is implied in this proposition. If God is supreme or "almighty," He Himself cannot be subject to any other being and is in a state of absolute freedom.

The theological concept of sovereignty has been secularised

11. On the problem of sovereignty in the federal State, see below, p. 166. On the reasons why the identification of positive sovereignty with internal sovereignty, and of negative sovereignty with external sovereignty, is too narrow and, therefore, likely to be misleading, see below, p. 174.

to describe by way of analogy the position of those who, in relation to their own subjects, claim to be "His lieutenants for the welfare of other men." [12] Every community which is not dependent on any other community has a sovereign in this sense.[13] It is irrelevant whether this is an individual, as in the days of absolutism, or a collective entity, as the Queen in Parliament in the United Kingdom.

In claiming supremacy for sovereign princes, the political science of absolutism safeguarded the overriding claims of God by the formula *Dei gratia*. The significance of this is its implication. These early scholars were not impressed by the supposed dilemma that sovereignty must be either absolute or nothing. They had sufficient elasticity of mind to realise that it was perfectly feasible to visualise, subject to God's absolute sovereignty, a more relative form of sovereignty exercised by their sovereign princes. Since the days of absolutism, the bearers of positive sovereignty have changed. The reality of this form of sovereignty is, however, as potent today as ever. Some theorists of federalism have claimed that, in the federal State, the phenomenon of positive sovereignty has been eradicated. Actually, the federal State succeeds merely in increasing the number of bearers of legal sovereignty by a system of checks and balances.

If two or more entities, each of which may desire to exercise positive sovereignty over the rest, happen to exist simultaneously, they must make their choice. It is between treating sovereignty as an absolute or relative in their mutual relations.[14] If sovereignty is to be absolute, this rules out the

12. Bodin, *Six livres de la république*, 1576, Bk. I, Ch. 10.
       On the origin of this terminology, *cf.* F. A. von der Heydte, *Die Geburtsstunde des Souveränen Staates*, 1952, p. 328 *et seq.* See also W. Ullmann, 64 *English Historical Review* (1949), p. 8 *et seq.* and below, note 18.
13. Even if one of the organs of a federal State does not usurp legal sovereignty, the reality of political sovereignty cannot be eliminated in the federal pattern. See *l.c.* above, n. 10, 1951, p. 88.
14. To simplify matters, absolute sovereignty in the theological meaning of the term is ignored in this juxtaposition. If it were to be taken into account, the situation would not be substantially altered. It would

co-existence of entities which do not accept any one in their midst as superior nor any common superior. Then, either one of these entities must succeed in attaining supremacy over the rest or all must agree to pool their sovereign rights and create a new bearer of positive sovereignty. The world State by conquest or consent illustrates positive sovereignty, treated as an absolute in the relations between a plurality of entities.

The other alternative is for the entities concerned to resign themselves to the necessity of co-existence as the overriding factor in their mutual relations. Then, they must be prepared to renounce or, at least, curb their aspirations for domination over each other. The patterns which, since the classical period of the *symmachies* of the Greek city States,[15] can be observed in the history of international relations preclude dogmatism on the minimum of equality which is compatible with co-existence. It would not, therefore, be advisable to generalise beyond this point: To the extent to which entities base their relations on the principle of equality—whether formal or substantive—sovereignty is transformed from an absolute into a relative. Correspondingly, the emphasis shifts from positive sovereignty to its implied negative.[16]

Negative sovereignty means non-recognition of any superior authority. On the level of legal relations, this situation may be expressed in terms of a right, or freedom, not to have to recognise any superior.[17] Moreover, if entities in this class recognise that certain objects are allocated to one rather than others among themselves and one another's supremacy over such

---

merely become necessary to distinguish between various degrees of relativity of sovereignty.

15. See further G. Ténékidès, *La Notion Juridique d'Indépendance et la Tradition Hellénique,* 1954. See also H. Triepel, *Die Hegemonie,* 1938, p. 355 *et seq.,* and B. Paradisi, *L'Amitié Internationale,* Hague Academy of International Law, Vol. 78 (1951), p. 329 *et seq.*

16. See above, p. 165.

17. *Cf.* for instance, the Letter of 1297 of the Count of Flanders on his Alliance with the King of England against the King of France (Rymer's *Foedera,* Vol. II, p. 737) and the Treaty of Alliance of the same year between the same (*ibid.,* p. 761). See also 25 B.Y.I.L. (1948), p. 55 *et seq.,* and von der Heydte, *l.c.* above note 12, p. 59 *et seq.*

objects, they thereby mutually recognise the exclusive character of this personal or territorial jurisdiction.

Once the possibility of relative sovereignty has been accepted, it is impossible to draw any line beyond which sovereignty becomes inalienable.[18] It then becomes entirely a
question of circumstances whether relations are kept on a
footing of negative sovereignty or whether positive sovereignty
is allowed to intrude again into such a nexus. In the latter
case, the resulting dependency may be restricted to the non-
legal field or even formalised in legal terms.

If hierarchical relations are of a *de facto* type, lawyers tend
to ignore them. If relations of this type are of a *de jure* character, their substantive analysis can still be avoided so long
as they are established by consent; for any inequality based
on consent is considered as leaving unimpaired the status of
legal equality, however formal or hypothetical this may be.
The four other forms of sovereignty serve to clarify these
facets of the phenomenon of sovereignty.

(b) *Legal and Political Sovereignty.* In any social environment in which the supremacy of law is normally assured,
self-limitation of the lawyer to the legal manifestations of sovereignty is not likely to present him with a manifestly distorted
view of the phenomenon of sovereignty. Yet, like any other
kind of blinkers, legal purism has its penalties. It fails to explain relevant problems of some moment.

One is that of the forcible replacement of one legal order
by another or, in other words, the validity of revolutionary

18. For a perceptive analysis of naturalist inhibitions and ideologies on this
point, *cf.* P. N. Riesenberg, *Inalienability of Sovereignty in Medieval
Political Thought*, 1956.

    On the somewhat pragmatic resuscitation in recent Soviet legal theory
of the notion of the inalienability of State sovereignty, and its extension
to nationhood, see I. Lapenna, *Conceptions Soviétiques de Droit International Public,* 1954, p. 228. For use of this terminology in Soviet practice, see Mr. Shepilov's Speech to the Supreme Soviet of February 12,
1957 (*The Times,* February 13, 1957): "The Soviet people have been
and remain opponents of Egypt's inalienable rights being curtailed by
removing the Suez Canal from under Egyptian sovereignty and establishing some sort of foreign administration for the waterway."

law. Another is the merely apparent elimination of sovereignty in the federal State.[19] Finally, situations of the ineffectiveness of the legal sovereign and the impotence of law in the face of "over-mighty subjects" can hardly be understood fully in terms of the categories of thought which are at the command of the analytical purist. How can he hope to cope with *de facto* rivals of the legitimate bearers of positive sovereignty? Still, these are exceptional situations, and if they occur, they are symptoms of a serious malaise in a body politic. It is, therefore, at least arguable that, in relation to mature legal systems, strict compliance with the postulate of the self-isolation of the legal element is more important than any resulting inability of lawyers to cope with other than typical or stereotype situations.

What may be a questionable postulate in mature systems of community law becomes a serious bar to the understanding of the meaning of sovereignty in totalitarian States and international law.[20] The reason is that, in the municipal law of advanced communities, rules of public policy prevent the worst excesses of extreme social inequality. International customary law does not know of any corresponding *ordre public international* [21] and must resign itself to the supremacy of the rule of force in international relations.[22] Admittedly, the contractual quasi-order of the United Nations is more ambitious, but not equally so in relation to all members of the United Nations. This privileged position of the select few—

19. See *l.c.* above, note 10, 1951, p. 87 *et seq.*
20. On the similarities between these types of law, see further *l.c.* note 10 above, 1951, pp. 216–17.

    Even on the purely analytical level, the interpretation of terms such as "political independence" in Article 10 of the Covenant of the League of Nations or "economic independence" in the Geneva Protocol of 1922 (*Austro-German Customs Union* case 1931—A/B 41) calls for awareness of the possibility that political (or economic) and legal independence are not necessarily synonymous terms.
21. See further *l.c.* note 6 above, p. 376 *et seq.* [and, further, 43 *Texas Law Review* (1965), p. 455 *et seq.*, or 18 *Current Legal Problems* (1965), p. 191 *et seq.*].
22. See further *l.c.* note 10 above, 1951, p. 202 *et seq.*

"enshrined" as it is in the Charter of the United Nations—
makes it even more necessary not to forgo voluntarily any
tool which is likely to provide more than a merely formalistic
answer to the mystery of this peculiar type of "sovereign
equality."

To see the relevance of these issues for purposes of legal
analysis does not require any consciously sociological treatment of international law. It suffices to be endowed with the
common sense and independence of minds such as Austin or
Oppenheim could claim their own.

In his Lecture on *Sovereignty*, Austin examined the position
of the French Government during the Allied occupation of
France in 1815. As the commands issued by the Allies to the
French Government and the latter's obedience were "comparatively rare and transient," Austin did not think that this
amounted to a state of subjection which was incompatible
with the continued sovereignty of the French Government.[23]
In a similar way, he analysed the position of the extremely
weak Saxon Government in relation to the members of the
Holy Alliance.[24]

In more general terms, Austin considered that, although
powerful States happen to be permanently superior, and
feeble States permanently inferior, so long as there is no habit
of command or obedience, hierarchical relations of this type
are compatible with the sovereignty of weak States.[25]

Austin qualified his analysis of the position in Saxony by
the significant proviso that, "in case the commands and submission were somewhat more numerous and frequent, we
might find it impossible to determine certainly the class of
the Saxon community. We might find it impossible to determine certainly where the sovereignty resided: whether the
Saxon Government were a government supreme and independent; or were in a habit of obedience, and therefore in

23. *The Province of Jurisprudence Determined,* Vol. I (5th ed. by Camp-
    bell), p. 222.
24. *Ibid.,* pp. 223 and 229.
25. *Ibid.*

a state of subjection, to the allied or conspiring monarchs." [26]

A borderline case which puzzled Austin was Prussia's predominance over the other members of the North German Confederation. It made Austin wonder whether this hegemonial relation had not engendered habits of command and obedience so as to leave Prussia alone in a state of sovereignty and reduce the others to one of subjection.[27]

Similarly, Oppenheim was too much a scholar and realist to be oblivious of the relevance for the study of international law of the power hierarchies in international relations. He took, however, the tenable view that the balance of power system of his time reduced sufficiently the discrepancies between greater and smaller States to provide for the indispensable minimum of social equality between the subjects of international law. In his view, the "first and principal moral" which the history of international law could teach was the need for such an equilibrium. In its absence, the omnipotence of an "over-powerful State," that is to say, its exercise of positive sovereignty over other States in disregard of international law could not be prevented.[28]

In a world in which discrepancies in power were less glaring than in our age, and a relatively effective system of balance of power appeared to neutralise any preponderance of power as, in fact, existed, it sufficed to point out that these conditions of international law in general, and legal sovereignty in particular, had to be borne in mind.

In the post-1945 era, three decisive changes have taken place. First, the process of concentration of power in international society appears to have reached its penultimate phase, and our bipolarised world is much more deeply divided than that of Austin or Oppenheim. Secondly, the discrepancies in power

26. *Ibid.,* p. 229.
27. *Ibid.,* p. 229, note 1.
28. *International Law,* Vol. I, 1905 (1st ed.), pp. 73–4.

It is instructive to compare Oppenheim's penetrating observations on this topic with the version which, since the 5th ed. (1937, pp. 80–1) has replaced the original text.

between the hegemonial States in each of the world's two halves and their "junior partners," "allies" or "satellites" are no longer of a merely quantitative character. The possession of such weapons as megaton bombs and ballistic rockets with nuclear warheads marks the dividing line between "over-powerful" States and the rest of international society. Thirdly, outside the deceptive orbit of the United Nations, "non-committed" countries are hardly a balancing third force, but objects of a continuous contest between the two world camps.[29] The somewhat anaemic character of legal sovereignty in international customary law, and of "sovereign equality" under the Charter of the United Nations, becomes fully explicable only against this sombre background of the overshadowing reality of political sovereignty in the nuclear age.

Paradoxical as it may appear, the rise of these new Leviathans has its compensations. The existence of hegemonial powers which, in their own orbits, are either immune from challenge or can crush resistance with impunity creates a stronger type of international quasi-order than that offered by the United Nations on the level of world society. Thus, it holds out the promise of types of international law which, in effectivity, may well compare favourably with universal international law.

Admittedly, in a split world, these types of international law are limited to the sectors of the world which are controlled by one of the hegemonial powers. It may also be conceded that a hegemonial power which wields such positive sovereignty over those under its sway is itself necessarily above the law. Yet, the fact that this was the position under the Tudor

29. See further *l.c.* note 10 above, 1951, pp. 113 *et seq.*, and 695 *et seq.*, and 36 *Grotius Transactions* (1950), p. 229 *et seq.* [and, further, 13 *Year Book of World Affairs* (1959), p. 236 *et seq.*, 15 *ibid.* (1961), p. 233 *et seq.*, and 21 *ibid.* (1967), p. 179 *et seq.*].

The description in the Speech of the Pakistan Prime Minister, Mr. Suhrawardy, at Dacca University of the hypothetical situation of the Baghdad Pact being restricted to its four Muslim members, and the United Kingdom excluded from it, deserves to be recorded: "Zero plus zero plus zero plus zero still equals zero" (*The Times*, December 17, 1956).

monarchs does not prevent English lawyers from treating the law of Tudor absolutism as a vital period in the evolution of English law. Finally, there are differences which ought not to be minimised between the two hegemonial powers. The one has had its task largely thrust upon her; exercises it rather as a trust than as a privilege; cherishes the values of the heritage of Western civilisation and is susceptible to public opinion at home and abroad. It suffices to say of the other that, in almost every respect, it is its opposite.

Yet when all this is said, the antipodes share a characteristic which, in order to understand sovereignty in contemporary international law and organisation, is more directly relevant. In their respective realms, any apparent subjection of either hegemonial power to law in its relations to its "allies" or "satellites" is purely self-willed and optional. In this respect, the attitudes taken by the Soviet Union and the United States towards the Optional Clause in the Statute of the World Court are symptomatic and not so different as, on the surface, may appear. The Soviet Union has never stooped to make a declaration under Article 36 of the Statute. The United States has done so, but excluding disputes which are essentially within her own domestic jurisdiction "as determined by the United States of America." [30]

(c) *Absolute and Relative Sovereignty.* The limitation of any form of sovereignty to its absolute extreme is as little justified as the attribution of a necessarily absolute character to any other notion. In fact, the very contrast of the sovereignty of God with any form of worldly sovereignty proves sufficiently the necessarily relative character of any type of sovereignty claimed by a temporal authority.[31] Nothing, for instance, prevents positive sovereignty from being "relativised" so as to assist in explaining what happens in the case of a limitation of negative sovereignty by international law.[32] Conversely, the term *dependence* need not be used exclusively in an absolute sense. If duly "relativised"—as its counterpart *inde-*

30. See further the writer's *International Law*, Vol. I, 1949, pp. 401–2.
31. See above, pp. 165–6.
32. See below, p. 174 *et seq.*

pendence—this term appears to fill a serious gap in terminological equipment.[33] Moreover, the distinction between forms of absolute and relative sovereignty makes it possible to find a useful place for interdependence. If dependence is not one-sided, but mutual, the substantive reciprocity of dependence is well expressed by the term interdependence.

The various states of absolute and relative sovereignty can then be tabulated in a simple scale:

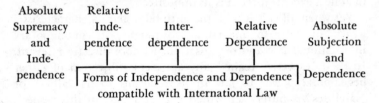

Absolute Supremacy and Independence	Relative Independence	Interdependence	Relative Dependence	Absolute Subjection and Dependence
	Forms of Independence and Dependence compatible with International Law			

III · The Forms of Legal Sovereignty

The description of supremacy and freedom in terms of jurisdiction and discretion in the legal sphere may be of apparent rather than real significance. If jurisdiction or discretion is overriding, it cannot be overruled. Conversely, if it can be overruled it cannot be overriding. In other words, whatever the illusions or inhibitions of individual bearers of overriding jurisdiction, this is likely to differ, at most in degree, but not in kind from sovereignty in the positive meaning of the term.

In the relations between subjects of international law territorial and personal jurisdiction—as these terms are employed in international law—are not forms of *positive* sovereignty, for they indicate independence from one another and mutually recognised areas of supremacy over *objects* of international law. Both are illustrations of *negative* sovereignty.[34] If, for instance, the death penalty is applied to the citizen of a sovereign State in his own country, this amounts to an exercise

33. See below, p. 178 *et seq.*
34. See above, p. 167, and further Rousseau, *l.c.* above, note 4, 1948, p. 220 *et seq.*

of territorial and positive sovereignty in the relations between the territorial sovereign and the condemned man. However, in the relations between the territorial sovereign and other subjects of international law, this State activity constitutes merely an exercise of negative sovereignty.

It is sometimes said that territorial and personal jurisdiction may be concurrently exercised. This is true, but only in the sense that several subjects of international law may simultaneously exercise their own exclusive jurisdiction, be it territorial or personal, over one and the same object of international law. Thus, a national abroad is subject to the territorial sovereignty of the place of his sojourn, but he may still be under legal obligations towards the sovereign of his home State. Yet, the fact that one and the same object is the addressee of commands from different sovereigns does not affect the exclusive character of relations which between either of the two sovereigns and the addressee partake of the character of positive sovereignty, but which in the mutual relations between these sovereigns illustrate the operation of two different forms of negative sovereignty.

It would be precipitate to assume that international law does not know of positive sovereignty. It operates through the medium of the compulsory and optional rules of international law which limit the scope of those governing territorial and personal sovereignty.[35] In every such case, one subject of international law acquires the right to command another subject to behave in accordance with the rule invoked. Whenever a new rule of customary law grows up, the existence of a general principle of law recognised by civilised nations is proved or a treaty obligation has been created, the field of negative sovereignty shrinks in favour of that of positive sovereignty.

If, for instance, a rule of international customary law or general principle of law recognised by civilised nations bids subjects of international law to treat one another's nationals in accordance with the minimum standard of international law—or a treaty embodies the most-favoured-nation standard

35. For these rules, see *l.c.* above, note 6, p. 214 *et seq.*

—the rule in question establishes, potentially until invoked and actually if invoked, a hierarchical relation of command and obedience between the subjects of international law concerned.

If the rule is of a unilateral character as, for instance, a crushing peace treaty which a victor imposes on the vanquished, it is easy to perceive the state of dependency created by the treaty. Similarly, a *societas leonina* on the Roman model or an international protectorate by which the "protected" State grants to its "protector" the right of exclusive international representation, appears to fit well into this pattern.

If two States conclude an alliance, the reciprocal character of the rights of positive sovereignty which one acquires over the other may be thought to cancel out the element of subjection. Yet, whether this reciprocity is real or merely apparent depends on the circumstances of each individual case. Reciprocity may be formal or substantive. While, in the case of a reciprocal alliance between a giant power and a dwarf State, formal equality is likely to disguise actual and one-sided dependence, the position is different in the case of an alliance between States of roughly equal strength.[36]

If legal rules form part of international customary law or are recognised as general principles of law, the element of substantive reciprocity, which takes the sting out of the exercise of positive sovereignty, is no less pronounced. Would it not, therefore, be advisable to be content with the simplicity of the traditional formulation, that is to say, the limitation of sovereignty by international law or, at least, the indubitably elegant phraseology of the supremacy of international law?

If full understanding of a problem can be combined with simplicity and elegance of exposition, this is the optimum that is attainable. In this particular case, however, both these formulations appear to explain singularly little of what actually happens when international law is supposed to become the active agent in limiting sovereignty or is poised in a position of supremacy over sovereignty dethroned. Actually, both

36. See above, p. 167 *et seq.*

these formulations may easily come to fulfil unintended ideological functions. The objective existence of international law is taken for granted as something beyond the need of proof. It would be more to the point to inquire whether it can be proved. This, however, is too big a subject to be treated incidentally in this paper.

In the case of rules of a universal, general or particular character, whatever is taken away from one subject of international law by way of limitation of the field of negative sovereignty accrues actually or potentially to others in the form of the acquisition of corresponding powers of positive sovereignty. In the case of rules of a unilateral character, however, as in the case of a one-sided treaty, the limitation of sovereignty by international law means a unilateral assumption of positive sovereignty over the obligated State. Admittedly, this positive sovereignty—like its negative counterpart—is of a relative character. The beneficiary cannot insist on any type of behaviour on the part of the obligated State, but merely on compliance with the rule. The more serious, however, the limitation of negative sovereignty is the wider and more absolute the scope of positive sovereignty becomes. In any case, if the relativity of negative sovereignty is accepted, that of positive sovereignty is no argument against its description in terms of sovereignty. Moreover, in one respect, the exercise of positive sovereignty is truly absolute. Its bearers are entirely free agents to invoke or waive observance of the rule in question.

This means that the whole of the interplay of the rules of international law [37] can be expressed in terms of the interplay of the forms of positive and negative sovereignty. Whenever negative sovereignty is limited by optional or compulsory rules of international law, it does not vanish. What happens is that potential or actual jurisdiction is transferred and, correspondingly, negative sovereignty is transformed into positive sovereignty. If any particular rule ceases to be operative, the process works in reverse Thus, positive and negative sovereignty are truly complementary terms.

37. See further *l.c.* note 6 above, p. 195 *et seq.*

Three doubts require, however, to be laid at rest. They relate to the character of prohibitory rules, the jurisdiction of international institutions and analogies from municipal law, which appear to militate against the analysis of rights under international law in terms of positive sovereignty.

(a) *Positive Sovereignty and Prohibitive Rules.* Who is the bearer of positive sovereignty in the case of prohibitory rules of international law? In the absence of such rules, a subject of international law may exercise its discretion as, for instance, regarding the exercise of its *jus ad bellum.* Once a prohibitory rule in this field comes into existence, does not the former right cease to exist? This is true but, even in this case, a transfer of jurisdiction and the creation of an area of positive sovereignty have occurred.

If a multilateral treaty, such as the Kellogg Pact, comes into force, and war other than in self-defence is outlawed, the parties to the treaty acquire rights of positive sovereignty in both their individual and collective capacities. Thus, in the example chosen, each of the parties may demand from all others compliance with the international quasi-order established. Yet, the former jurisdiction to wage war for other than defensive purpose has not vanished. It now rests with the collectivity of the parties to the treaty, for they are free at any time to unmake the treaty by *contrarius actus* and to hand back their joint jurisdiction to each of the participants. In the case of rules of international customary law and general principles of law recognised by civilised nations, *mutatis mutandis,* the same applies. Whether the prohibitory rule is invoked by an individual subject of international law or is waived by the collectivity of these subjects, in either case they exercise positive sovereignty. Yet, while in the one case it is relative, in the other it is absolute.

(b) *Positive Sovereignty and the Jurisdiction of International Institutions.* Does the view of the necessarily complementary character of the forms of positive and negative sovereignty explain the jurisdiction exercised by international institutions?

All international institutions are optional and, of necessity, exercise only the authority which is delegated to them by their members. They may do so expressly or tacitly, or merely acquiesce in an arrogation of jurisdiction on the part of an international institution. Claims made on behalf of any international institution to be entitled to exercise jurisdiction over non-members can be supported only if the exercise of this jurisdiction rests on consent, acquiescence, recognition or estoppel of the non-member concerned.[38] Thus, the acquisition of any jurisdiction by international institutions rests necessarily on acts of transfer from their member States.

Actually, the constituent instrument of any international organ lends itself readily to this interpretation. In the field in which the members decide to limit their sovereignty, each of the members acquires potential rights of positive sovereignty against all other members. By consenting to the establishment of an international institution, each member must be taken to have transferred these rights to the institution in question. Thus, the functional jurisdiction exercised by international institutions is merely the sum total of the pooled and delegated rights of positive sovereignty which result from the transfer of rights from the members to these organisations. Subsequent agreements concluded by international institutions with each other or sovereign States do not add any new feature to the picture, for whatever powers international institutions exercise is purely derivative.

(c) *Municipal Law Analogies.* The explanation of limitations of sovereignty by rules of international law in terms of the creation of areas of positive sovereignty is likely to meet with some psychological resistance from the municipal lawyer. He may wonder whether an explanation of limitations of the freedom of action of a citizen by the Common Law or statutory law in similar terms would make sense. The simple answer is that it would not. The reason is that the two situations are not analogous, for nothing is likely to prove more misleading than analogies from one type of law to another. In particular, this applies if two types of law are so different as the mature laws of highly integrated communities and the law of a loosely organised international society.[39]

In the Queen in Parliament, English law has its composite

38. See further the writer's *International Law,* Vol. I (3rd ed.), Ch. 25.
39. See further 2 *Current Legal Problems* (1949), p. 103 *et seq.*

bearer of absolute and positive sovereignty. It, therefore, has neither need nor room for additional bearers of relative and negative sovereignty.[40] The initial hypothesis of international law which relates to the co-existence of sovereign States is that these recognise one another as bearers of relative, and negative, sovereignty. Areas of positive sovereignty must, therefore, necessarily be carved out from the existing fields of negative sovereignty. Moreover, in the absence of a superior bearer of absolute sovereignty, none other than the subjects of international law, and any derivative organs which they choose to create, are available as bearers of such positive sovereignty as, in this way, may come into existence in international law.

Another difference between municipal law and international law, which is closely related to the existence of an absolute and positive sovereign in the former, and its initial absence in the latter, is the existence of rules of public policy in municipal law and their absence in international customary law.[41] Emphasis on potential and actual dependence as is implied in the concept of positive sovereignty is more necessary in a legal system in which subjects are so little protected against their own weakness and folly as in international customary law. They are free, as they choose, to limit their own sovereignty in favour of other subjects of international law. They may even validly consent to their own relegation to mere objects of international law.

Affirmation of this type of positive sovereignty does not appear to run counter to any of the governing rules of international customary law. None of the rules of international customary law sets any limits to the alienable character of sovereignty. The validity of treaties by which, as in the case of international protectorates, relations of dependency under international law are created does not depend on conditions which differ from the requirements of other consensual engagements. What distinguishes a "protected" State under international law from a colonial protectorate is merely the intention of the parties that the treaty be subject to interna-

40. On the position in a federal State, see above, note 13.
41. *Cf. l.c.* above, note 6, p. 376 *et seq.* [and *l.c.* above, note 21].

tional law, and the continued recognition of the "protected" State as a subject of international law by the protecting power and third States.[42] So long as the international personality of the dependent State continues, the exercise of any amount of positive sovereignty by one subject of international law over another is fully compatible with these relations remaining governed by international law.

In any case, the attempts made by the World Court to cope with the problem of limitations of sovereignty on the assumption that any such limitations relate merely to the *exercise* of sovereign rights, but leave unimpaired a somewhat hypothetical status of independence appear slightly artificial.[43] It would make it necessary to allow for the existence of a number of ghosts of a "hollow sovereignty" [44] and to introduce yet another pair of variants of sovereignty, that is to say, formal and substantive sovereignty.

Probably for tactical reasons, the World Court did not wish to state bluntly the true position. Germany was bound by the Peace Treaty of Versailles of 1919, not because this left her independence intact, but because, under international customary law, every subject of international law may forgo its independence and enter into relations of dependence. The Court's doctrine also fails to explain the problem of the dependent and non-sovereign subject of international law.

To be content to explain any kind of limitations of sovereignty on the ground of the growing "interdependence of the peoples of the world" [45] might be in the spirit of San Francisco. This might also prove more acceptable to the ideological outposts of both hegemonial powers and their junior partners or

---

42. On the attempt to relegate *inter se* relations between protecting powers and protected States to the plane of municipal law, *cf. l.c.* above, note 38, Ch. 5. *Cf.* also the apt formulation in the Final Declaration of the Tangier Conference of 1956 (Cmnd. 60—1957, p. 9) that the Sultan of Morocco had "recovered" the totality of his powers.
43. *Cf.* the *Wimbledon* case (1923), A 1, p. 25. See also B 10, p. 21, and B 14, p. 36.
44. Judge Hudson's Sep. Op. in the *Lighthouses in Crete and Samos* case (1937), A/B 71, p. 127.
45. Article 76 (b) of the U.N. Charter.

satellites, for this terminology has the inestimable asset of hiding tactfully the real character of relations in which interdependence appears suspiciously akin to dependence.

The choice of dependence as descriptive of relations in which the beneficiary of rules commands and their addressee obeys is embarrassing because it states an inconvenient truth. It, however, avoids the evasiveness of the doctrine evolved by the World Court. It appears to provide a uniform explanation of the increasing number of *de facto* and *de jure* hierarchies in international relations and makes unnecessary any embarrassed exception for dependent States. In order, however, not to lead to any overstatement, this notion requires one qualification. If exercised on a footing of substantive reciprocity and mutuality,[46] positive sovereignty is compatible with relations between equals and, then, is so relativised as to justify the use of the term *interdependence*.

Emphasis on dependence as the typical consequences of the exercise of positive sovereignty in international law underlines the overriding trend in our bipolarised world society: its growing stratification and, concomitantly, the increasing importance of hierarchical relations on the world scene. In particular, this applies to the decisive relations between each of the world powers and its junior partners or satellites.[46a] If words are meant to express truth rather than hide it, it is advisable to put the emphasis on matters essential rather than peripheral. At the same time, this does not exclude expressing relations which deserve a different description in terms of either independence or interdependence.

IV · USES OF THE FORMS OF SOVEREIGNTY

To understand both the potentialities and limitations of the forms of sovereignty, it is necessary to elaborate more articulately the specific character of the phenomenological categories employed in this paper.

Every such phenomenon is an abstraction from real-

---

46. See above, p. 174.

[46a. See further *l.c.* in note 3 above (1967), p. 179 *et seq*.].

ity.[47] The only legitimate purpose of distinguishing various forms of a phenomenon is to use them as means of classification. These forms are convenient means of coping with individual manifestations of more abstract notions on lower levels of abstraction than those congenial to most social phenomena. Thus, they are valuable aids to more concrete thinking on particular facets of such phenomena.

The forms of a phenomenon may be likened to trays on which relevant data—facts or trends—are sorted out. Frequently, all that is required to perform this task is a sound instinct and common sense. It would not be fair, however, to ask anybody to take on trust any allocation of particular data. The selective tests employed must be rationally verifiable. Like other criteria, they vary according to the object and purpose of any examination. This is true of the forms of sovereignty as much as of those of any other phenomenon.

Probably the least reliable test would be the explanation offered by any party which is directly or indirectly interested in any socially relevant set of facts. The social functions fulfilled by such manifestations and their actual effects offer less suspect guidance. These functions are primarily determined by the character and degree of cohesion of the social environment in which a phenomenon manifests itself. Thus, both these conditioning factors are highest on the list of tests which serve to assist in allocating particular data to the most significant forms of their phenomenon.

Within the compass of this paper, it is not possible to attempt more than to illustrate shortly the application of these primary tests. Actually, this is probably as much as is required, for another object of this technique is to enable anybody who has convinced himself of the helpfulness of this method to analyse for himself any other manifestations of the phenomenon of sovereignty which may attract him.

(a) *The Character of the Surrounding Social Relations.* In any "pure" community in the technical meaning of this term, it would be likely that the exercise of any sovereign rights

47. On legal abstractions in particular, see *l.c.* above, note 6 [and further the present writer's *The Inductive Approach to International Law* (1965), p. 72 et seq.].

were as much in performance of duties as of rights and, primarily, in the interest of the community concerned. In a "pure" society, the opposition presumption would apply. This means that, in any actual social nexus, the verdict on the character of any exercise of sovereign rights is likely to be decisively influenced by the relative admixture of "society" and "community" elements in the structure of the group concerned.[48]

Thus, if any particular manifestation of sovereignty in contemporary international affairs is at issue, its accurate interpretation is likely to depend largely on an adequate assessment of its social environment, that is to say, present-day world society. The experiences gained during the last few years appear to have done little to shake the analysis of international relations in the nuclear age, both inside and outside the United Nations, in terms of power politics in disguise.[49] One thing only has become still plainer than it was before. The validity of the maxim "The greater the truth, the greater the libel" is not confined to English Criminal Law. In a field which is honeycombed with precariously entrenched ideological positions and frequented by amateurs and professionals in the game of flying their kites of escapism, this is not altogether surprising.

It appears but consistent with the tradition established in the teaching of international law and relations at University College London to choose as illustrations manifestations of sovereignty in recent years which—in the eyes of what Oppenheim ventured to call diplomatic international lawyers—would be best covered with oblivion. From this point of view, a comparison of three apparently unrelated manifestations of sovereignty, the suppression of the Hungarian October Revolution of 1956, the Anglo-French expedition to Port Said of the same year and the *coup d'état* in Guatemala of 1954, is not uninstructive.

48. See further 2 *Current Legal Problems* (1949), p. 103 *et seq.*, and *l.c.* above note 10, 1951, p. 12 *et seq.*
49. See further *l.c.* above note 10, 1951, p. 695 *et seq.* [and 21 *Year Book of World Affairs* (1967), p. 179 *et seq.*].

Even in dealing with topics of so explosive a character, it would be possible to be commendably "discreet" or, in other words, to limit oneself to the "safe" and, therefore, meaningless aspects of these events. All that would be necessary would be to confine the discussion to the legal form of sovereignty and refrain from evaluating the implications of these legal findings. Each of these acts, if attributable to subjects of international law other than the territorial sovereign,[50] amounts to an intervention, that is to say, an invasion of the area of negative sovereignty. Unless undertaken with the consent of the territorial sovereign or justified by an enabling rule of international law, any such intervention amounts to an illegal act.

It would be hard to find a legal justification for the first of the two Russian interventions, that is to say, the overthrow of the Nagy Government by the Russian forces stationed in Hungary. The second Russian intervention, which may have taken place at the request, or with the *ex post facto* approval, of the Russian-established Kadar Government, presents greater difficulties, for the nominal bearer of Hungarian sovereignty who was at least the outward beneficiary of this intervention would be the last to complain of any breach of sovereignty.

Assuming—although, for the time being this view rests merely on indirect evidence—that the United States, Nicaragua and Honduras had "co-operated" in making possible the Guatemala *coup d'état,* this was as much—or as little—an illegal interference with Guatemalan sovereignty as the second Russian intervention in Budapest.[51] Once the revolutionary mili-

---

50. In this respect, the only controversial case is that of the Guatemala *coup d'état.* It appears, however, established that the Guatemala revolutionaries used the territories of two neighbouring States, both members of the United Nations, as bases and operated with aeroplanes of United States manufacture. See further *The Annual Register of World Events,* Vol. 196 (1954) p. 329 *et seq. Cf.* also A. van Wynen Thomas and A. J. Thomas, *Non-Intervention,* 1956, p. 161 *et seq.;* the fair selection of extracts from the discussions in the Security Council in L. B. Sohn, *Cases on United Nations Law,* 1956, p. 371 *et seq.,* and the curious Report by Her Majesty's Minister at Guatemala, Cmd. 9277 (1954).

  [See also *l.c.* in note 3 above (1959), p. 236 *et seq.*]

51. *Ex abundanti cautela,* it may be added that, in terms of humanity or in-

tary junta was in power, the new bearers of Guatemalan sovereignty were as anxious as the Kadar Government to "heal" whatever hypothetical breach of international law might have occurred.

In the case of the Anglo-French expedition to Port Said, an enabling rule which could be invoked to justify this ill-fated venture would be Article 51 of the Charter of the United Nations. The ground of intervention would then have been collective defence of Israel against the series of armed attacks which, over a prolonged period, Egypt had launched by infiltrating irregulars (*fedayeen*) from the Gaza Strip and elsewhere.[52]

What results does this trilogy yield? In the cases of the intervention in Budapest and Guatemala, the new bearers of territorial sovereignty were only too willing to grant the requisite consent and, thus, to square political reality and the requirements of international law. So long as third powers did not draw from the dependence of these governments on the interventionist powers the conclusion that the dependent States had ceased to be subjects of international law [53] or the substituted governments were not entitled to be treated as either *de facto* or *de jure* governments of sovereign States, the actual lack of independence of these governments did not matter. What, then, became decisive was the consent, approval or acquiescence of these dependent governments.

The Anglo-French intervention did not lead to the establishment of a new bearer of Egyptian sovereignty. As the Egyptian Government contested the legality of the intervention, and neither side was prepared to submit the issue to legal adjudication, the position remained necessarily inconclusive in law. If, however, the Anglo-French action had led to the es-

---

humanity, legally and sociologically comparable acts may still deserve very different assessment. We are not, however, concerned here with the possible and, in other contexts, relevant distinction between barbarous and civilised forms of intervention.

52. See further the writer's Letter to the Editor of *The Times*, November 8, 1956. [See further *l.c.* in note 13 above (1965), p. 175 *et seq.*].

53. See above, p. 177.

tablishment of a new Egyptian Government on the Churchill-
ian model of 1942,[54] it would have become indistinguishable
in law from those of the Soviet Union and the United States.
It, therefore, appears that, on the level of international law
as applied in the *direct* relations between members of the
United Nations, an initially illegal intervention can become
legal by dint of the successful establishment of a more pliable
bearer of sovereignty in another member State and the acquiescence of other member States in the breach of the relevant
Principles of the Charter of the United Nations.

On the level of the United Nations organs which concerned
themselves with these cases, these issues took on more sophisticated appearances. In the Guatemala case, the existence of
two international institutions with competing jurisdictions—
the United Nations and the Organisation of American States
—made it possible for action in both to be delayed until the
coup d'état had succeeded, and the new bearer of Guatemalan
sovereignty ratified the intervention.

In the case of the Russian interventions in Hungary, the
General Assembly of the United Nations passed recommendations in which it affirmed the illegality of these interventions
and exhorted the Soviet Union to desist from further interference with Hungarian domestic matters. Unless, however,
the General Assembly refuses to treat the Kadar Government
as effectively representing one of the "sovereign and equal"
members of the United Nations, it will find it increasingly
difficult to refuse to recognise that the utter dependence of
the government of one member State on that of another is
incompatible with the principle of the "sovereign equality"
of the members of the United Nations.

In the case of the "armed conflict" in the Near East, the
General Assembly did not even attempt to explore the pos-

54. *Cf. The Observer* (newspaper), May 26, 1946, and *Survey of International Affairs*, Vol. I: *The Middle East in the War* (2nd rev. impr.),
1953, p. 208 *et seq.*

On the threat to withdraw recognition from the King of Greece in
exile to induce him to acquiesce in the regency of Archbishop Damaski-
nos, *cf.* Sir Winston Churchill's Letter of December 30, 1944 (Churchill,
The Second World War, Vol. 6, 1954, p. 279).

sibility that, under Article 51 of the Charter, the action taken by Israel and the Anglo-French intervention might be justifiable. It passed resolutions which took for granted the illegality of the action taken by the three Powers.

In law, the inconclusive debates in the Security Council on the Guatemalan *coup d'état* and the resolution passed by the General Assembly on Hungary and the Near East amounted very much to the same thing, for all these resolutions were but recommendations. In each case, however, what happened and did not happen did not lack metalegal significance. The reactions of the other members of the United Nations made it possible for the interventionist powers to gauge accurately whether other States would desire to fall back on their own reserve powers of collective defence under Article 51 of the Charter or, in other words, wish to recover their freedom of action.

Viewed in the light of the pattern of political sovereignty, it becomes intelligible *why,* in a system of power politics in disguise, some interventions are successful and, ultimately, tend to become legalised and *vice versa.* In the case of Guatemala, it was clear that the Soviet Union did not seriously challenge the exercise of political sovereignty by, and on behalf of, the United States inside the Western hemisphere. Moreover, this *coup d'état* had the sympathy of the greater number of the members of the Organisation of American States and the Western powers at large. Thus, in fact, the United Nations had to accept a new type of Monroe Doctrine, which equated the discreet exercise of positive sovereignty by one of the hegemonial powers inside its undisputed orbit with the principle of "sovereign equality" in the Charter of the United Nations.

Conversely, over Budapest, the United States made it plain that it would not use the Platonic condemnation by the General Assembly of Russian intervention in Hungary as a justification for a counter-intervention of her own with incalculable consequences. Thus, again, recommendations of the General Assembly masked discreetly the constitutional inability of the United Nations to prevent or redress the exercise of political sovereignty by one of the hegemonial powers within its own power radius unless the other world power is prepared to make the issue a *casus belli*.

By way of contrast, the Near Eastern intervention under- lined the consequences of the assertion without the consent of their hegemonial power of political sovereignty by States within the purview of one of the world powers. It exposed this intervention to the full onslaught of the other hegemonial power. The exercise of its full weight by the one, and the pronounced passivity of the other, super-power gave an ap- pearance of effectiveness to the relevant resolutions of the Gen- eral Assembly and enabled it boldly to proclaim its rejection of an Anglo-French Monroe Doctrine in the Near East.

Thus, these cases of intervention illustrate well the meaning of sovereign equality in the Charter of the United Nations. In principle, sovereign equality is incompatible with the uni- lateral assumption of political sovereignty by one member of the United Nations over another. If, however, one of the world powers takes such action, and the other tacitly concedes the "essentially domestic" character of this exercise of jurisdiction —or, with the tolerance of at least one of these powers, any other State acts in their image [55]—it becomes evident that, under the Charter of the United Nations, some of its members are more sovereign and equal than others. The scope of their exercise of positive sovereignty, and the degree of the depend- ence established in this way, are the measure of the relevance of viewing such relations in terms of political and positive sovereignty.

In cases in which a hegemonial power is allowed to substi- tute with impunity bearers of sovereignty in other member States, Paragraph 7 of Article 2 of the Charter of the United Nations comes to fulfil a new function. Once the *fait accompli* has been accomplished, the clause tends to operate retroac- tively in favour of the factual monopoly of hegemonial inter- vention. In situations of this type, the international quasi-order of the United Nations becomes ineffective and gives way to

55. From this point of view, it is worth while examining whether, in rela- tion to Kashmir, an Indian Monroe Doctrine is in the making.

sectional, but more effective international orders enforced by sovereigns who, in fact, are *legibus soluti.*

In the relations between "ordinary" members of the United Nations, "sovereign equality" means reciprocal respect for the legal and negative sovereignty of member States. In those, however, between the "overmighty" members and others in a state of *de facto* dependence, it means exactly the opposite, that is to say, sovereign inequality and acceptance of the political and positive sovereignty of those above the law of Charter.[55a]

Awareness of the scope in the United Nations for the existence of relations on such a footing of dependence indicates the danger for accurate analysis which would result from acceptance of any of the more "modern" alternative terms such as interdependence, active and peaceful co-existence or other similar appellations. They are appropriate only to designate relations of truly mutual dependence. If, in relation to contemporary world affairs, these terms were used exclusively to point out goals not yet attained on a global scale, they would be beyond reproach. If, however, they are equated indiscriminately with the highly ambivalent reality of the United Nations, their abuse is hard to avoid. They tend to become either euphemistic disguises of less attractive, but more real relations of an essentially hierarchical character or purely verbal forms of escapism.[55b]

(b) *The Intensity of the Surrounding Social Relations.* Emphasis on the ideological and utopian elements in the interpretation of world affairs in terms of interdependence rather than dependence is open to an intrinsically irrelevant, but nonetheless favoured form of criticism. It is supposed to be unhelpfully destructive and oblivious of, in a "long view of the matter," more important constructive trends in international society.

Is not the scope of international law continuously widening?

55a. *Cf.* L. C. Green, "The Double Standard of the United Nations," 11 *Year Book of World Affairs* (1957), p. 104 *et seq.*

[55b. See further *l.c.* in note 3 above (1959) and *l.c.* in note 13 above (1965), p. 72 *et seq.*].

In Professor Jessup's terminology, is there really any intrinsic difference between Morocco's desire for separation from France—meanwhile fulfilled—and Mary's urge to be liberated from Frank at Reno or elsewhere? Have not relations with a foreign element between individuals, between corporations and between corporations and governments and those between subjects of international law at least a decisive negative element in common? Is not the choice of the applicable law frequently governed by considerations which make its application one *ab inconvenienti?* Would it not be preferable that the choice should be made by reference to intrinsically more congenial criteria, and these were elaborated in a new branch of "transnational" law? Is there not a growing "inter-penetration" of international and municipal law, and are there not encouraging signs of the growth of an international co-operative law? [56] In short, as matters appear to look from the international hothouses of New York and Geneva and the old world quietude of the Hague Peace Palace, should not the emphasis be put on what may "properly" be regarded as a "progressive" view of international law and organisation? [57]

Admittedly, elements of scepticism and faith, constitutional or professional, enter into any qualitative assessment. Yet, are generations of international lawyers who are but repeating in different words what they have said in previous pre-war periods and, on fundamentals, have been so often disappointed in their own expectations, and have disappointed others with their earlier prognoses,[58] entitled to be again taken on trust? For what evidence can they adduce for their protestations of faith?

The issue is not merely one of possible disagreement on the conditioning effect of world power politics on international

---

56. For representative and instructive illustrations of this attitude, *cf.* C. W. Jenks, 31 B.Y.I.L. (1954—published 1956), p. 1 *et seq.;* Ph. C. Jessup, *Transnational Law,* 1956; K. Loewenstein, 48 A.J.I.L. (1954), p. 222 *et seq.,* and W. Friedmann, 50 *ibid.* (1956), p. 475 *et seq.*

57. Sir Hersch Lauterpacht, 32 B.Y.I.L. (1955–56), p. I [and further *l.c.* in note 13 above (1965), pp. 1 and 115 *et seq.*].

58. See further 9 *Current Legal Problems* (1956), p. 235 *et seq.*

law and organisation. The self-styled "progressive" school of
thought appears to suffer from a noticeable proneness to over-
generalisation in an understandable tendency to underpin its
somewhat irrational optimism. By way of an antidote, it may
be advisable to insist politely but firmly on the need for more
concrete thinking and to provide further assistance towards
this end.

Are the trends which, for instance, are supposed to be indicative of the increasing scope of international law or the
growing inter-penetration of international law and municipal
law really characteristic of international law at large? Are
they not tendencies which, at the most, can be discerned only
in international law as applied on certain levels of international integration? A few illustrations must suffice to bring
out the relevance of this criterion, at least in relation to contemporary manifestations of sovereignty.

On the level of international customary law, a distinct movement from positive, to negative, sovereignty is discernible. The
rules underlying the principles of consent, good faith, international responsibility and freedom of the seas appear especially affected by this trend towards negative sovereignty.[59]

59. See further *l.c.* above, note 6, p. 195 *et seq.*
   On the questionable assumptions that to throw in doubt the juris-
   dictional immunities of foreign States amounts to another blow against
   the privileged position of the State as compared with the individual
   and contributes to the extension of the rule of law, symptomatic doctrinal attempts have been made to whittle down to insignificance such
   consensus as, in diplomatic and judicial practice, still exists on this issue.
   See, for instance, H. Lauterpacht, 28 B.Y.I.L. (1951), p. 220 *et seq.* While
   these assumptions, however unjustified on a world scale, may appear
   progressive, they are, in fact, merely indicative of a trend from positive,
   to negative, sovereignty in international law. This technique of presen-
   tation of topics permits a remarkable combination of extreme "ideal-
   istic" argumentation with unswerving support of negative sovereignty.
   The method is applicable, and has been applied with a measure of
   success, to topics as varied as the expropriation of foreign property; the
   continental shelf; the legality of the bribery of members of enemy
   forces and the compatibility of the use of the hydrogen bomb with the
   rules of warfare. See further 5 *Current Legal Problems* (1952), p. 308
   et seq., and 8 *ibid.* (1955), p. 229 *et seq.* [and the present writer's *The
   Legality of Nuclear Weapons* (1958)].

It would, however, be unwarranted to draw general conclusions from international law as applied on the level of lowest international integration in favour of an unqualified thesis of negative sovereignty triumphant. At the same time, applied to the relations between the two world camps, this view of the matter would be, at least relatively, less inaccurate than that of sovereignty evanescent.[60]

On the level of international law as applied inside the United Nations, it appears essential to distinguish between different types of relations:

(1) Relations in which permanent members of the Security Council, with their privileges, are involved.

(2) Relations between hegemonial powers and others inside their own world camp.

(3) Relations between members of one of the world camps and "non-committed" members of the United Nations and between "non-committed" members of the United Nations.

(4) Relations governed by the Optional Clause of the Statute of the World Court.

Within the compass of this paper, it is not feasible to work out in detail the average correlations of these types of relations and particular manifestations of sovereignty. It may, however, be helpful to state at least some of these correlations in the form of tentative working hypotheses.

In relations of types 1 and 2, the forms of political and positive sovereignty tend to be preponderant. Relations of type 3 provide illustrations of the possibility of a different type of political sovereignty: small-power lawlessness. In a broad belt, covering the world frontier between the two global camps from North Africa to South-East Asia, the somewhat hypothetical freedom of "non-committed" countries to opt for the Communist world camp and the chance to prove their nuisance-value in the General Assembly has put a premium on members of the United Nations in this area. With calculable lack of risk, they become increasingly accustomed to hold

60. See further *l.c.* above, note 29 [and further *l.c.* in note 3 above (1967), p. 179 *et seq.*].

Western powers and investors to ransom. The expropriation
of the Anglo-Iranian oil refinery at Abadan was the beginning
of a disturbing chain reaction. Acquiescence of the Western
powers in this relapse into lawlessness disguises only thinly
the anarchic and pristine form of sovereignty which raises its
head in this strategic no man's land between East and West.[60a]

In the General Assembly of the United Nations, shifting
combination of small-power groupings produce their own type
of perversion of Paragraph 7 of Article 2 of the Charter.[61]
Their own particular brand of purported political and positive sovereignty consists in a morbid disdain [62] for a clause
which, in a world of increasing stratification, might form
some, however precarious, protection against world-power
hegemony.

It would be pleasing to be able to contrast relations pertaining to type 4 with the other three types of relations on the
level of the United Nations and hold them out as shining
illustrations of relations in which the international judiciary
does its utmost to preserve a calculable balance between negative and positive sovereignty on the legal level. Advisory
Opinions, such as those on *Interpretation of Peace Treaties
(Second Phase*—1950) or *Reservations to the Genocide Convention* (1950), not to speak of the hardly disguised exercise
in law-making of the Judgment in the *Anglo-Norwegian Fish-
eries* case (1951), provoke rather a different line of thought.[63]
These decisions indicate the scope of the discretionary powers
which, on the basis of the consent of the parties and the application of wide and elastic rules of international law, international judicial institutions are able to arrogate to themselves.

Findings which vaccilate so incalculably between the most

[60a. See further *l.c.* in note 13 above (1965), p. 175 *et seq.*].

61. See above, p. 189.

62. See further United Nations, *Repertory of Practice of United Nations
Organs*, Vol. I, 1955, p. 55 *et seq.*; Professor Rousseau's Report to the
Institut de Droit International, 44 (I) *Annuaire* (1952), p. 137 *et seq.*;
the discussion on the Report 45 (II) *ibid.* (1954), p. 108 *et seq.*, and
T. Komarnicki, 60 R.G.D.I.P. (1956), p. 550 *et seq.*

63. See further 4 *Current Legal Problems* (1951), p. 1 *et seq.* and *l.c.* above,
note 38, *passim*.

meticulous respect for negative sovereignty and outright judicial legislation come dangerously close to the dispensation of positive sovereignty between litigants. The fact that less than half of the members of the United Nations are signatories to the Optional Clause, and most of these do not appear unduly anxious to submit contentious disputes to the World Court, appears to confirm acute awareness of this situation in the chancelleries of the powers.

Analysis of the constitutions and, still more, the actual attainments of the Specialised Agencies of the United Nations proves equally suggestive. It invites further consideration whether it would not be advisable to add another pair to the six forms of sovereignty, that is to say, the distinction between real and apparent transfer of positive sovereignty. In two different types of international institution this transfer is real enough, but they are hardly typical of world organisation at large.

The one is illustrated by the North Atlantic Pact and the Warsaw Pact.[64] The other is the type of supra-national institution on the model of the European Coal and Steel Community, the functional substitute for the political federation of States which become increasingly conscious of the fact that, in isolation, they are no longer "viable."

In both cases, the institutions created wield unmistakably political and positive sovereignty.[65] Hegemonial leadership,

64. For a vivid account of the Russian attempts made since the end of the Second World War to establish their political, military and economic hegemony over Yugoslavia, *cf.* V. Dedijer, *Tito*, 1953, p. 317 *et seq.*

65. The commitment undertaken by the United Kingdom not to withdraw from the Continent the effective strength of the United Kingdom forces assigned to the Supreme Allied Commander, Europe, "against the wishes of the majority of the High Contracting Parties [of Western European Union] who should take their decision in the knowledge of the views of the Supreme Allied Commander, Europe" (Article VI of Protocol II on Forces of Western European Union, October 23, 1954—Cmd. 9498 (1955)), and the attitude taken by Western European Union towards the British request for consent to considerable withdrawals proves that it is no exaggeration to describe such jurisdiction in terms of positive sovereignty. By way of contrast, the United States remains a free agent regarding the strength of its forces stationed in Germany (see further *The Times,* March 15, 1957).

in the one case, and anticipation of ultimate amalgamation, in the other, explain why these high levels of international integration have been attained. Then, it becomes less far-fetched to speak of legal and negative sovereignty becoming increasingly meaningless, and the borderline between international law and municipal law being correspondingly blurred. If this is so, it is not because, in these relations, sovereignty in its most innocuous and defensive form is ousted, but because it gives way to sovereignty of a more virile type. Political and positive sovereignty claims its birthright of overriding competence.

Ivor Wilks

A NOTE ON
SOVEREIGNTY

In this note I shall offer an analysis of one aspect of an extremely powerful doctrine of political theory—the doctrine of sovereignty.

I

In the latter half of the sixteenth century Jean Bodin said, "There must be a sovereign in every state," and thereby gave political thought a New Look. In what lay the novelty? Certainly Bodin coined a new word, "sovereign," yet this alone did little more than improve the linguistic apparatus available for talking about a notion already quite familiar to writers on politics and law in earlier times.[1] It was not this that made the New Look. The real novelty lay in the fact that Bodin's assertion was not the empirical "There *always happens to be* a sovereign in every state," nor even the theocratic "God creates a ruler in *every* state in His own (sovereign) image," but rather the paradoxical "There *must be* a sovereign in every state." For in this Bodin confronted his contemporaries with an assertion exhibiting the features typical of a philosophical para-

From *The Philosophical Quarterly,* vol. V, no. 21 (October 1955), pp. 342–47. Reprinted by permission of the author and the publisher.

1. See, for example, Otto Gierke, *Political Theories of the Middle Ages,* translation by Maitland (Cambridge 1900), p. 35 *et seq.* Also compare Bodin's notion of the sovereign as "unrestrained by law" with the familiar Roman maxim—*Princeps legibus solutus est.*

dox. The assertion was, on the one hand, so obviously false: one had only to consider the protracted struggles *for* sovereignty apparent in so many states. Yet, on the other hand, once stated, it was so obviously true—indeed, so self-evidently true that it has been the cornerstone of political theory ever since. Bodin had no wish to deny any of the familiar facts of political life, but he did wish to provide new ways of talking about those familiar facts and to stimulate new ways of looking at them. And this Bodin did, not so much through his clarification of the notion of sovereignty, but rather by his persistent suggestion of the "mustness" of the sovereign. In this lay the real novelty of his doctrine.

But what sort of "must" was the "must" in "There must be a sovereign in every state"? That it was a "must" of definition is a matter of history, not of logic. Thus Bodin's own definition of the state included the notion of sovereignty—"La République est un droit gouvernement de plusieurs ménages et de ce qui leur est commun avec puissance souveraine" [2] —and so did that of an array of subsequent writers.[3] Two sovereigns, two states, was the underlying theme—or else, of course, a Hobbesian "state" of nature where life was nasty, brutish, and short.

To recognise that the assertion, "There must be a sovereign in every state," was analytic, however, only serves to point the way to a more fundamental, non-historical, inquiry: granted that the tendency to make the concepts of the state and the sovereign function together has characterized political theory ever since Bodin wrote, then what rationalization can be given of this tendency?

II

Attention has recently been drawn to the suggestion that "many fundamental concepts of modern political theory are nothing but 'secularised' theological concepts." [4] If the claim

2. Jean Bodin, *Six Livres de la République* (1576) I, i.
3. See Gierke, *Natural Law and the Theory of Society,* translation by Barker (Cambridge 1950), p. 40 and p. 235, n. 35.
4. A. P. d'Entrèves, *Natural Law* (1951), p. 69.

that the concept of the sovereign is a secularised version of the concept of God is too strong, however, at least it may be said that the analogy between the sovereign in his state and God in His universe is scarcely one that could have escaped writers of the sixteenth and seventeenth centuries. The analogy had been a familiar one to earlier writers. St. Thomas Aquinas, for example, was well aware of it: "A king, then, should realise that he has assumed the duty of being to his kingdom what the soul is to the body and what God is to the Universe." [5] Yet in writers in the post-Bodinian tradition, the analogy is seldom explicitly made. Perhaps as a result of this one does not find in these writers what might be of special relevance to an investigation of the "mustness" of the sovereign—namely, any clear development of arguments for the existence of a sovereign within any state, parallel to the well-known arguments for the existence of God. But one does find hints—hints, for example, of an ontological argument. "In temporal matters," suggested James I, "how can one be sovereign, that may be fleeced of his temporalities by any superior power?",[6] and in like vein Hayward asks, "For how should he be esteemed a sovereign who in the greatest actions and affairs of state acknowledgeth the jurisdiction of another greater than himself. . . .?" [7] Note in both writers the very significant use of "how"—the "how" of "How can one conceive that. . . . ?" It is not quite an ontological argument for the existence of a sovereign in every state that is revealed here, but the right language is being employed. It is not a far cry from it to an Anselmian-type ontological argument via the impossibility of conceiving the non-existence of a sovereign (i.e. of "that body in the state than which no more powerful body can exist"). Such an Anselmian-type argument would turn on the supposed internal contradiction in the concept of a non-existent sovereign, since an existent sovereign would always be, in the nature of the case, more powerful. A corresponding

5. See *On Princely Government*, chs. 12 and 13.
6. James I, *The Right of Kings*. See *The Political Works of James I,* ed. C. H. McIlwain (1918), p. 170.
7. Sir John Hayward, *A Report on a Discourse, etc.* (1606), p. 11.

Spinozistic-type argument might run: "Inability to exist is want of power. A more powerful body in the state may prevent the existence of a less powerful body. But no body in the state could prevent the existence of the sovereign. Therefore a sovereign must exist in every state." [8]

Whilst the possibility of constructing such ontological arguments may provide a partial explanation of the immediate success of Bodin's doctrine of sovereignty, the flaws in such arguments are now so well recognised that they need not detain us here.

III

From the ontological argument attention naturally turns to the possibility of a cosmological-type argument for the existence of a sovereign in every state. Such an argument may clearly be constructed on the pattern of the first three of St. Thomas's Five Ways, i.e. the three ways that depend upon the rejection of an infinite regress. Using this device St. Thomas argues from the occurrence of motion to the existence of a first unmoved mover ("and this everyone understands to be God"), from causality to a first uncaused cause ("generally termed God"), and from contingency to a first necessary being ("and this all men speak of as God").

Applying this pattern of argument to our "secular" use, two specimen proofs of the existence of a sovereign in any state may be offered.

Prima Via: The Argument from Limitation

It is evident that in any state there are bodies whose power is limited by that of higher bodies.

But an infinite regress of limited powers is impossible.

---

8. Compare these arguments with Hobbes, *De Corpore Politico*, Pt. II, Ch. 1, 19: ". . . he that in a commonwealth is punishable by any, or that assembly that is dissolvable, is not sovereign. For a greater power is always required to punish and dissolve, than theirs who are punished and dissolved; and that power cannot be called sovereign, than which there is greater."

Therefore there must exist in any state a body whose power is unlimited, i.e. a first unlimited power.

And this all men speak of as the sovereign.

Secunda Via: The Argument from Derivation

It is evident that in any state there are bodies whose authority is derived from that of higher bodies.

But an infinite regress of derivative authorities is impossible.

Therefore there must exist in any state a body whose authority is not derivative, i.e. a first non-derivative authority.

And this all men speak of as the sovereign.

It will be clear that, in our present context, problems arising from the use of the terms "power" and "authority" need not arise. The key terms in the two ways are "limited" and "derivative," just as the key terms in the first three ways of St. Thomas are "moving," "caused," and "contingent."

IV

It would now generally be agreed that whatever is the status of these cosmological-type arguments, it amounts to something less than proof.[9] And there the matter might rest were it not that arguments of this type, more or less thinly disguised, appear to play a considerable part in certain contemporary politico-legal theories. The "pure theory of law" associated particularly with the name of Kelsen may, in this respect, be taken as representative.[10]

Laws, for Kelsen, are ought-statements, though quite distinct from moral ought-statements in virtue of their characteristic connection with sanctions. Kelsen describes them as

9. See, for example, E. L. Mascall, *Existence and Analogy* (1949), p. 78: ". . . the process (i.e. the cosmological argument) by which we go on to affirm the existence of God is hardly to be described as a 'proof' in the usual sense of that term." Compare with Kant, *KRV* 606: "Speculative reason seems in this case [i.e. the cosmological argument] to have brought to bear all the resources of its dialectical skill to produce the greatest possible transcendental illusion."

10. See *Hauptprobleme der Staatsrechtslehre* (1911), and *Allgemeine Staatslehre* (1925).

norms. A legal system is an "exclusive" or closed system, since
a legal norm cannot be derived from a moral norm, nor from
nature statements, such as sociological generalisations about
how people do in fact behave. A legal norm can only derive
from another legal norm, and any two legal norms may be
related either by subordination ("is derived from") or, conversely, superordination ("is the source of"). Thus an Act of
Parliament may be superordinate to an Order in Council,
but subordinate to the Constitution. Clearly, however, an
infinite regress of superordinate or subordinate norms is impossible. Thus Kelsen is led to speak of every legal system as
containing one norm such that no other norm is superordinate
to it, though many norms may be subordinate to it. This norm
Kelsen describes as the "Grundnorm" of the system, and
handles it as corresponding to the traditional political concept of the sovereign—"The legally admissible, and indeed
indispensable, basic norm has no positive content. It has no
a priori content whatsoever. . . . In one place it names an
autocrat as the supreme authority, in another the people."

In effect, then, Kelsen presents us with a transition from the
existence of subordinate laws to the necessity of a first non-
subordinate law [11]—and this, we are told, all men will recognise as a law naming the sovereign.

V

What, then, can we now say about the "must" in "There must
be a sovereign in every state"? The substance, as opposed to
the form, of our argument from derivative authorities I take
to be this: that no system of derivative authorities (i.e. one
containing an axiom to the effect that for any *x*, if *x* is an

---

11. The prototype of this transition, as applied to laws, is perhaps to be
    found in Kant's notion of the first non-duty-bound member of the king-
    dom of ends—"Duty does not apply to the sovereign in the kingdom of
    ends, but it does to every member of it and to all in the same degree"
    (*Metaphysic of Ethics*). Explicit use of the infinite regress device is
    apparently made by Petrazhitsky; see N. S. Timasheff, *An Introduction
    to the Sociology of Law* (1939), p. 264.

authority, then there is a further authority y, such that x derives from y) can be a complete or closed system. To say that a system of authorities is complete or closed is incompatible with saying that it is entirely a system of derivative authorities. A similar interpretation is to be given to the argument from limited powers. And Kelsen's account would likewise turn upon the incompatibility between speaking of a complete (pure) system of laws, and speaking of every law in that system as subordinate to a further law. The use of the reference to the impossibility of an infinite regress is just one form in which this basic point may be cast. But in no case is one confronted by any attempt at *formal* proof; one is simply invited to "see" the point.

It might be said that the type of argument under consideration has the status of an intuitive "proof." This seems unobjectionable. If x is a law in system S, then we can speak of the source of x. But the source of x will be a further law, and accordingly we can speak of the source of the source of x. . . . One sees intuitively that S cannot be a complete system. Or, to reverse the point, if one has an incomplete system of subordinate laws, then one can see intuitively that such a system can never be completed by the use of further subordinate laws, but only by the use of a statement that belongs to (or is provable or decidable in) a different system. Thus, in Kelsen's system of legal norms such that each derives from a further legal norm, the system is complete only in virtue of its containing one statement that is not, strictly, a legal norm, since it does not derive from a further legal norm—and this statement is a political statement meaning some body as sovereign, testable only outside the system in which it occurs.

Taking the substance of our cosmological-type arguments for the existence of a sovereign in every state in this way, their intuitive content appears to be analogous in certain respects to Goedel's formalized proof that for every system of sufficient complexity (roughly, sufficiently complex to contain arithmetic), there exist well-formed expressions of that system that can neither be demonstrated nor refuted in it, but only in a higher system. That this analogy is not purely fortuitous is

suggested by the fact that, just as Goedel's proof is closely connected with certain paradoxes of self-reference ("syntactical
antinomies") such as the paradox of the liar, Grelling's antinomy, and Richard's antinomy,[12] so it is possible to construct
comparable paradoxes that bear an obvious connection with
the type of argument that we have been considering. The following is an example of such a paradox.

At noon on January 1st, 1980, Ruritania is invaded by
enemy forces and completely occupied in a matter of hours.
On January 2nd members of the Ruritanian government, who
have gone into hiding preparatory to an attempt to escape
into exile, hold a secret meeting. At this meeting, as a source
of embarrassment to subsequent puppet governments, a law is
passed to the effect that: "No laws passed in Ruritania after
noon on January 1st, 1980, and before the liberation, shall be
valid." The members of the old government feel that they
have accomplished a subtle act of statecraft, until it is pointed
out to them that if what they passed is a law, then it is not
a law, and only if it is not a law can it possibly be a law.

Considering such a paradox as this, its connection with what
I have taken to be the substance of the cosmological-type arguments becomes clear. For corresponding to seeing the point
of these arguments, one sees that the way out of the paradox
is via some discussion in political rather than formally legal
terms. The suggestion that, for example, since Ruritania was
effectively occupied on January 1st, sovereignty passed to the
occupying power, and hence the old government meeting on
January 2nd possessed no legislative powers—such a suggestion
would clearly be *the sort of* consideration relevant to an attempt to resolve the paradox.

VI

The doctrine of sovereignty has held a central place in political thought for something approaching four centuries.

12. See Carnap, *The Logical Syntax of Language* (English translation by
    Smeaton, 1937), pp. 211–22; Mostowski, *Sentences Undecidable in For-
    malized Arithmetic* (1952), p. 4 *et seq.*

There is little sign today that its usefulness is diminishing. It has been the main purpose of this note to suggest the basis of one aspect, *but one aspect only,* of this doctrine, namely, the basis of the belief that there *must* be a sovereign in every state, or, in other words, the basis of the belief that a doctrine of sovereignty is indispensible to political theory. It is suggested that this belief is ultimately to be linked, as a special case, with a feature of the logic of formal systems of a certain complexity, of which systems of derived authorities, limited powers, and subordinate laws, are all examples. It has been considered beyond the scope of this note to inquire in what directions the traditional doctrine of sovereignty might be modified or refined in the light of its logical basis.

six

PHILOSOPHIC
COUNTER-PROPOSALS

W. J. Rees

THE THEORY OF
SOVEREIGNTY RESTATED

There is a tendency among present-day political theorists to work without the aid of the concept of sovereignty. This is due partly to the logical difficulties inherent in the concept, and partly to the fact that certain modern political developments, such as the growth of democracy, federalism and public law, have made the concept a difficult one to apply in present conditions. The purpose of this article will be to re-examine the traditional use of the concept, and to inquire whether it still cannot be used in such a way as to avoid the objections now usually raised against it.

I

The strength of the logical objection to the traditional theory can be seen if we merely examine the following traditional questions: (1) Is it necessary that there should be a sovereign, or an ultimate source of authority or power, in every state? (2) Is it necessary that the authority or power of the sovereign should be indivisible? (3) Is it necessary that the authority or power of the sovereign should be unlimited? and (4) Where is the sovereign located? It is notorious that no unambiguous answer is possible to these questions. What then is the point of asking them, and what is the point of a concept which merely enables us to ask pointless questions? Nor is the criti-

From *Mind*, vol. LIX, no. 236 (October 1950), pp. 495–521. Reprinted by permission of the author and the publisher.

cism obviously exaggerated. The evidence of some three and a half centuries of political theory is largely on the side of the critics.

There are, however, two different reasons why it may not be possible to give a straight answer to a seemingly straight question. In the first place, the question may not be a genuine question. This may be either because it involves a logical contradiction, e.g. What is there outside the universe? or because we do not know what information would be relevant to determining the answer to the question, e.g. Is everything twice as big to-day as it was yesterday? But in the second place, the question may be more than one question. This would be the case when the terms in which the question is stated are capable of having more than one meaning, e.g. "Is justice the interest of the stronger?" where "justice" may mean "legal justice" or "ideal justice," and where the answer may be different according to the sense in which the word is used.

The traditional questions about sovereignty, it seems to me, are questions of the latter and not of the former kind. They cannot be satisfactorily answered, not because they are not genuine questions, but because each question consists of several questions which have never been clearly distinguished. Once the proper distinctions are drawn, therefore, they may be replaced by other questions to which unambiguous answers can always be given. To show that this is so, all that is necessary is to analyse the possible meanings of the terms we are using.

In the traditional questions about sovereignty, the words which have been most often used ambiguously are the words "sovereign" and "state." My first task, therefore, must be to analyse the different meanings which different philosophers, and sometimes the same philosophers, have given to these two words. I shall take, first of all, the word "sovereign."

1. The word has been used by some as equivalent to a *supreme legal authority*. Those who have used the word in this way have not usually thought it necessary to define what they mean by authority, or to say how authority is to be distinguished from power or influence. It is clear, however, from

the way in which they have written, that they have meant to draw some important distinction between these concepts. "Let us notice in the first place," writes Lord Lindsay, "that the doctrine of sovereignty is properly concerned with the question of authority. It is not properly concerned with questions of force or power as such." [1] This is predominantly the sense in which the word was used by John Austin, and by the lawyers of the Austinian school. I shall call this, sovereignty in the legal sense.

A word of further explanation, however, is needed. Theorists who have adopted the doctrine of the separation of powers have used the word "sovereign" to mean either (*a*) a supreme legislative authority, as for instance in the case of Dicey, or (*b*) a supreme legislative or executive authority, as in the case of Lord Bryce. Those who have denied the separation of powers, on the other hand, have used the word to mean (*c*) a supreme legal authority, irrespective of whether it is the authority of a Parliament, a Ministry, or a Court; that is, they have used it to mean what would, on a separationist view, be regarded as a supreme legislative, executive or judicial authority.[2] In order to avoid over-burdening the present analysis, and in order also not to prejudge the case for or against the doctrine of the separation of powers, I shall use the words "supreme legal authority" in this latter sense. I shall use them, that is to say, in what a separationist may regard as a generic sense, and what an anti-separationist may regard as the only appropriate sense. This will preclude any direct discussion of sovereignty in senses (*a*) and (*b*) above, but that will not affect my general argument. If the separationist view is the correct one, and if clear answers can be given to the traditional questions, using the present generic sense, then the same answers can always be given to the same questions, using senses (*a*) or (*b*). If, however, the separationist view is not the correct view, then the need to discuss senses (*a*) and (*b*) does not arise in any case.

1. *The Modern Democratic State*, vol. i, pp. 217–18.
2. *Cf.* Finer: *The Theory and Practice of Modern Government*, vol. i, chap. 1.

2. The word "sovereign" has been used by others to mean a *supreme legal authority in so far as it is also a completely moral authority*. This is sovereignty as understood by Rousseau and the Hegelians. "The Sovereign," says Rousseau, "merely by virtue of what it is, is always what it should be." "Sovereignty," says Bosanquet, "is the exercise of the General Will," which "is expressed in law, in so far as law is what it ought to be." [3] It is, therefore, a species of sovereignty in the previous sense. For that reason, it is not always clear that a person who uses the word in this way is using it necessarily in a way which is different from the previous one. But we can, in fact, be sure that a different sense is involved wherever there is clear evidence that the writer would, in addition, deny the title of sovereign to a supreme legal authority which is not, in his opinion, a completely moral authority. When the word is used in this way, I shall say that it is used in the moral sense.

3. For another group of philosophers the word has meant *a supreme coercive power exercised by a determinate body of persons possessing a monopoly of certain instruments of coercion*. They have not usually defined what they mean by coercive power, nor clearly stated how it is to be distinguished from legal authority or political influence. But it has been generally understood that power in this sense is to be distinguished from legal authority at least in one respect, namely, that its exercise may sometimes be extra-legal. In this sense, the sovereign is a determinate body of persons capable of *enforcing* decisions against any likely opposition, no matter who *makes,* or *otherwise carries out,* those decisions. Usually such a body consists of a professional police or a standing army; usually, too, the decisions which it enforces are those of Parliaments, Ministries and Courts, but they may be the analogous decisions of persons who have no legal authority to make such decisions, although such persons may acquire such legal authority in virtue of their decisions being enforced, e.g. the dissolution of the Long Parliament by Cromwell, or the overthrow of the Directory by Napoleon. This use of the

3. *The Philosophical Theory of the State,* pp. 232 and 107.

word "sovereign" is implied in Lord Bryce's concept of the Practical Sovereign, which he defined as "the strongest force in the State, whether that force has or has not any recognized legal supremacy." [4] T. H. Green also wrote as if he thought the word should ordinarily be used in this or some similar sense: "the term 'sovereign' is best kept to the ordinary usage in which it signifies a determinate person or persons charged with the supreme coercive function of the state." [5] I shall call this, sovereignty in the institutionally coercive sense.

4. The word has again been used by some as equivalent to a *supreme coercive power exercised habitually and co-operatively by all, or nearly all, the members of a community.* Locke speaks variously of this kind of supreme coercive power as "the force of the community," "the force of the majority," and "all the force of all the people," in such a way as to imply a distinction between this and the coercive power of a professional police or a standing army.[6] T. H. Green, although he did not favour the usage, held that the word *could* be used in this, or a very similar, way. "A majority of citizens *can* be conceived as exercising a supreme coercive power. . . . But as the multitude is not everywhere supreme, the assertion of its sovereignty has to be put in the form that it is sovereign 'de jure'." (p. 109.) This is also a meaning of the word which has sometimes, though not necessarily always, been implied both by those who have spoken of the "sovereignty of the people," and by those who have spoken of the "tyranny of the majority." When the word is used in this way, it will be convenient to say that it is used in the socially coercive sense.

5. It may now be noted that these four different senses of the word "sovereign" refer to supreme authorities or powers, each of a different kind. But the fact that they are sovereigns of a different kind does not mean that they cannot, in some cases, be subordinated one to another according to some principle of subordination other than those already indicated. Some philosophers have, indeed, held that they can be so

4. *Studies in History and Jurisprudence*, p. 511.
5. *Lectures on the Principles of Political Obligation*, p. 103.
6. For examples see *Treatise*, Book II, paras. 3, 88, 89, 96, 130, 131.

subordinated, and have tried to show accordingly which of these sovereigns is "really sovereign." By so doing, they have used the word "sovereign" in yet another sense. They have used it in a sense which is equivalent to what one might call the *strongest political influence,* where political influence is to be distinguished, in some way yet to be determined, both from legal authority and from coercive power. Many things may be regarded as sovereign in this sense, but usually this kind of sovereignty has been attributed to the popular majority, irrespective of whether the popular majority be also regarded as the coercive sovereign or not. The following examples from Locke and Dicey will indicate how the concept has been generally used. "Though in a constituted commonwealth," writes Locke, "there can be but one supreme power, which is the legislative, to which all the rest are and must be subordinate, yet the legislative power being only a fiduciary power to act for certain ends, there remains still in the people a supreme power to remove or alter the legislative, when they find the legislative act contrary to the trust reposed in them." (para. 149.) "The plain truth," says Dicey, "is that as a matter of law Parliament is the sovereign power in the state. . . . It is, however, equally true that in a political sense the electors are the most important part of, we may even say are actually, the sovereign power, since their will is under the present constitution sure to obtain ultimate obedience." [7] This I shall call sovereignty in the influential sense.

6. There is, finally, a usage of the word "sovereign" which would make it equivalent to a *permanently supreme authority, power or influence*—the significant word in this case being the word "permanent." It seems to be a matter of custom among political theorists to make statements such as the following: "Force is not sovereign in the state, for no state can be perpetually ruled by force alone." Those who make such statements as this would not usually deny that a state may for some time be ruled by force alone; force may well be sovereign for some time, assuming some meaning of the word "sovereign" already given. But if now the title of sovereign is to be denied

7. *The Law of the Constitution,* 8th edn., p. 73.

to a "sovereign" of this kind, clearly the word has once again shifted its meaning. It has shifted its meaning to the extent that a sovereign, in any of our previous senses, is no longer to be called sovereign unless it continues to exist for an indefinitely long time. Duguit says of Bodin, for instance, that "he defines sovereignty as 'the absolute and perpetual power in the state'"; [8] and Professor Laski, with this definition apparently in mind, argues against Bodin as follows: "The government which acts as its (Professor Laski means the state's) sovereign organ never, as a matter of history, has the prospect of permanence if it consistently seeks to be absolute. Civil War and Revolution in the England of the seventeenth century, 1789 in France, 1917 in Russia, are all of them footnotes to the problem of sovereignty." [9] I shall call this, sovereignty in the permanent sense.

So much for the word "sovereign." It is necessary now to consider the word "state."

The word "state" has been used by philosophers in at least three different ways. (1) To some, it has meant a *politically organized society.* "The state," says Sorley, "is not something separate from the citizen, and it is not something separate from the community or society to which it belongs. It is this society organized as a whole and able to act as a unity." [10] This is the sense of the word "state" which we usually have in mind when we are dealing with matters of international politics, e.g. when we speak of small and large states, backward states, industrial states, European states, etc. (2) To others, it has meant a *politically organized society in so far as it is ideally organized.* This, in the main, is the Hegelian use of the term. "By the State, then," says Bosanquet, "we mean Society as a unit, recognized as rightly exercising control over its members through absolute physical power." (p. 184.) Since this is a species of the state in the previous sense, it is not always clear that a person who uses the term in this way is using it in a sense which is different from the previous one.

8. *Law in the Modern State,* trans. F. and H. Laski, p. 9.
9. *Grammar of Politics,* p. 49.
10. Creighton and others: *The Theory of the State,* p. 32.

But, as with the moral sense of the word "sovereign," we can
be sure that a different sense is involved whenever the writer
is prepared to deny the title of state to a politically organized
society which is not, in his opinion, ideally organized. (3)
More often in ordinary speech, however, and sometimes in
political theory, the word "state" has meant *government as an
institution.* "The state," says Professor R. M. MacIver, "exists
within society, but it is not even the *form* of society"; it is
"a structure not coeval and coextensive with society, but built
within it as a determinate order for the attainment of specific
ends." [11] This is the sense of the word which we usually have
in mind when we are discussing matters of domestic politics,
e.g. when we speak of state enterprise, state employees, the
revenues of the state, the machinery of the state, etc.

It may be that the words "sovereign" and "state" have been
used in some senses other than these which I have indicated,
but these at least are definite, it seems to me, as far as the
history of political theory is concerned. Admittedly some of
these senses are arbitrary, in that they are not the senses which
are implied in the common use of the words by persons who
are not political theorists; but to determine which is arbitrary
and which is not is a question which need not concern us
here, since it would not in any case affect any of the conclusions which may be derived from the foregoing analysis.

We are now in a position to answer the first of the traditional questions about sovereignty, namely, Is it necessary that
there should be a sovereign in every state?

1. If we are using the word "sovereign" in the legal sense,
it is not *logically* necessary that there should exist a sovereign
in every state, on any of the three definitions of the word
"state," since it is clearly not self-contradictory to say that there
does not exist in a state a supreme legal authority. But it
is, however, *causally* necessary that there should exist a sovereign in every state, on any of our three definitions. I am
now using the word "cause" in the sense in which it is normally
used in the practical sciences, and which has been defined
by Collingwood to mean "an event or state of things which

11. *The Modern State,* pp. 5 and 40.

it is in our power to produce or prevent, and by producing or preventing which we can produce or prevent that whose cause it is said to be." In this sense it is causally necessary that a sovereign should exist in every state, since, in practice, government can only be carried on by means of laws, and laws can only be effectively administered if there exists some final legal authority beyond which there is no further legal appeal. In the absence of such a final legal authority no legal issue could ever be certainly decided, and government would become impossible.

2. If, however, we take the word "sovereign" in the moral sense, and if, in addition, we use the word "state" in its second, or Hegelian, sense, then it is *logically* necessary that there should exist a sovereign in every state. For if the supreme legal authority which exists in a "state" is not a completely moral authority, that "state" is not an ideally organized society, that is, it is not a state on the present definition. This is an analytical proposition derived solely from the definitions of the terms used. But on any other use of the word "state," of course, it is neither logically nor causally necessary that there should exist in any state a sovereign in this sense.

3. It is not *logically* necessary that there should exist in a state, on any of the three definitions, a sovereign in the coercive sense, since again, it is not self-contradictory to say that there does not exist in a state a supreme coercive power. But it is, nevertheless, *causally* necessary, in the present state of society, that there should exist in the state—senses (1) and (2) —a sovereign either in the socially coercive or in the institutionally coercive sense. Since it is a fact that many men in their present state are prone to disobey the law, it is necessary, if laws are to be effective, that they should be capable of being enforced. But laws can only be enforced in one of two ways: either by the habitual and co-operative exercise of coercive power in support of the law by indeterminate but exceedingly numerous persons in society, or else by the exercise of coercive power by a determinate body of persons, who are fewer in number, but who possess a monopoly of

the instruments of coercion. Assuming, for the time being, that these two ways represent genuine practical alternatives, it is not causally necessary that there should exist in the state, as now defined, a sovereign in both the above senses, but only that there should exist a sovereign in the one sense or the other. But if, however, we are using the word "state" in the third sense, the same facts would need to be stated rather differently. In this case we should have to say that it is causally necessary that an institutionally coercive sovereign should exist in the state, if there does not exist in society a sovereign of the socially coercive kind. That is, the state must possess a monopoly of the instruments of coercion, as long as there does not exist in society a sufficiently large number of persons capable of co-operating to enforce the state's decisions.

4. If now we use the word "sovereign" in the influential sense, it is neither logically nor causally necessary that there should exist a sovereign in every state. This is true on any use of the word "state," since the strongest political influence may be exercised by bodies which exist, or events which occur, outside the boundaries of the state, e.g. the influence of another powerful state, or of international economic events, etc. If we use the word "state" in sense (3), moreover, there is the additional reason that the strongest political influence may be that of public opinion, which itself lies outside the state as the state is now being defined.

5. It is, finally, neither logically nor causally necessary that there should exist in the state, on any of the given definitions, a sovereign in the permanent sense. In order, for instance, that the King in Parliament may be the legal sovereign to-day, it does not seem to be either logically or causally necessary that he should continue to be the legal sovereign for an indefinitely long time.

Summing up now the above argument, it is possible to say (a) that it is necessary, *in the sense of logically necessary,* that there should exist a sovereign in every state, if we use the word "sovereign" in the moral sense and the word "state" in the sense of a political society ideally organized. It is also possible to say (b) that it is necessary, *in the sense of causally necessary,* that there should exist a sovereign in every state, if we use the word "sovereign" in the legal sense or generically in the coercive sense, and if we use the word "state" in any of the three senses indicated. On no other usages of the words "sovereign" and "state" can it be said to be necessary that a sovereign should exist in every state.

The three remaining traditional questions may be dealt with more briefly, since we shall no longer be concerned with the variations in the meaning of the word "state." The answers may be given in three groups corresponding to the three traditional questions.

1. To the question, Is it necessary that the sovereign, if it exists, should be indivisible? the following answers may be given: (*a*) If by the word "sovereign" we mean the legal sovereign, it is in one sense logically necessary that the sovereign should be indivisible, since it would be self-contradictory to hold that there could be more than one final decision on any one legal question; but it is neither logically nor causally necessary that the sovereign should be indivisible in the sense that every legal question should be finally decided by one and the same legal authority. This is equally true, if by the word "sovereign" we mean a moral sovereign, since sovereignty of this kind is only a special case of sovereignty in the legal sense. (*b*) The same would also be true, *mutatis mutandis,* if by the word "sovereign" we meant the institutionally coercive sovereign, the socially coercive sovereign or the influential sovereign. It is, in one sense, logically necessary that these sovereigns should be indivisible, since it would be self-contradictory to say of any two coercive powers which were of the same kind, or of any two political influences, that they were both at one and the same time the strongest. But it is neither logically nor causally necessary that these sovereigns should be indivisible in the sense that the power or influence in question may not be divided between two or more bodies. (*c*) If, however, we use the word "sovereign" in the permanent sense, no questions about indivisibility arise, other than those already answered in connection with its other meanings. The

additional qualification of permanence now introduced does
not affect the present issue.

2. The answers to the third of the traditional questions,
namely the question, Is it necessary that the authority or
power or influence of the sovereign should be unlimited? will
depend on what political theorists have meant when they
have used the word "unlimited." The word has been used in
at least two different ways. (a) Some have used it as equivalent
to "omnipotent." [12] When it is used in this way, it is clearly
neither logically nor causally necessary that sovereignty, in
any sense, should be unlimited. In the United States, for instance, there exists no legal authority which can legally deprive any State within the Union of its equal representation
in the Senate. Standing armies everywhere are dependent
on other persons for their supplies of arms and equipment,
and the larger the army the greater its dependence, in this
respect, on the rest of the population. Equally, there are few
political groups which can successfully influence legislation
without compromising to some extent with rival groups. On
no usage of the word "sovereign," therefore, is it necessary
that sovereignty should be unlimited in this sense. (b) The
word "unlimited" has often been used, however, in a weaker
sense, to mean "exceedingly great" or "superior to any
other." [13] When the word is used in this way, it is logically
necessary that sovereignty, in any sense of the word, should
be unlimited. But to say that it is, is now to utter rather a
pointless tautology. It is simply to say that a supreme legal
authority must be supreme, and so on, *mutatis mutandis,* for
any other use of the word "sovereign."

3. The fourth of the traditional questions, namely, Where
is the sovereign located? may now be easily dealt with, since
it resolves itself into a series of entirely empirical questions
requiring straightforward historical, legal or sociological answers. It is not necessary here, therefore, to establish what
the correct answers are in this case, but merely to indicate

12. E.g. Laski, op. cit., pp. 51–3; Popper, *The Open Society and its Enemies,*
    vol. i, p. 107.
13. E.g. Bryce, op. cit., pp. 522–23; Laird, *The Device of Government,* pp.
    83 ff.

what kinds of answers would be appropriate. It would be appropriate, for instance, though not necessarily true, to say that the sovereign was located in the King in Parliament, or the Cabinet, or the House of Lords (legal or moral sense), or in the bulk of the people or in the army (coercive sense), or in the electoral majority or in the economically dominant class (influential sense), or nowhere, because no such sovereign at present exists (moral or permanent or any other sense). Needless to say, this question, or rather these series of questions, may still be difficult to answer, but if so, that it now due to insufficient empirical evidence, rather than to any ambiguity or other logical impropriety in the question. Not all questions which are difficult to answer are logically improper questions.

Answers have now been given to the traditional questions about sovereignty. If these are satisfactory, and I trust they are, then the traditional questions are not pointless questions, however much they may require analysis, and the theory of sovereignty may still be used in such a way as to present at least a consistent theory of politics.

II

The analysis which has now been given, I submit, removes the ambiguities in the traditional theory. Unfortunately, however, it does so only at the expense of making the theory so complicated that it is no longer economical or serviceable to use. The dilemma with which we are faced, therefore, if we wish to retain the concept of sovereignty, is very great. If we preserve the traditional simplicity of the concept, it is too ambiguous to be of service, but if we draw the distinctions necessary to avoid these ambiguities, the analysis of the concept becomes so complicated that its use is no longer helpful. Is there, then, any way of overcoming this difficulty? Is it possible to recommend a use of the concept which will both remove the ambiguities of the traditional theory and preserve it as a useful instrument of political analysis? It seems to me that this is possible, and I shall now endeavour to show how I think this can best be done.

In the first place, the use of the word "sovereign" in the permanent sense may, with every advantage, be abandoned altogether. If the word "permanent" is taken literally to mean "lasting for an indefinitely long time," then this usage is objectionable for two reasons. (1) If we are referring to states which have existed in the past, the concept is so imprecise that no two historians could easily agree as to whether or not a sovereign in this sense did or did not exist in any given state. Did such a sovereign exist, for instance, in the Roman Empire? Some would say not. (2) If we are referring to contemporary states, if it is impossible to *know* that a sovereign in this sense exists in any state, for even though it is conceivably possible that some existing "sovereign" may last for an indefinitely long time, it cannot possibly be *known* that it will. Nor is it easy to see what other use of the word "permanent" would justify the retention of the concept. It may be, of course, that some theorists have meant by "permanent" the same thing as "stable," but, although it is causally necessary that a sovereign should be stable, this does not justify a separate use of the word "sovereign." The fact that a certain characteristic belonging to a thing is a *causally necessary* characteristic, in the sense of causal necessity used here, does not justify our making it a *definitional* characteristic of that thing. A well-drained soil is necessary to grow most plants and vegetables, but the fact that it is not well-drained does not mean that we no longer call it soil.

In the second place, the concept of the sovereign as the moral sovereign may also be abandoned without loss. All the issues which can be discussed with the help of this concept can be discussed more adequately and more usefully with the aid of the concept of obligation. If we define the state in such a way as to identify it with the ideal state, then we can quite logically speak of the sovereignty of the state in the moral sense, but this simply means that we are defining the state and the sovereign in such a way that no organization is a state, and no authority a sovereign, unless we recognize a moral obligation to obey them. There is nothing logically objectionable about this, so long as it is understood that this is simply a way of approaching the problems of political obligation. But in practice this method of approach is objectionable for two reasons. (1) Since the definition of the state is arbitrary, the method is liable to slip from being a method of approaching problems of political obligation to being a method of justifying any state or political régime which happens to exist. This occurs whenever the meanings of the words "state" and "sovereign" slip from their announced meanings into one or other of their more familiar meanings. (2) It tends to prejudge certain questions of ethical theory. The concept of the sovereign as a moral authority tends to establish a strong *presumption* in favour of the view that there are certain moral standards which are the same for all persons, at least within any given political group. But although it may well be true that an objective theory of some kind in ethics is the correct one, this is a question to be examined in the light of our moral experience as a whole, and not one to be prejudged in the interest of a political theory.

This leaves four other concepts, the value of which needs now to be determined.

There is no doubt that the concept of legal sovereignty is valuable in any discussion of the legal aspects of the state's activity. On any definition of the state, as we have seen, it is causally necessary that a sovereign of this kind should exist in every state, and the question, Where is the legal sovereign located? is a fundamental question for every lawyer. Indeed, no contemporary political theorist seems to be prepared to deny the utility of the concept in this limited field, and those who have attacked the use of the concept have done so simply because its utility is confined to this particular field. Since its utility is confined to this field, it is argued, the concept is worthless for more general political purposes. This is a criticism which may fairly be levelled against anyone who maintains that this use of the word "sovereign" is its only "proper" use, and who then ignores its other, allegedly "improper" uses. For, in that case, the theory of sovereignty becomes predominantly a legal theory without relevance to political issues, except in so far as these also happen to be legal issues.

But suppose we allow, as certainly we should, that there can be more than one "proper" use of the word "sovereign." What then becomes of this criticism? A theory of sovereignty which permits a number of proper usages of the word "sovereign," may easily allow that the concept of legal sovereignty is only useful within a limited field, without thereby limiting its own utility to the same field.

But there is a further requirement which needs to be met if the concept is to be worth using at all, and that is to define more precisely what is meant by supreme legal authority. To exercise authority, in its widest sense, is to determine a person's actions in certain intended ways by means of a rule. It is possible, however, to distinguish different kinds of authority by distinguishing the different ways in which different rules, and sometimes the same rules, may oblige a person to act. In this way, the following kinds of authority may be distinguished: (1) authority of a moral kind, where a rule obliges a person to act in virtue of its being accepted by his own conscience, (2) authority of a customary kind, where a rule obliges him to act in virtue of his desire not to incur the disapproval of some other person or persons, e.g. the authority of a tribal chief or of a father of a family, and (3) authority of a coercive kind, where a rule obliges a person to act in virtue of its being enforced, usually with a penalty attached, in the event of disobedience. There are, however, two further subspecies of this latter kind of authority: (a) authority of the kind where the rule is usually enforced by a coercive power, but not by a supreme coercive power, e.g. the authority of a schoolmaster (in some respects), of a trade union, or of an umpire at a cricket match; and (b) legal authority in the strict sense, where the rule, whether it takes the form of a written regulation or of an unwritten convention, is enforced either directly by the exercise of a supreme coercive power, or indirectly by a serious threat of the exercise of such power, e.g. the authority of a king, of a parliament, or of a judge. Legal authority, therefore, is one species of authority, and, when exercised, may be defined as the determination of a person's actions in certain intended ways by means of a law, law being defined as an unwritten convention or a written regulation, enforceable either directly by the exercise of a supreme coercive power, or indirectly by a serious threat of the exercise of such power. From this standpoint the definition of what is meant by the exercise of legal sovereignty presents no further difficulty. To exercise legal sovereignty, or supreme legal authority, is to determine the actions of persons in certain intended ways by means of a law as previously defined, where the actions of those who exercise the authority, in those respects in which they do exercise it, are not subject to any exercise by other persons of the kind of authority which they are exercising.

The definition of law given above is not yet entirely satisfactory since the concept of supreme coercive power, as yet undefined, occurs in the definition. This will be remedied in due course. Leaving the matter for the time being in abeyance, the definitions now given differ in two respects from the definitions given by Austin: (1) the definition of law is wider and designed to include customary law as well as case law and statute law, and (2) legal sovereignty is defined in terms of law rather than vice versa. The latter point has important implications, in that it enables us to reduce constitutional law, as it exists in either the United States or in Great Britain, to positive law. This is theoretically important, since it enables us to bring the theory of legal sovereignty into line with the more fundamental aspects of constitutional and federal government. Moreover, it enables us to do this without necessarily abandoning the command theory of law, since anyone who wishes to hold that theory may still claim that, although judges and legislative assemblies say what the rules are, it is the command of the *coercive* sovereign (*not* the legal sovereign, as Austin seems to have thought) which gives those rules the status of law.

As to the concept of coercive sovereignty, it is clear that this is no less important than the concept of legal sovereignty. Where it is necessary that a legal sovereign should exist, it is also necessary, as we have seen, that a coercive sovereign should exist. There is, in fact, a functional connection between them. Human nature being what it now is, it is necessary, if certain rules are to be obeyed, that they should be capable of being enforced; and, in order that they may be capable of being enforced, it is necessary that there should exist some body of persons sufficiently strong to enforce such rules against any likely opposition within the community. It is this functional connection which was recognized in our definition of law and of legal sovereignty, both of which were defined, at least partly, in terms of supreme coercive power. There is little doubt, it seems to me, that the utility of the concept is great, and that its use in political theory is fully justified.

There are separate objections, however, which might be raised against both what I have called the institutionally coercive sovereign and the socially coercive sovereign. These require to be considered.

It might be objected that the concept of the institutionally coercive sovereign is itself ambiguous. As it has been usually employed, this is certainly a fair criticism. Very often, the sovereign in this sense has been understood to be, not the army or the professional police, but the person who has the legal or effective control of the army or the police, i.e. not Cromwell's army, but Cromwell. This is a practice based on one of two different kinds of confusion. The first is the identification of a whole with a part, or of a group with a member. When the army, commanded by Cromwell, enforces the decisions of Parliament, Cromwell is a *member* of the coercive sovereign and may himself be called sovereign only by a metaphor. The second confusion is to identify coercive sovereignty with legal sovereignty. When Cromwell's army enforces the decisions of Cromwell as against the decisions of Parliament, or even the decisions of Parliament as dictated by Cromwell, Cromwell is not the coercive sovereign; he is simply appropriating legal sovereignty. Provided these two confusions are removed, however, the concept is no longer ambiguous.

The utility of the concept of the socially coercive sovereign might be questioned on the ground that no such coercive power can in fact exist. There is no doubt, however, that there have been historical examples of a supreme coercive power of this kind, notably the police system known as the frankpledge system in medieval England, and similar systems elsewhere. There are, nevertheless, fairly definite conditions under which a coercive power of this kind may be exercised. It can be exercised only, (1) if all or nearly all adult men can be effectively organized for police duties, (2) if all or nearly all men have access to certain kinds of arms and are trained in their use, and (3) if there do not exist serious social cleavages within the community. Where any one of these conditions, and more especially the third, is lacking, law can only be maintained in the last resort by a professional police or armed force. Very often, however, the two coercive systems may exist side by side within the same community. It is often the case, as in England for many centuries, that the socially coercive power performs the coercive functions necessary in the case of those breaches of the law on which society is not deeply divided, such as crimes committed against the common law in times of peace, while the institutionally coercive power is held in reserve to deal with possible large-scale breaches of the law, such as a riot or a threatened revolt or uprising. Of more theoretical interest, it is the existence side by side of these two coercive systems which enables us to regard customary law as genuine law, and thus justify the wide definition of law previously given.

There is no doubt, therefore, that these two concepts of coercive sovereignty are useful. Since they represent, however, two species of a single genus, the theory of sovereignty may be simplified without loss of comprehensiveness or clarity, if we use the word "sovereign" in a generic sense only. Traditionally, in order to simplify the theory, it has been the custom to confine the use of the word "sovereign" to one or other of the relevant species. This is what was recommended by T. H. Green, for instance, when he said that "the term 'sovereignty' is best kept to the ordinary usage in which it signifies a determinate person or persons charged with the supreme coercive function of the state." But this is simply a further example of the common error of assuming that some one possible meaning of the word "sovereign" is a "proper" meaning, while all other possible meanings are to be ignored. In this case, indeed, the error is committed twice over. Not only is it assumed that one generic usage rather than another (i.e. the coercive rather than the legal usage) is the proper usage, but also it is assumed that, within this genus, the word is properly confined to one of the species. There is no solution of our problem along these lines. The only solution lies in accepting both usages, or, if the requirements of simplification are over-riding, in accepting only a generic usage. In this case, there is everything to be said for retaining only the generic usage.

This means that it is necessary now to define what is meant by supreme coercive power, and, in particular, to distinguish coercive power from legal authority and from political influence. To exercise power, in a social and political sense, is to determine the actions of persons in certain intended ways. There are, however, different species of power, and these may be distinguished according to the means used to determine persons' actions. We thus have the following species. (1) Power in the sense of authority, especially legal authority, where the means used is the formulation of, or the reference to, a rule of law, e.g. "the powers of the President," "the powers of local authorities," etc. This species of power we have already considered. (2) Coercive power, where the means used consists either in the direct use of physical force, or else in a serious threat of the use of force, e.g. "the power of the police." (3) Power in the sense of influence, where the means used may be any means other than the employment of a rule of law or of physical force, e.g. "the power of the priest." In all these cases, of course, one often finds, in addition, figurative expressions in which the power is ascribed to the means used rather than to the persons using it, e.g. "the power of the law," "the power of the bayonet," "the power of money," etc.

It is now possible, however, to define coercive power. Coercive power, when it is exercised, is the determination of a person's actions in certain intended ways, either by the direct use of physical force, or else by a serious threat of the use of force. Only a further step is therefore necessary in order to define what is meant by the exercise of coercive sovereignty. A person or a body of persons may be said to exercise coercive sovereignty, or supreme coercive power, if it determines the actions of persons in certain intended ways by means of force or the threat of force, and if the actions of the persons who exercise the power, in those respects in which they do exercise it, are not themselves capable of being similarly determined.

This leaves one more concept to be considered, namely, that of the influential sovereign. The most serious objection which might be raised against the retention of this concept is that it is seldom possible to determine the existence of an influence, and never possible to determine its strength, even when we know that it exists. In the case of legal authority and coercive power we can directly observe certain written rules and punitive instruments; we can observe the ways in which these are being used, and thereby discover chains of authority and power. But how does one determine the existence of an influence and, more especially, the strength of an influence? The objection is one of fundamental importance, since, if there is no means of doing this, the concept is obviously pointless.

It does not seem to me, however, that this objection is finally convincing. The determination of degrees of influence is a job which economists, historians, anthropologists and politicians have often to undertake, and one which they often undertake quite successfully. There are two ways in which this can be done. (1) By means of experimental methods, i.e. by deliberately changing the supposed determinants with the view to observing the concomitant changes, if any, in the behaviour of the persons whose actions are supposed to be influenced. In order to test the extent of the influence which slum surroundings have upon children, it is possible to remove a number of children from these surroundings and observe the changes, if any, in their behaviour. (2) By means of historical abstraction, i.e. by abstracting past variations in the supposed determinants and correlating these with the variations, if any, in the behaviour of the persons or bodies of persons whose activities are supposed to be influenced. In order to determine the influence of economic factors on the techniques of instrumental music, it is not necessary to change the economic system here and now; it is possible by means of abstraction to isolate past economic changes and to correlate these with past changes, similarly isolated, in techniques of instrumental music. In order to determine degrees of political influence, however, it is true that the first of these methods is rarely applicable, since, although the determinants of political influence are capable of being changed, they are seldom if ever capable of being changed experimentally. The changes once carried out are not reversible, so that they cannot usually be carried out at all unless there exists a widespread desire to abandon the older state of affairs for good. But the method of historical abstraction is generally applicable and its practical possibilities are greater the greater the accumulation of historical knowledge. There does not seem to me, therefore, to be any valid objection to the use of the present concept on the ground that it is not possible to determine degrees of political influence.

There are, in addition, strong positive reasons for retaining the use of the concept. Questions about influence are as important in politics as questions about legal authority and coercive power. Are the decisions of the legislature, for instance, primarily determined by the interests of a social class, or by the state of trade, or by the opinion of the majority of the electorate formed independently of class interest and in ignorance of world conditions, etc., etc.? All these questions, and many others like them, are questions about political influence. Generalized, they amount to the one question, Where is the influential sovereign located? What the correct answer to this question may be is, of course, a different matter, but that the question itself is an important one seems to me to be beyond doubt. It is important because a correct answer to it would enable one to intervene more effectively in political affairs. If we wish to determine what Acts of Parliament shall be passed, without being ourselves Members of Parliament, it is important to know which is the most effective way of doing so, whether to try and convince the majority of the electorate, or to try and convince or overthrow the ruling class, or to do something else.

There is, however, one important qualification which needs to be stated if the concept is to be successfully used in this way, namely that the strongest political influence has to be a domestic and not a foreign influence. When the persons, or bodies of persons, who exercise a certain influence within a state, normally reside outside that state, then either it is impossible for any citizen to affect their actions or else, if he can do so, he can usually do it only through the legislature. In either case, his knowing where the strongest political influence lies, will not help him to determine the activities of the legislature. The concept is useful, therefore, only when the actions of the legislature can be regarded as being predominantly determined by the actions or wishes of persons who normally reside within the state, whether they be the whole people or a part of them. Its utility is clearest, of course, where there exist political conventions expressly designed to secure the supremacy of a certain kind of influence, as when a government is given a "mandate" in an election; but its utility may be equally great in practice where there exist no accepted political conventions of this kind, as when the government is, in fact, an instrument of an oligarchy or a priesthood.

Since we must, therefore, as it seems to me, accept the concept, it now remains to define it. This is a difficult matter, since the concept is a residual concept and can only be defined negatively in terms of other concepts. I propose, however, to construct a definition in the following way. To exercise influence, as we have seen, is to determine a person's actions in certain intended ways, by some means other than by a rule of law or a threat of force. But in order that any influence may be regarded as a political influence, it must be an influence on politics, and to say that anything is an influence on politics is to say that it determines the actions, jointly or severally, of the legal and coercive sovereigns. For instance, cer-

tain elements of a country's culture, such as knowledge of the
country's history, can often in this sense be a means of political influence, in a way in which other elements of its culture, such as a knowledge of mathematics or a taste for good
music, very seldom can be. To exercise political influence,
therefore, is to determine in certain intended ways the actions, jointly or severally, of the legal and coercive sovereigns,
provided always that their actions are determined by some
means other than by a rule of law or a threat of force. It is
now possible to define what is meant by the exercise of sovereignty in the influential sense. To exercise sovereignty in
this sense is to exercise political influence, as now defined, to
a greater degree than anyone else, provided that those who
exercise it normally reside within the state whose legal or
coercive sovereign they are supposed to influence.

Before leaving these definitions, there is one further point
to be made. The definitions now given do not define sovereignty, but the exercise of sovereignty; that is, they define
different kinds of events or occurrences. Words like "sovereignty," "power," "authority," and "influence," however, have
this peculiarity, that when used in a sentence they do not in-
form us of any events now happening or about to happen,
but of the probability of such events under certain understood conditions. In this respect, they resemble the names of
dispositions. To say that x is sovereign, for instance, is to
say, among other things, (1) that if a new law were to be
enacted, and if no revolution occurred in the meantime, etc.,
then x would enact it (legal sense); or (2) that if an uprising
were to take place, and x was not itself disaffected, etc., then
x would suppress it (coercive sense); or (3) that if a new law
were to be enacted, then x would determine the kind of law
which the legislators would enact (influential sense). To say
that a certain body of persons is sovereign, therefore, is not
to say that it now determines the actions of persons in certain
intended ways, etc., but that it recurrently succeeds in doing
this under certain understood conditions, and will continue
to do so under the same conditions in the future. This is the
element of truth in the otherwise misleading view that sov-

ereignty implies permanence. Sovereignty does imply recurrent activities of a certain kind under certain understood conditions, but it implies nothing about the duration of the conditions. It is also the much larger element of truth in the still somewhat misleading view of Austin, that sovereignty implies *habitual* obedience on the part of the bulk of the subjects. To say that sovereignty implies habitual obedience is false, if by "habit" we mean a disposition of which the occurrent manifestations are voluntary and automatic, as in the case of smoking and swearing. Sovereignty does, however, imply recurrent acts of obedience, as distinct from habitual obedience in the strict sense, and to this extent Austin was right. Once we understand the proper logical function of words like "sovereignty," "power," "authority," etc., we can easily embrace the element of truth in these views, without at the same time committing ourselves to the errors which they have helped to propagate.

III

We are now in a position to deploy the results of the above discussion. The main purpose of the discussion so far has been to simplify the theory of sovereignty as analysed in the first part of this paper, while at the same time avoiding the logical ambiguities of the traditional theory. This has been done by reducing the six concepts, mixed up in the traditional theory, to three concepts, now systematically defined and analysed. These three concepts, taken together, constitute an analysis of the concept of power as used in political theory. If this analysis is in general correct, then the applicability of the theory of sovereignty to modern political conditions should follow as a matter of course. A test of its correctness, therefore, is whether its applicability to these conditions does in fact follow.

The usual objections raised against the theory of sovereignty on the score of its inapplicability to modern political conditions, are the following: (1) that the theory is inapplicable to the most important political developments of the last hundred years, namely, political democracy, political federalism, and public law as represented in welfare legislation; (2) that it is incompatible with belief in international law, and (3) that it is powerless as a theoretical device to safeguard the individual against despotism. I shall now briefly consider whether the above analysis of the concept does in fact meet these objections.

In the case of democracy, not only is the theory outlined above consistent with the facts of the case, but it enables a classification of democratic systems which, in itself, it seems to me, is both interesting and useful. If democracy is defined as majority rule, we may distinguish the different species of democracy by distinguishing the relations which may exist (1) between the majority and the legal sovereign, and (2) between the majority and the coercive sovereign. In both cases, there are two relations which may exist between them: (*a*) the majority may itself constitute the sovereign or (*b*) it may be the strongest influence on the sovereign (i.e. may itself constitute the influential sovereign). These are the relations commonly referred to, more especially when used with reference to the state's legal functions, as direct democracy and indirect democracy respectively. Since, however, every state has both legal and coercive functions, and since either function may be characterized by either of these two relations, we have four ideal forms of democracy, as follows: (1) Direct legal and direct coercive democracy, e.g. the political organization of some highly developed tribal societies; (2) Direct legal and indirect coercive democracy, e.g. the political organization of some of the Greek city states; (3) Indirect legal and direct coercive democracy, e.g. the state of affairs existing on the American frontier during the last century, approximately; (4) Indirect legal and indirect coercive democracy, e.g. Parliamentary democracy where it exists at its best. Whatever the merits of this classification, it demonstrates, at least, that the theory of sovereignty now presented is fully applicable to the general conditions of political democracy.

We may turn, then, to the argument from federalism. This has been held to be fatal, in particular, to the concept of legal sovereignty. Where in the United States, for instance, is the legal sovereign located? One school replies that the legal sovereign is the constitution; but since the constitution can be legally amended by both Houses of Congress acting in conjunction with three-fourths of the States of the Union, this is hardly plausible. Another school consequently replies that the legal sovereign is both Houses of Congress acting in conjunction with three-fourths of the States of the Union. But since this body has acted as a body only on twenty-one occasions in a hundred and sixty years, and since both Houses of Congress, in any case, derive their own legal existence from the constitution, this is even less plausible. The question is clearly an embarrassing one, and becomes even more embarrassing once it is realized that there is nothing in the nature of the dilemma which makes it one peculiar to federal states. It is a dilemma which arises whenever we have to deal with legal systems which distinguish between ordinary law and constitutional law, whether the constitution be federal or otherwise. What, then, is the answer to this dilemma?

There is, of course, a perfectly simple answer, namely: that in constitutions of this kind—and in almost any constitution, for that matter—there exist at least two supreme legal authorities, one having supreme authority in one set of decisions, on one level of generality, and the other supreme authority in another, on a different level of generality. The traditional objection to this straightforward answer has been that legal sovereignty is not, in that case, necessarily indivisible. But as has been previously shown in this article, the phrase "sovereignty is indivisible" can mean in this context two quite different things. In one sense it is logically necessary that sovereignty should be indivisible, namely in the sense that it would be self-contradictory to hold that there could be more than one final decision on any one legal question, but it is neither logically nor causally necessary that the sovereign should be indivisible in the sense that every legal question should be finally decided by one and the same legal authority. Although traditional theory was right, therefore, in holding that sovereignty is in some sense indivisible, it is not indivisible in the sense necessary to sustain the above objection. In which case, there is no further difficulty.

The argument from welfare legislation has again been held, with greater apparent justification, to be fatal to the concept of legal sovereignty. The argument is put by Duguit as follows (p. 31):

> If the state is not sovereign in one only of its activities it is never sovereign.
>
> Yet in those great state services which increase every day—educational, the Poor law, public works, lighting, the postal, telegraph and telephone systems, the railways—the state intervenes, but it intervenes in a manner that has to be regulated and ordered by a system of public law. But this can no longer be based on the theory of sovereignty. It is applied to acts where no trace of power to command is to be found.

In this statement, two criticisms of the theory of legal sovereignty are implied. In the first place, it is implied that since all welfare legislation *legally* binds the government to provide certain services for the community, such a government can no longer be regarded as *legally* sovereign. Secondly, it is implied that the theory of legal sovereignty requires one to hold a command theory of law, whereas in welfare legislation there is, in fact, no trace of command to be found.

The first of these criticisms is much the more important of the two. To meet it at all, it is necessary seriously to face the question: How can a supreme legal authority be *legally* subject to its own rules? Hitherto it has been well-nigh universally held that to admit the implication in this question would be tantamount to asserting a self-contradiction. All political theorists have found it logically necessary, therefore, either to deny the existence of legal duties on the part of the government so as to be able to maintain its legal sovereignty, as with Austin, or else to deny its legal sovereignty in order to assert its legal duties, as with Duguit. But neither of these standpoints appears to me to be in the least plausible. In fact, it is quite clear that both standpoints are the opposite poles of one and the same antinomy, and one of the chief merits which can be claimed for the theory of sovereignty now presented here is that it enables us to discover the conceptual source of this antinomy and thus to dispose of it once and for all. The antinomy arises from a failure to distinguish between legal and coercive sovereignty. If these two concepts are identified, it does become logically self-contradictory to hold that a supreme legal authority can be legally subject to its own rules. For if a genuine sovereign is, by definition, a composite sovereign having both legal and coercive functions, and if this composite sovereign prescribes rules to itself, then either those rules cannot be enforced against the sovereign, in which case they are not genuine laws, or else, if they are genuine laws and can be so enforced, the so-called sovereign is not a genuine sovereign. But if the concepts of legal and coercive sovereignty are not identified in this way, this self-contradiction does not arise and the antinomy disappears. For in this case, the rules prescribed by the legal sovereign to itself may be enforced against itself by the coercive sovereign, and may thus be correctly called laws, while the legal sovereign, which is thus subjected to its own rules, is subjected only in virtue of the enforcement of the rules by the coercive sovereign and not in virtue of their prescription, in which case it is still no less sovereign legally. In short, just as the distinction between the legal and coercive sovereigns enabled us to show how constitutional law can be positive law, so also it enables us to show how a supreme legal authority can be legally subject to its own rules. To this extent the argument from welfare legislation can be turned into an argument in favour of the theory of sovereignty presented here.

The second criticism is less important, and there are, in any case, two replies which may be made to it. In the first place, although it is logically necessary that a person who holds a command theory of law should also hold a theory of sovereignty of some kind, since the existence of a command implies the existence of a commander, there is no such necessity for a person who holds a theory of sovereignty to hold a command theory of law. Even if it is true that the rules of a supreme legal authority cannot be correctly interpreted as commands, this is not the slightest evidence for believing that they are not the rules of a supreme legal authority. In the second place, even if one were obliged to hold a command theory of law, this need no longer be embarrassing. On the above theory of sovereignty, an advocate of the command theory of law need no longer argue that acts of welfare legislation consist of commands issued by the legal sovereign, whether addressed to itself or to anyone else. He can now argue that in so far as these rules are genuine laws and not self-imposed moral precepts, they consist of the commands of the coercive sovereign addressed to the legal sovereign. This is at least plausible. Indeed, on this view, it can hardly be now said that the existence of welfare legislation presents any serious difficulty for a command theory of law.

And now the argument from international law. It has been said that the growth of international law is incompatible with the sovereignty of the state, but this is a vague criticism, and in order to give it some precision it is necessary to clarify its terms. It is necessary, in particular, to distinguish two uses of the word "law." It may mean (a) a body of rules enforceable by institutions having supreme coercive power, i.e. positive law in the strict sense; or it may mean (b) a body of formal and solemn agreements, usually between states, the maintenance of which is solely dependent upon the recognition of an interest or a duty by the contracting parties. I shall call it agreement law. The argument that the growth of international law is incompatible with the sovereignty of the state may, therefore, mean any one of four different things. It may mean (1) that the existence of a supreme legal authority within a state is incompatible with the existence of a world positive law; or (2) that it is incompatible with the existence of an inter-state agreement law; or (3) that the existence of an inter-state agreement law is incompatible with the existence within a state of a sovereign in the influential sense; or (4) that the existence within a state of a sovereign, whether in the legal, coercive or influential sense, is a practical obstacle to the free development of inter-state agreement law and/or universal positive law. What now, then, may be said of these four arguments?

Of the first argument, namely that the existence of a supreme legal authority within a state is incompatible with the existence of a world positive law, there are two things to be said. (*a*) Since such a thing as a world positive law does not as yet exist, any incompatibility which there may be between its own existence and that of a supreme legal authority within a state, does not, in present circumstances, argue the non-existence of the supreme legal authority. (*b*) Even if a universal positive law did exist, its existence would be incompatible, not with the existence of a supreme legal authority within the state, but with the existence of *more than one* legally sovereign state, which is quite another matter. Of the second argument, that the existence of a supreme legal authority within the state is incompatible with the existence of an inter-state agreement law, it must be said that this is no argument at all. The alleged incompatibility simply does not exist. If two bodies, both of which are legally sovereign within different territories, reach certain solemn agreements with each other, it is simply false to assume that they thereby cease to be legally sovereign within their own respective territories. The third argument, however, is valid criticism of most traditional theories of sovereignty. It is often true, although not always, that the existence of an international law is incompatible with the sovereignty of the state in the influential sense. The existence of an international agreement may in practice be as binding upon a government as any positive law, although in a different way, and to ignore this would be to ignore a fact of very great political importance. Whether it is so or not, however, is an empirical question. It is entirely a question of fact whether the strongest influence on the legal sovereign is an international or a domestic influence. But assuming that it is in fact an international influence, this implies no criticism of the theory of sovereignty advocated here, since it is not essential to this theory to hold that it is either logically or causally necessary that there should exist in any state a sovereign in the influential sense. The fourth argument was the argument that the existence of sovereignty in any sense is a practical hindrance to the free development of inter-state agreement law and/or universal positive law. In this case, the contention itself may well be both true and important, but even if true it does not in the least deny the existence within the state of a sovereign in any of the senses indicated. The fact, if it is a fact, that these things hinder the growth of international law, is no proof, unfortunately, that these things do not exist.

Lastly, is it true that the theory of sovereignty is powerless to safeguard the individual against despotism? Undoubtedly, as against much the greater part of traditional theory, this charge is justified. The traditional theory has been extremely liable to slip into one of two positions, either (1) of identifying sovereignty in a legal or coercive sense with sovereignty in a moral sense, or (2) of ignoring sovereignty in the influential sense. The first standpoint is exemplified in the Rousseau-Hegel-Bosanquet tradition, the second in the Bodin-Hobbes-Austin tradition. The effect of the former was to prejudge all questions of political obligation in favour of the despotic claims of the state, while the effect of the latter was to put the law and the coercive forces of the state, for theoretical purposes, beyond the possibility of control by society. The one told the subject, in effect, that he ought to have absolute government because it is good for him, the other that he must have absolute government if he is to have any government at all. Either standpoint is vicious, whether from a theoretical or a practical point of view. But, equally clearly, neither standpoint is essential to a theory of sovereignty. They are simply by-products of ambiguities in the statement of the theory, and can be easily removed once the proper distinctions are drawn. The purpose of this article has been to draw these distinctions, and thus to safeguard the theory against this as well as the other charges.

Yves R. Simon

SOVEREIGNTY IN DEMOCRACY

The subject of sovereignty is one that every treatise or text-book of political science, no matter how elementary, has to discuss. Consequently, the state of the question in our academic and scholarly circles is particularly bad. With problems of extreme difficulty, the worst that can happen is that hasty and mediocre writers should feel obliged to contribute treatments for the satisfaction of not very exacting and not very industrious readers. True, the case of common teaching would not be so bad if great books had not set an example of uncertainty. This is not due entirely to the difficulties of the question; it is also due to the confusing influence of historical circumstances. The discussion of sovereignty often arouses passions which make a philosophic treatment impossible and substitute for it—most of the time surreptitiously—vindications of existing conditions or exhortations for the bringing-about of a new state of affairs. The writings of King James contain the ideology of British absolutism. More shockingly, Bossuet burdened posterity with a theory in which it is easy to recognize the ideology of the great historical movement which culminated in the monarchy of Louis XIV. Late eighteenth-century theories of sovereignty express the struggles fought by the American people against the British Crown or by the French bourgeoisie against king, nobility, and established church. The impression left by the literature

From *Philosophy of Democratic Government* by Yves R. Simon (The University of Chicago Press, Chicago, 1961), pp. 144–60; 176–94. Copyright 1951 by The University of Chicago. Reprinted by permission of The University of Chicago Press.

on sovereignty is gloomy: distortion due to practical concerns can be feared almost everywhere.

Such factors of confusion make it particularly important to state the problem in simple and clear terms. The common experience of civil societies shows that men obey other men. Disobedience is not infrequent, but it is impressively out-weighed by obedience in any society that has not reached the last stages of disintegration. We have to interpret this great fact of political obedience. On what ground do some men claim a right to be obeyed? What are the reasons why they are not always disobeyed? Many would answer that they do not want to go to jail or to be shot down, and some theorists would maintain that fear and self-interest account sufficiently for the fact of obedience in civil society. Any human experience, any knowledge of history, evidences the shallowness of this explanation. The relationship which obtained between the police and the bootleggers in the era of prohibition exemplifies a situation in which fear and self-interest alone motivate obedience. Such a situation does not characterize civil society, it means the end of it. Things take place in civil relations, not exceptionally but regularly, as if some men had the power of binding the consciences of other men. The factual behavior of men in society testifies to the regular operation of an ethical motive of obedience. Not only in persons of lofty morality but also in those classified as average citizens there is a certain awareness of being obliged to obey public powers, at least a vague feeling that, things being what they are, men commonly considered as the agents of society have a right to give orders within the limits of their legally formulated functions. Now the proposition that a man can bind the conscience of another man raises a very great difficulty: far from being obvious, it is altogether devoid of verisimilitude. This is the very essence of the problem which we propose to examine; on the one hand, it seems to be impossible to account for social life without assuming that man can bind the conscience of his neighbor; on the other hand, it is not easy to see how a man can ever enjoy such power.

THE COACH-DRIVER THEORY

There is a way out. The difficulty can be explained away. It would vanish if it were possible to show that a man is never bound in conscience to obey another man. There is a theory according to which civil obedience is but an appearance and an illusion. If only traditional violences and superstitions were checked, the illusion would disappear and social relations would reveal their true nature, to the great benefit of all. Then it would become clear that the claim of man to be obeyed by his neighbor is in all cases unwarranted and deceitful. We obey ourselves alone. I really obey myself alone, and this is all that society needs and wants me to do. In society I remain as free as in solitude. Great caution must be used in giving this theory a name. No doubt Rousseau has written, about freedom and civil obedience, things which mean that, in the state as he conceives it, citizens are their own masters and obey but themselves. The theory we are in the process of describing represents an aspect of Rousseau's political philosophy; but to describe it, with no qualification, as Rousseau's theory of sovereignty might involve a risk of oversimplification.

This theory holds that the government is the servant of the people; but the same view is accepted in extremely diverse systems of political thought. It holds, further, that the men in power are delegated by the people, that they are given definite missions by the people, and that in the fulfilment of their missions they remain strictly subordinated to the people that delegated them. Thus the governing person is a leader entirely under the control of those whom he leads. Authority belongs not to the leaders but to the led. Or perhaps it should be said that real leadership, the one which is inseparable from authority, belongs not to the government but to the governed. *In so far as the governing person is considered a leader, his is a leadership without authority.* Because he is, in a way, leader, he seems to have the power of directing judgments and wills, of binding consciences—in short, he seems to exercise authority. Such appearance is commonly exploited by tyranny. In truth, however, authority remains in the hands of the governed, since it is only by virtue of their will and of the missions given to persons of their own choice that the government exercises leadership.

To call this the "theory of the sovereignty of the people" involves intolerable confusion, for the same expression can be used, and is used very commonly, to designate a widely different philosophy of civil authority. There is, in the theory under consideration, something distinctive and unique which ought not to be missed by the expression meant to designate it; it is the statement that obedience of man to man, in political society at least, is mere illusion and violence, that the citizen ought to obey himself alone, and that the leadership exercised by the governing personnel involves no authority. The expression "sovereignty of the people" does not bring forth this essential element of the theory. A proper name for it is suggested by Paul-Louis Courier, a liberal, a rebel in the petty bourgeois style, a Voltairean, a humanist in perpetual revolt against church and state. He wrote that in a liberal state of affairs the government is like a coach-driver, hired and paid by those whom he drives.[1] The coach-driver leads his patrons indeed, but only where they want to go and by the ways of their own choice. The theory which reduces the role of the government to that of a leader without authority could appropriately be called "the coach-driver theory." Merely to assert that sovereignty belongs to the people is not precise

---

1. Paul-Louis Courier, *Lettres au rédacteur du Censeur*, Lettre X, 10 mars 1820 (*Œuvres* [Paris: Firmin Didot, 1845], pp. 62–63). This letter is concerned with the freedom of the press; the writer describes in humorous fashion the evils that its adversaries expect of it: "If this abuse [i.e., the freedom of the press] should endure, every undertaking of the court would be controlled beforehand, examined, judged, criticized, estimated. The public would consider all business as their own; everything would arouse their contemptible interest; they would check the records of the treasurer, supervise the police, and scoff at the diplomatic service. In one word, the nation would manage the government after the fashion of a coach-driver whom we hire and who is supposed to lead us, not where he wants, not how he wants, but where we intend to go and by the way that we find convenient. This is a thing horrible to imagine, contrary to the divine right and the capitularies."

enough; for it is not obvious, it is not even certain, that the sovereignty of the people suppresses obedience. By likening the government to a coach-driver, doubts are eliminated. Primitives traveling in a civilized country—as they used to do in eighteenth-century fiction—would perhaps believe that the driver of the coach is the real master and takes the persons on the back seat where he pleases; a similar illusion has been exploited by men in power throughout the history of mankind. It is only of late that the spell has been broken and that the governing personnel have been identified for what they are: purely instrumental characters whose duty it is, even when they shout orders, to fulfil the orders given them by the governed.

In the work of Rousseau the coach-driver theory is so supplemented as not to disclose too shockingly its paradoxical simplicity. Yet Rousseau has probably done more than anyone else to spread the ideal of an organization capable of doing away with the ethical substance of authority and obedience.[2] Persons concerned with real liberty soon recognized that the sovereignty of the people, as it appears to the readers

2. J.-J. Rousseau, *The Social Contract* ("Everyman's Library" [New York: E. P. Dutton & Co., 1930]), Book I, chap. vi: "The problem is to find a form of association which will defend and protect with the whole common force the person and goods of each associate, and in which each, while uniting himself with all, may still obey himself alone, and remain as free as before." Book II, chap. i. "I hold then that Sovereignty, being nothing less than the exercise of the general will, can never be alienated, and that the sovereign, who is no less than a collective being, cannot be represented except by himself: the power indeed may be transmitted, but not the will." Better than any of the political writings of Rousseau, the *Émile* shows that the all-important thing is to substitute submission to impersonal forces for obedience to persons. See Augustin Cochin, *La Crise de l'histoire révolutionnaire* (Paris: Champion, 1909), p. 49: "Such is the precise and new meaning of the 'war against the tyrants' declared by the Revolution. It does not promise freedom in the ordinary sense of the word, i.e., independence, but in the sense in which Rousseau understands this word, viz., anarchy, deliverance from all personal authority, whether that of the lord to whom respect is due or that of the demagogue who exercises fascination. *If one is obedient, it will never be to a man but always to an impersonal being, the general will*" (italics mine).

of Rousseau, supplied tyranny with a new vindication of unprecedented efficaciousness. Rousseau and his admirers prac- perhaps less interested in what actually happens in social prac- tice than in the purely interior and entirely spiritual process of interpreting relations among men. If a disciple of Rousseau has to choose between an unpleasant situation imposed upon him without any consent of his own and a pleasant situation to be accepted voluntarily out of a sense of obedience, he chooses the former as more consonant with his notion of lib- erty. The coach-driver theory exercised great influence upon the French Revolution, upon French democracy throughout its history, and upon all democratic movements inspired by French examples. It did not play a decisive part in the early ages of American democracy; the concept of natural law was then too strong to allow the voluntarism of such a theory to unfold its consequences and reveal its principle. From the time of Andrew Jackson on, the coach-driver theory has been an ideological factor of some importance in American history. It never won in America the same position of unquestioned supremacy that it did in several Latin countries.

This theory flatters an instinct of disobedience from which no human heart is entirely free. When this instinct is unin- hibited, it may lead to anarchism. But if it is kept under control by an interest in good manners and a sense of respecta- bility, it finds a fitting outlet in the coach-driver theory. Fur- ther, this theory draws considerable power from its apparent ability to explain a number of phenomena pertaining to regular democratic practice. Think, in the first place, of the direct government of the people by themselves as practiced, for instance, in New England towns and in some Swiss can- tons. Although such government without a distinct personnel is seldom possible, it is reasonably held to constitute the funda- mental pattern of democratic government. The archetype of democracy is a government without a distinct governing per- sonnel, without any representative assembly. No representa- tion is needed: the people gather, and they are the government. But, without using any distinct governing personnel, democ- racy may use agents. The people's assembly may appoint managers who are not really men in authority; they are merely instruments, and authority remains entirely in the hands of the people. Such agents, managers, or secretaries employed by the people's assembly receive orders and do not—in spite, perhaps, of certain appearances—give orders of their own. They can be properly likened to coach-drivers who take the orders of their patrons and lead them where they want to go. Against this background of direct democracy let us consider a democratic organization such as ours, with a distinct governing personnel, elected legislative assemblies, and an elected president. Outwardly, at least, there are resemblances between this governing personnel and the managers hired, after the fashion of a coach-driver, by direct democracy. We elect our representatives on the basis of their programs. By doing so, do we not order them to lead us where we want to go, that is, to the objective described in the program of our choice and through the ways recommended by the program that we have chosen? When new elections are held, we express either our satisfaction by re-electing our representative or our dissatisfaction by voting for his opponent; it looks very much like hiring again, or refusing to rehire, an instrumental character according as he has fulfilled properly, or failed to fulfil, the orders that he was given. A number of less fundamental but very significant democratic practices seem to be properly accounted for by the coach-driver theory. Think of the many means of pressure used by the electorate, between election periods, in order to have their will carried out. To write to your congressman that you want him to support a certain measure is perfectly intelligible if your congressman is, like the secretaries and managers of a direct democracy, a pure instrument that has no orders to give but only orders to take.

In order to test the coach-driver theory of sovereignty, we shall consider the case in which it seems to work most plainly and from which it drives most of its energy and prestige, viz., the case of a small community practicing direct, nonrepresentative government. Here are a few hundred farmers. Consider them, first, while they are not in session. Each of them, a private citizen, toils in his own field and minds his own business. When the assembly convenes, these men undergo a qualitative change. One hour ago they were scattered in their fields. Right now they have gathered for purposes of public business; they are no longer a collection of private citizens minding their own affairs, they are the people minding common affairs. It is crucially important to understand the qualitative nature of the change. *Between these few hundred farmers scattered in their fields, busy with their own private affairs, and the same farmers gathered in an assembly in charge of the community's affairs, the qualitative difference is just as great as between the President of the United States and any of us United States citizens.*

The best way to understand this qualitative difference is to consider the basic problem of civil obedience in relation to an assembly inclusive of all the people. The coach-driver theory serves the ideal of a situation such that each should remain, in society, as independent as in natural solitude and obey but himself. Does such a situation obtain in direct democracy? *Apparently* it does. These men who issue rules for common action by majority vote do not obey anybody except themselves. Suppose, first, for the sake of clarity, that the vote is unanimous; then everybody can say that the law is his own law and that, by obeying it, he obeys only himself. Suppose, then, that there is no unanimity but that I am among the majority; again I can, apparently, boast that the law which I shall obey is my own law and that, by obeying it, I obey only myself. But what happens when I am in the minority? Here lies the real test, and from the interpretation of my situation as member of a minority I shall infer conclusions concerning the proper interpretation of my situation as member of a majority or of a unanimous assembly.

Suppose that throughout a long period I was among the majority. What am I going to do the day I find myself in the minority? I may refuse to obey the law that I did not approve and declare myself a rebel; but then it will be clear that I have always been a rebel. A conspicuous rebel as member of a minority, I was already a rebel when I was member of a majority or of a unanimous assembly, since, even then, I was determined to disobey whenever I should happen to disagree. I never was a law-abiding citizen; I never abided by the law, except by accident. This makes it plain that the coach-driver theory does not supply a satisfactory explanation for the basic facts of political behavior even under the circumstances which would be most favorable to its operation, if such a theory ever could work. In a direct democracy where, by hypothesis, there is no distinct governing personnel, distinct persons are not governors but mere agents, purely instrumental characters. There is no question of obeying them, except possibly in incidental fashion, in the way in which the police chief would obey his subordinates in the enforcement of a traffic regulation that he made and that he can change. Such purely instrumental characters do not hold authority, *but the fact that authority is not held by any distinct persons does not mean that it is not held by anybody.* . . . the requirements of the concept of authority are entirely fulfilled in the case of a community governing itself directly, without any distinct governing personnel. Authority is not lacking; it resides in the community. The few hundred farmers meeting in assembly are, as a body, essentially distinct from what they were before they assembled and will be as soon as they return to private citizenship. Meeting in assembly, they are the government, and to this government each of them, on returning to private citizenship, owes obedience, regardless of what happened to him as a member of the people's assembly. Whether he belonged to a unanimous assembly, to the majority, or to a minority is entirely incidental. The thing that matters is that he is bound by the law that the people, acting as their own government, passed. Whether he voted for or against it makes absolutely no difference; he is subjected to it and ought to abide by it. This is the only way to interpret the fundamental data of political life so far as law and obligation are concerned. The coach-driver theory renders these data unintelligible by reversing relations between the essential and the casual. A citizen is considered law-abiding if, and only if, he considers his obligation independent from his personal opinion. If the law was passed in spite of his wish, his duty to abide by it may be unpleasant, but it is just as clear as if he had voted for it. In the coach-driver theory, on the contrary, my personal consent to the law is essential. I feel obligated to abide by the law if, and only if, I wanted the law to be what it is. Clearly, I abide by the law not on account of its essence as law but because of my incidental approval of it. If the coach-driver theory should ever be received in a spirit of strict consistency, society would soon be destroyed by secession. But this theory does not need to be applied with strict consistency in order to be effective.

What generally happens is that the dissenter performs the acts prescribed by the law which he disapproves, but in a purely utilitarian fashion, merely in order to spare himself and others the inconveniences following upon the breaking of the law. Thus outward anarchy and the violent disruption of society are avoided. External order is not delivered up to the fortuitousness of unanimity. But the inner dispositions of minds and hearts toward the law are subjected to such fortuitousness; this weakens dangerously the unity of society and corrupts the character of political life by substituting a law of utility and force for the law of voluntary co-operation whenever I happen not to be in the majority. In a direct democracy as well as in any other organization the nature of society demands that man should obey man. The artifice calculated to do away with obedience threatens directly the principle of authority in its most essential functions . . . we saw that the need for government is so rooted in the nature of society that government would be needed even in the ideal case of a society made only on enlightened and virtuous people. If government, as distinct from unanimity, is made necessary by the very nature of things, the obligation to obey has its roots in the nature of things, in the very nature of man and of human society. It is completely independent of my casual belonging to the majority or the minority. This is why the coach-driver theory is unlikely to be very popular where there is a strong belief in a law of nature independent of the whims of man.

Back to our initial question, let us remark, again, that

there is something paradoxical about one man's having the power to bind the conscience of another man. Of course, a man cannot do such a thing. God alone can. And God can bind a man to obey another man. This he did by the creation of the human species, which is naturally social and political; for the necessity of government and obedience follows from the nature of community life.[3]

DIVINE RIGHT

Let us now turn to the subject so confusedly described as the "theory of divine right." The expression "divine right" is just as confusing as the expression "sovereignty of the people"; neither should be used except when the context removes all ambiguity.

The so-called "theory of divine right," as it has been known to the Western world ever since the seventeenth century, is related to the history of Christianity in such fashion that it does not seem possible to give an exposition of it except in terms of Christian history. According to Christian faith, God became man, and before he left this world he founded a society designed to maintain his life in men. The first leaders of this society were designated by him. Among them he distinguished one, Peter. Concerning the supremacy of the latter, disagreement came to a showdown early in the sixteenth century; from then on, part of the Christian world ignored the notion of one supreme leader appointed by Christ. Simul-

3. Leo XIII, *Diuturnum* ("On Civil Government") (1881), trans. presented by Joseph Husslein, S.J., in *Social Wellsprings: Fourteen Epochal Documents by Pope Leo XIII* (Milwaukee: Bruce Publishing Co., 1940), p. 52: "But now, a society can neither exist nor be conceived in which there is no one to govern the wills of individuals, in such a way as to make, as it were, one will out of many, and to impel them rightly and orderly to the common good; therefore God has willed that in a civil society there should be some to rule the multitude. . . . But no man has in himself or of himself the power of constraining the free will of others by fetters of authority of this kind. This power resides solely in God, the Creator and Legislator of all things; and it is necessary that those who exercise it should do it as having received it from God."

taneously, the other part of the Christian world became more and more articulate and firm in its acknowledgment of the supremacy of Peter and his successors. According to the upholders of Peter's supremacy, the head of the church enjoys a power which comes from God directly. The first person to hold this power was, moreover, designated by Christ himself. Here (i.e., in the case of Peter) we can speak of power by divine right with perfect propriety; for this power is in no way from man, it is from God alone, and even its conjunction with the particular person who holds it is effected by God. In the case of Peter's successors, the person is designated by man, the conjunction between power and person is effected by man, but power continues to be from God directly and exclusively. The successor of Peter, as well as Peter himself, is vicar of Christ and in no way whatsoever vicar of the church. Men have nothing to do with his power, except so far as the designation of the person is concerned. In spite of this designation by man, the expression "power by divine right" is perfectly appropriate.

We are considering here a spiritual society, a society which describes itself as not concerned properly and directly with temporal affairs, a society whose main ends are found in another world and in a future life, a society whose proper life and main ends are held to be supernatural. The Gospel states the principle of a distinction between this spiritual or supernatural society and the state or temporal society: There are, according to the Gospel, things that are Caesar's and things that are not Caesar's. But, between these two orders of things, the relation is such that the distinction, though intelligible and clear, cannot always work plainly. In centuries of universal faith as well as in times of widespread disbelief, clashes are frequent between the two powers. One effect of these uncertainties and adventures is that some ascribe to one power peculiarities, features, characteristics, and prerogatives proper to the other power. Not infrequently, people dreamed of a church organized and governed according to the pattern set by the temporal society. And not infrequently, people dreamed of a temporal power enjoying dignities similar to those of the church. We find in the Middle Ages theories implying that the pope is the vicar of the church as well as the vicar of Christ. History also records theories according to which the king is not the vicar of the people but only the vicar of God.[4]

Some extremists went so far as to maintain not only that the power of the king is directly from God but also that the designation of the king is effected divinely. The most paradoxical among these eccentrics was Filmer, who said that kings and governors inherited from the patriarchs an authority received from Noah, from Adam, and ultimately from God.[5] Such a reading of history probably did not convince many people. On the other hand, the notion that great leaders, great makers of history, are singled out by God and taken into governing positions through methods distinct from the ordinary course of providential government is not uncommon. Strikingly, momentous instances of such a belief can be found in times and places where religious faith is not particularly warm or orthodox. We have only to think of Napoleon and Hitler. Of little importance in this history of political philosophies, the theory of divine designation sometimes played a decisive part in political history. Its power is great when it assumes the form of a myth capable of supplying a people, in the midst of exalting emotions, with a practical explanation of its manifest destiny.

The theory implying both (1) that the power of the temporal ruler is directly from God and (2) that God himself designates the person of the temporary ruler deserves to be called the "divine-right theory" in the most proper sense. Next to it comes the theory which, though acknowledging that the designation of the king, as well as that of the pope (with the exception of the first pope), is effected by men, maintains that the power of the king, as well as that of the pope, comes directly from God. This theory could also be described with propriety as a theory of divine right, but the usual expression, "designation theory," is specific and satisfactory. The designation theory is a more moderate, less paradoxical form of the divine-right theory; it holds that in temporal power the

---

4. See *The Political Writings of James I,* with an Introduction by C. H. McIlwain (Cambridge: Harvard University Press, 1918).
5. Robert Filmer, *Patriarcha,* published only in 1680.

only thing traceable, *in any sense,* to human power is the
designation of the ruling person.

THE TRANSMISSION THEORY

Another theory holds that the first bearer of civil authority
is not the king or any governor but the people as a whole, the
civil multitude. Whenever there is a distinct governing personnel, men have done two things and not one, as in the case
of the pope: they have *designated* the ruling person, and they
have *transmitted* to him the power given by God to the people. Let us emphasize that *transmitting* does not mean the
same as *giving.* To say that God alone gives authority is the
same as to say that God alone can bind the conscience of man.

The transmission theory is commonly attributed to Thomas
Aquinas. True, the question does not belong to his *Problematik*
and is not treated explicitly in any part of his work. The best
approximation to a treatment of it is found in the *Treatise on
Laws* of the *Summa theologica.* After having shown that law
is a product of the reason—more precisely, a premise of practical argumentation (a.1)—and that it is essentially relative
to the common good (a.2), Aquinas poses the question *Whether
the reason of any man is competent to make laws?* The answer is commanded by the principle of proportion between
end and cause. Since the end is the common good, the efficient
cause ought to be, proportionately, the multitude or a person
"holding the part of," "acting instead of," "being in charge
of," the multitude. "Now to order anything to the common
good belongs either to the whole people or to someone who
is the vicegerent of the whole people. Hence the making of
a law belongs either to the whole people or to a public per-
sonage who has care of the whole people." [6] In a later question

---

6. *Sum. theol.* i–ii. 90. 3: "Ordinare autem aliquid in bonum commune
   est vel totius multitudinis, vel alicujus gerentis vicem totius multitudinis. Et ideo condere legem vel pertinet ad totam multitudinem,
   vel pertinet ad personam publicam, quae totius multitudinis curam
   habet; quia et in omnibus aliis ordinare in finem est ejus, cujus est
   proprius ille finis."

of the same treatise he shows that custom can obtain the force of law; an objection to this statement is derived from the public character of the lawmaker: ". . . the framing of laws belongs to those public men whose business it is to govern the community . . . but custom grows by the acts of private individuals. . . ." Here is the answer of Aquinas (trans. A. C. Pegis):

> The people among whom a custom is introduced may be of two conditions. For if they are free, and able to make their own laws, the consent of the whole people expressed by a custom counts far more in favor of a particular observance than does the authority of the sovereign, who has not the power to frame laws, except as representing the people. Therefore, although each individual cannot make laws, yet the whole people can. If, however, the people have not the free power to make their own laws, or to abolish a law made by a higher authority, nevertheless, among such a people a prevailing custom obtains the force of law insofar as it is tolerated by those to whom it belongs to make laws for that people; because by the very fact that they tolerate it, they seem to approve of that which is introduced by custom.[7]

There cannot be any doubt that the transmission theory is in full agreement with the nation of political authority expressed here by Aquinas. These texts are most simply and directly interpreted by the theory that power belongs primarily to the people, who can use it to make laws for themselves, and that, if and when power lies in the hands of a distinct person, this person has the character of "one who substitutes

---

7. *Ibid.* 97. 3, ad 3: "Multitudo, in qua consuetudo introducitur, duplicis conditionis esse potest. Si enim sit libera multitudo, quae possit sibi legem facere, plus est consensus totius multitudinis ad aliquid observandum, quod consuetudo manifestat, quam auctoritas Principis, qui non habet potestatem condendi legem, nisi inquantum gerit personam multitudinis; unde licet singulae personae non possint condere legem, tamen totus populus condere legem potest. Si vero multitudo non habeat liberam potestatem condendi sibi legem vel legem a superiori positam removendi, tamen ipsa consuetudo in tali multitudine praevalens obtinet vim legis, inquantum per eos toleratur ad quos pertinet multitudini legem imponere; ex hoc enim ipso videntur approbare quod consuetudo introduxit."

for the people." The expression *gerens vicem* might suggest
the coach-driver theory; but this is ruled out by Aquinas'
general views on obedience and authority. Thus it can be said
that his only existent expressions on the subject of the origin
of political power support the transmission theory. Yet, because these expressions amount merely to a few sentences,
because the problem is not fuly disengaged, and because the
alternative solution (i.e., the designation theory) is not en-
visaged, to state with qualification that the transmission theory
is that of Aquinas would perhaps be more than the texts
warrant. . . .

AUTHORITY IN DEMOCRACY

Among the obnoxious simplifications which fill the treatises
of political science, let us single out the proposition that the
divine-right theory is theocratic and the sovereignty-of-the-
people theory democratic. If theocracy means the ruling of
temporal society by the spiritual power, no theory of divine
right is theocratic. The common view that every lawful authority holds from God the power of binding man's conscience
is not theocratic but rather dismisses all theocratic claim by
supplying the temporal power with a complete justification.
And King James's theory is shrewdly calculated to exclude
all threat of theocracy by setting, between the king and God,
a relation equal to that which obtains between the pope and
God (at least equal, for the privilege of hereditary transmission can make it even better). As to the expression "sovereignty of the people," we know that it may refer to the coach-
the so-called "sovereignty of the people," for there cannot be
driver theory, in which case there is nothing democratic about
democratic government when the very essence of government
is negated; this lust for a situation in which the need of society for leadership would be satisfied without the leader
(who may well be the community itself, expressing itself
through majority vote) being endowed with any authority
does not pertain to democracy any more than to any other
regime, although it is in the democratic framework that it

expects satisfaction, so that democracy is particularly exposed to its destructive power. If, on the other hand, the expression "sovereignty of the people" refers to the transmission theory, it should be mentioned that this theory was never understood to hold for democracy alone. Historians often described the views of Bellarmine and Suarez as expressions of the democratic theory of sovereignty; yet neither of these thinkers meant to recommend democracy. They both had in view principally the monarchical governments of their time; and against the disorderly claims of emerging absolutism they meant to define general conditions of political sovereignty holding for every political government, whether democratic or not.

This point should be stressed: the transmission theory is not understood by its proponents to be distinctly democratic. It is distinctly *political,* no more.[8] The implications of its *political* character are three: (1) it concerns the state, i.e., the complete or perfect *temporal* community; (2) it concerns the fully *legitimate* government of such community rather than what we call a *de facto* government, which must be obeyed for the single reason that, under the circumstances, disobedience would entail more inconvenience than obedience; (3) it concerns, finally, a government which is *political* in the sense defined in the second chapter of this book, viz., in the sense in which a political system is understood to imply a degree of autonomy and a legally defined power of resistance in the hands of the governed. If a despotic regime happens to be legitimate (as in the case, mentioned by Suarez, of a rule resulting from just conquest and not yet sanctioned by popular consent), the transmission theory of sovereignty does not apply fully; true, the normal characteristics of temporal society are but partly realized; for a society which can be lawfully ruled in despotic fashion is one that has not yet attained maturity as a complete temporal society or one that has lost the privileges of maturity through some perversion.

8. The "free people" of which Aquinas speaks (i–ii. 97. 3, ad 3) seems to be a people subjected to *political* government in the sense defined in chap. ii.

When the concept of temporal government is realized with all its implications, the transmission theory of sovereignty holds, regardless of whether government is democratic, aristocratic, monarchical, or mixed. It implies that the governed consent to the government which is theirs, but it does not imply that this consent is necessarily exercised in the democratic procedure of election. The constitutional powers of the British king and those of the French president are similar in several respects: the French president is elected by the people, though indirectly; the British king is designated by heredity; both enjoy the consent of the majority. In the case of the president, this consent is expressed by election; in the case of the king, without any election. Notice that the popular consent given to the British king without any voting procedure is at least as genuine, sincere, profound, and unmistakably established as the consent given, through election, to the French president. The transmission theory implies that the power which primarily belongs to the people and has been transmitted by it to a distinct governing personnel can be withdrawn from unworthy rulers. . . . whether the regime is democratic or not, the transmission theory holds that the people, after having transmitted power and having placed itself in a position of mandatory obedience, retains a power greater than the power transmitted; this power is to be exercised when, and only when, the governing personnel are gravely unfaithful to their task. Consider, for the sake of clarity, the case of a monarchy according to the old pattern, i.e., that of a monarchy associated with few, if any, democratic elements; according to the transmission theory, the people enjoys, in such a system, a power greater than that of the king; what difference and what relation are there between this power of the people in a nondemocratic state and the power of democratic control?

The transmission theory holds that the people still possesses, after transmission has been effected, a power greater than that of the governing personnel; yet, in an aristocratic or monarchical regime this power cannot be lawfully exercised except in extreme cases: this is not democratic control, which is periodically exercised without there being anything abnormal or extraordinary about the circumstances. The British can vote Mr. Churchill out of power without even implying that they are dissatisfied with his record; they may merely mean that, after the war has been won, they intend to turn to tasks for which another administration is better qualified. The common right of deposition, which the transmission theory grants to every politically organized people, cannot be lawfully exercised without extraordinary circumstances, without dire and immediate threat to the common good. Thus, between the two, the difference is obvious. It can be illustrated by a comparison with the laws concerning the ownership of earthly goods. Anyone, no matter how destitute, may become lawful owner of a loaf of bread in case of extreme necessity. Yet there is a great difference, with regard to the use of wealth, between the man who can acquire it by regular means, i.e., by paying for it, and the man who can acquire it only in extraordinary circumstances and through the extraordinary privileges of extreme necessity. The people who transmitted power within democratic forms exercise, whenever election time comes, a power which may be likened to that of the regular owner over his regularly possessed goods. The people who transmitted power to a hereditary king and depose their ruler on account of high treason or some extraordinary mismanagement exercise a right that can be likened to that of anyone to make use of earthly goods, in an extreme emergency, to preserve his life or that of those who belong to him.

No matter how clear the difference between the common right of deposition and the democratic right of control, it is hardly possible to give much thought to the former without inclining toward the establishment of the latter. If people envisage the removal of their ruler as a contingency likely to occur in not extremely rare cases, they are logically inclined to promote institutions that can handle the procedure of deposition in nonrevolutionary fashion; such institutions, almost inevitably, turn out to be the beginning of democratic control. But what are the peoples who fail to realize that the removal of bad rulers is a thing necessary in not exceedingly rare cases?

Such peoples are those among whom a mythical representation of the governing personnel prevails, as in traditional Japan and also in nontraditional countries where many persons have come to believe that the genius of history is embodied in a definite party. Since there can be no question of deposing the genius of history, there is no use contemplating circumstances under which it might be necessary to get rid of such a party. Let the conclusion be that the concept of popular control inherent in the transmission theory and inseparable from it favors the promotion of democracy, although it is not distinctly democratic and finds application in every fully political system.

The features characterizing the behavior of sovereignty in democracy are still to be disengaged. Let us use, as a starting point, the trivial consideration that democracy alone admits of nontransmission of power. If the people, having received sovereignty from God, refrains from taking the human measures necessary for the establishment of monarchy or aristocracy, it finds itself constituted as a democratic society by its very abstention. Nontransmission of authority means democracy in its most typical form. Although a regime implying no transmission of power and no distinct governing personnel is a rare occurrence, it is plain that direct rule of the whole community through majority vote is the archetype of all democratic institutions and the fundamental pattern which must be referred to whenever there is a problem of understanding the democratic element in a mixed society.

What characterizes the democratic condition of sovereignty is that, in a democracy, sovereignty is never completely transmitted. But let us first consider in what sense sovereignty can be said to be completely transmitted in a nondemocratic regime. If the nondemocratic regime is political in the full sense of the term, the people remains capable of exercising a power superior to that of the king; but the act of transmission implies that such power can be exercised only under extraordinary circumstances and on account of a dire threat to the welfare of the community. Under normal circumstances the transmission of power to the king precludes the exercise of this popular power which is greater than that of the king. According to the theory of Cajetan, the king deposed by the people is deposed by a power superior to his; thus it would not be appropriate to say that, under extreme circumstances, the power transmitted to the king reverts to the people; for the deposition of the king as described by Cajetan, in a sharp contrast with the deposition of the heretical pope, implies the exercise of a power superior to that of the king; it implies that, *while the king is still in power,* another power superior to his, viz., the power of the people, steps in and puts an end to the power of the king. Are we back to the coach-driver theory? The temptation is great to say that the transmission of power is ungenuine and merely apparent. If the people retains a power superior to that of the king, it looks very much as if the king were only a secretary or manager hired by the people. To this difficulty let it be answered that, in order for the transmission of power to be genuine, it suffices that the superior power of the people should be suspended by the act of transmission and should remain suspended until circumstances of extreme seriousness give back to the people the right to exercise it. While royal power is normally exercised, the people remains in possession of a power superior to that of the king; otherwise, it could not, under extreme circumstances, depose the king by virtue of a power superior to his. *But the act of genuine transmission suspends the exercise of the people's power; subjection to the king is genuine; subjects are bound in conscience to obey the genuine power of the king.* The proper effect of the extraordinary circumstances under which the people can depose the king is to make it again lawful for the people to exercise a power which it never ceased to have but which could not be lawfully exercised under normal circumstances. The key to the interpretation of the case is the notion that the actual possession of a power does not necessarily entail the right to use it actually and that the suspension of the right to use a certain power does not necessarily entail the loss of this power. The following example may help to explain this important point.

Let us think of a constitutional ruler to whom the constitution gives extraordinary powers (e.g., that of issuing laws without parliamentary vote) in emergency situations. When an emergency materializes, what is it, precisely, that happens? Extraordinary powers are given to the governor not by the emergency but by the constitution. But the constitution gave such powers under such limitations that any claim to exercise them outside the emergency situation would be high treason. What the emergency effects is the releasing of powers given by the constitution under the provision that they are emergency powers and, consequently, cannot be lawfully exercised except in an emergency. Similarly, the people who transmitted power to a king would be guilty of criminal disobedience if they decided to depose the king for no extraordinarily grave reasons. It would be like a constitutional ruler fancying to exercise emergency powers when there is no emergency. Thus the superior power retained by the people does not jeopardize the genuineness of the transmission. Transmission is so genuine as to bind the superior power of the people, to tie it up in such a way that extraordinarily serious circumstances alone can untie it. The situation, so interpreted, does not resemble the relation symbolized by the coach-driver any more than a constitutional ruler endowed with emergency powers resembles an absolute despot.

This is, briefly, the sense in which transmission of power is complete in a nondemocratic regime. Its completeness does not mean that the power of the people ceases to be superior to that of the king. Such superiority cannot cease. It is due to the very nature of civil society and to the privilege of the civil multitude as first bearer of God-given power. In this very precise sense the sovereignty of the people is inalienable.

What distinguishes democracy is that in a democratic regime transmission of sovereignty is incomplete even in the sense in which it would be complete if the regime were nondemocratic. In other words, over and above this nontransmissible power that the people retains under all circumstances,[9] the people, in a democracy, retains the exercise of powers

9. Again, we are considering a people satisfying the conditions of *political* government.

which are transmissible and would be transmitted if the regime were not democratic. *Democracy never transmits the whole of the transmissible powers. Every democracy remains, in varying degree, a direct democracy.*

Let us briefly survey the features which evidence, in common democratic practice, the partial nontransmission of sovereignty. If government by distinct personnel is made democratic by the control of the people over the governing personnel through the procedure of periodical election, the very definition of democracy (indirectly exercised) points to merely partial transmission of sovereignty. It cannot be said that sovereignty is entirely transmitted to distinct personnel when the basic understanding is that this personnel will render accounts at the end of a determinate period and be reinstated or not by act of the people's sovereignty. But, in addition to the basic procedure of control over the governing personnel through periodical election, democratic practice always retains some aspects of direct democratic government. One of these practices is the obligation of submitting some particularly important laws (e.g., constitutional dispositions) to referendum. Another one, so common that without it democracy, at least in modern societies, is inconceivable, and so broad in its scope as to affect all aspects of political life, is the power of public opinion.

This is one aspect by which normal democratic practice bears resemblance to the coach-driver system. On account of this resemblance, this aspect of democratic practice can favor the inconspicuous corruption of democracy into masked anarchy. What are we requested to do when organizations pray that we bombard our congressman with letters to the effect that we want him to vote in such and such fashion? Bombardment of congressmen by letters from the electors may be interpreted in either of two ways, and this is why it is always a risky method. It may be interpreted as meaning that power of legislation and control over the executive has never been genuinely transmitted to the United States Congress, that this power has been retained by the people, and that, accordingly, congressmen are merely managers hired by the people for the enforcement of their will. This interpretation, familiar to all demagogues, violates the Constitution of the United States and constitutes an appeal to rebellion. It is fitting to recall here Bellarmine's proposition that the people is not morally free to transmit or not to transmit power. As explained, this proposition does not necessarily signify that Bellarmine ignores the lawfulness of direct democracy. It means that, when circumstances are such that a distinct governing personnel is needed, the people is obligated to create such a governing personnel and to transmit authority to it. Transmission of authority is not necessary under all circumstances. *There are circumstances under which a community can do without distinct governing personnel, but the thing which is never ethical and never political is insincere, ungenuine, unfaithful, apparent, and not real—in short, treacherous—transmission of authority.* A king may not be restricted by constitutional control; but, if he is, he cannot ignore constitutional control without violating the constitution and deserving the most severe punishment. Similarly, a people may not transmit sovereignty; it may, if circumstances allow, govern itself directly by majority vote and know of no distinct personnel except managers. But when circumstances demand that power be transmitted to a distinct governing personnel, when this demand of the common good has been sanctioned by fundamental law, every attempt at corrupting transmission of power into an ungenuine process is sheer revolt against the fundamental law of the country. Provided that those things are understood, public opinion has a noble part to play in the operation of democratic government.

The truth is that in every democracy, at least under modern conditions, the people retains the character of a deliberating assembly. The constitutional tradition of Great Britain provides for two assemblies, the House of Lords and the House of Commons; but a less articulate part of the constitution gives considerable power to a third assembly, viz., the people, as able to express its thoughts and wills through the common channels of public opinion. The Constitution of the United States was written with a higher degree of self-consciousness;

yet it includes an unwritten part which gives considerable
power to a third assembly, viz., the people of the United
States. That the powers of this informal assembly should not
be mentioned in any formal document is easy to understand
and entirely normal. But, because of the informal character of
this assembly and of the unwritten character of its powers,
great uncertainties inevitably ensue, and it is in the shadow
of these uncertainties that democratic government ceaselessly
undergoes the temptation of being corrupted into a coach-
driver system. Again, all the essential features of government
are found in a direct democracy. In a society ruled by majority
vote, without distinct governing personnel, everyone is bound
to obey; it is only by accident that one happens to be in the
majority and to follow one's own judgment as one acts according to the decision of the majority. *Nontransmission of
power does not destroy the essence of government; but ungenuine transmission does.* We mentioned earlier that a citizen
of a direct democracy who is determined to abide by the law
only when the law is what he wants it to be always behaves
as a rebel, never as a law-abiding citizen, even when he performs—in a purely material sense—the actions prescribed by
the law. Similarly, ungenuinely transmitted sovereignty implies constant rebellion, even when the laws and decrees
issued by the governing personnel are complied with. Practices
calculated to assure the influence of the people on the policies
of actually elected assemblies and executive agencies are ambiguous and risky, which does not mean that they are not necessary and important. So long as letters addressed to congressmen,
press campaigns, petitions, and street demonstrations are
merely the expression of opinions held by the consultative assembly established, in unwritten fashion, by every democratic
constitution, all is normal and sound. If, on the other hand,
such expressions of opinion are calculated to deprive the men
in power of their right to command, of their duty to have a
judgment of their own, of their responsibility, of their conscience; if such practices are calculated to change, through
threat and bribe, into mere secretaries or managers or mes-
sengers or mandate-holders or coach-drivers, men who know

that they are under obligation to exercise authority, to have a prudence of their own and to make use of it, to be governors and not mere managers; men who know that, as a consequence of transmission, they cannot give up the character of holders of authority without criminal failure to fulfil their task: such practices mean rebellion and treachery established at the core of political life. They tend to corrupt political life into a competitive system where all moral idea is absent. Promises, formal and informal bribes, threats of all kinds, not excluding physical ones, and soon slander and calumny become determining factors in public life. In such confusion there is no guaranty that the majority's wishes should prevail; it is all a question of force, and the greater force may not be on the side of the majority. In most cases it is more likely to belong to the minority—often a handful of particularly rebellious characters—who control the means of pressure. Practices calculated to make the transmission of sovereignty ungenuine do not lead the people to any sort of direct democracy but rather to oligarchic situations that are totally unwished for, except by their beneficiaries.

It would be very helpful, if it were at all possible, to formulate rules and criteria concerning those practices which, if our analysis is correct, can be either an important phase of democratic life or sheer rebellion, destructive of democracy and of political relations. One proposition can be safely uttered: in such matters quantity is of decisive importance, and the species of an action changes according as this action is of moderate, or of extreme, intensity. The situation of a congressman who receives, once in a while, letters in which a few electors voice their opinions seems not to differ, except quantitatively, from that of the congressman who is constantly disturbed by telegrams, telephone calls, and special deliveries. In fact, as often happens in human affairs, a change in quantity entails here a qualitative change, and nobody can say exactly where the qualitative change has taken place. (Changes that take place surreptitiously are always suspicious.) If some circumstances ever make it necessary to wage an extremely intensive campaign of opinion, those circumstances are not of the same kind as the circumstances which justify a campaign of moderate intensity.

Let us try, further, to define the qualitatively different characteristics of moderate and intensive campaigns. With due allowance for the element of relativity implied in all such considerations, let it be said that the moderate campaign implies merely a determination to have a certain opinion known and taken into consideration. An intensive campaign, on the other hand, means determination to assure the victory of an opinion. How, an assembly whose opinions are merely to be taken into consideration is a consultative, deliberative, or advisory assembly; but one whose opinions are meant to be final decisions, delivered for purposes of realization to executive agencies, is more than a consultative assembly, it is a legislating and governing one. In short, considering that in every democracy the people retains the character of an assembly that has normally a part to play in the government, let it be said that the transmission of sovereignty to a distinct governing personnel leaves to the people the character of a merely consultative assembly. Granted that, in addition to the Senate and the House, formally established by written constitution, the democratic organization of the federal government actually comprises a third assembly, informally constituted and not mentioned in a written document—that of the people of the United States— let our conclusion be that, whereas the first two assemblies are endowed with the power of decision, the third one is merely consultative in character. Campaigns of opinion, when they become intensive, treat the people as if it were possessed with a power of decision. This is the meaning of the qualitative change corresponding to the change of intensity: a moderately intensive political campaign treats the assembly of the people as a consultative assembly; an extremely intense campaign of opinion treats the people as an assembly endowed with a power of decision. A congressman who receives, once in a while, letters that let him know how various groups of electors feel about impending legislation and executive policies is a man in power who receives advice from people normally endowed with an advisory function. A congressman bombarded with telegrams, phone calls, and special deliveries, even if those messages contain no threats and no bribes, is treated as a man in charge of enforcing decisions described to him as made by the third assembly, that of the whole people. But if the assembly of the people retains a power of decision and if its power of decision is understood to overrule the judgment of the Congress, then sovereignty has not been transmitted to the Congress in a genuine way. In order for campaigns of opinion to avoid the character of rebellion, it is necessary that they should treat the assembly of the people as a merely consultative assembly. Then they will be but moderately intensive.

It remains to be considered whether it is ever lawful for a people that has transmitted authority to claim more than the character of a consultative assembly, to claim a power of decision. The answer is not dubious: after authority has been regularly transmitted, the people can make decisions only when it can and ought to exercise this power which is greater than that of the governing personnel and which cannot be transmitted. One way to exercise this power is by deposing the governing persons; this is an extreme procedure, almost never necessary in a democracy, since democratic institutions subject the governing personnel to periodical re-examination. Another procedure is intense opinion pressure. To conclude: Intense campaigns of opinion, which imply that the people has the power of decision, are lawful only when circumstances are so grave as to give the people a right to exercise, albeit in limited fashion, the power greater than that of the governing personnel which was suspended, but not nullified, by the act of transmission.

It should now be possible to analyze the expression "government by the consent of the governed"—a historic and glorious expression which will never fall out of use. It has several meanings, which cannot be distinguished in political speeches or even in statements of principles. Such is the paradox of political notions considered in their sociological existence; for it is in a state of confusion that they are most active and produce their most important effects. About all the clarity that these subjects admit of will be procured if instruments of clarification are available to whoever needs and cares to use them. To work out such instruments and see that they are kept in good order is what political philosophers are paid for.

1. The proposition that government requires the consent of the governed may mean that political association is an act of the reason and of the will; that political society is not brought about by instinct and infra-rational forces but by rational judgment and free will and, more precisely, by the good use of reason and freedom and by the qualities which render such use steady, i.e., wisdom, justice, and friendship. So understood, the theory of government by the consent of the governed expresses a truth of great profundity and consequence. It is particularly important to recall it and to understand it in a time like ours, since the social sciences, understandably, are influenced by the successful pattern of the physical sciences and consequently tend to represent human societies as a product of nature, in the sense in which nature means univocal determination and is spoken of in opposition to free will. The naturalistic concept of political society does not proceed only from the deterministic philosophy of human nature generally associated with materialism and positivism; it proceeds also from a conservative and traditionalistic reaction against the political voluntarism which has been and remains at work in the ideological and emotional movements connected with Rousseau and the French Revolution. In their righteous opposition to propositions which seemed to describe political society as a work of human arbitrariness, some traditionalists so emphasized the natural character of society as to make it appear a product antecedent to any activity of reason and freedom, a product, accordingly, foreign to morality, at least so far as its basic constitution is concerned.

2. The notion of consent of the people may refer to the designation of the governing personnel. What is signified, then, is that political leaders are not self-appointed but are designated by the people according to procedures which admit of great variety and of which the least formal are not necessarily the least genuine. Under extraordinary circumstances,

when elections and even regular consultations of public opinion are impossible, a handful of men may declare that they are the government and not the rebels. Think of the circumstances which led to the constitution of governments-in-exile during the occupation of Europe by the Nazis. In order for such a creation of leadership to be better than sheer rebellion, the indispensable condition is that there be, in the historical situation, a demand for such creation. This demand may be at variance with the conscious wishes of the majority. Thus, initially, a governing agency may exist and operate without the consent of the people. Plainly, it does not possess fully the character of a government until the self-appointed leaders are confirmed in power by popular consent. So long as such consent has not been expressed, the men who claim authority do not possess, except in a rudimentary and uncertain fashion, the prerogatives of a political organization. A committee which claims to be the government, whose purposes and activities seem to be borne out by the historical situation, but which has not yet been confirmed by any expression of popular consent, is one of these nontypical forms that history produces in times of crises and revolutions. In order to behave properly toward such nontypical forms, either by recognizing them or by opposing them, individuals need an unusual amount of lucidity; they have to make a clear decision in a situation which is not clear. They have to draw a definite line of action in a situation which is not definite. The virtue which produces such lucidity when all is dark is the fortitude of the heroes.

3. The proposition that government requires the consent of the governed may mean that the leaders of temporal society do not receive their power directly from God and that political power does not reside in any distinct governing personnel unless it has been transmitted to them by the people. So understood, the theory of government by consent of the people would be identical with the transmission theory as opposed to the designation theory. A difficulty arises with regard to situations in which plainly lawful government is exercised without the governed having effected any transmission of power. Think, for instance, of the power exercised in conquered

territory by the conqueror; if the war was fully just, this power is also fully just, though badly exposed to abuse. Or think of some barbarous population reluctantly controlled by a colonizing power. In spite of frequent and grave abuse, it would be absurd to deny that power exercised under such circumstances may be perfectly lawful. It may be lawful indeed, but not political. It is paternal authority, substitutional authority, in the sense of our first chapter.

4. The proposition that governments derive their powers from the consent of the governed may imply a demand for the periodical exercise of popular consent through the phases of political life. So understood, this proposition refers to the peculiar situation of sovereignty in democracy; it may even be considered the very formula of democratic government. If it is posited that consent of the people ought not to be given once and for all but should be elicited anew as political life goes on, there are only two possibilities, viz., direct democracy and control of the people over the governing personnel through the procedure of periodical election, that is, representative democracy.

5. The formula under consideration may signify determination to avoid complete transmission of authority. In this case it refers, again, to a situation which is not common to all lawful and political governments but proper to democracy. It refers to the fact that every democracy is, in a measure, a direct democracy and that in every democracy the people at large retains the character of a deliberative assembly which participates in the government by voicing its assent or dissent in several ways. Referring to what was said above of the people's assembly in indirect democracy, let it be mentioned that, so understood, the theory of government by the consent of the people must be held with discrimination and awareness of the risks.

6. The theory of government by consent of the people may mean that, all other things being equal, persuasion is a better instrument of government than coercion. It implies, then, that every government has a duty to seek the maximum of voluntary co-operation, to explain its purposes and methods, to

educate the governed, to appeal indefatigably to whatever element of good will can be found in them, and never to resort to
coercion unless persuasion proves impossible. Such interpretation is entirely wholesome and necessary, provided that it is
unmistakably maintained that the use of coercion is fully
legitimate whenever persuasion fails to accomplish some necessary purpose.

7. In the six preceding senses the notion of government by
the consent of the governed expresses either (*a*) an essential
condition of lawful government, (*b*) a condition proper to political government precisely considered as political, or (*c*)
some condition proper to democracy. But in a seventh sense
the formula is understood to mean that the governed are
never bound except by their own consent, that they never
obey except inasmuch as they please to obey—briefly, that
they are never obligated to obey. So understood, the theory
that government demands the consent of the governed expresses neither a political nor a democratic necessity but mere
revolt against the laws of all community.

seven

THE
HISTORICAL
VIEWPOINT

F. H. Hinsley

THE CONCEPT OF SOVEREIGNTY
AND THE RELATIONS
BETWEEN STATES

Men do not wield or submit to sovereignty. They wield or submit to authority or power. Authority and power are facts as old and ubiquitous as political society itself; but they have not always enjoyed the support or suffered the restraints that the theory of sovereignty seeks to construct for them. Although we speak of it as something concrete that may be lost or acquired, eroded or increased, sovereignty is not a fact. It is an assumption about authority—a concept men have applied in certain circumstances to the political power that they or other men were exercising.

Applied to a body politic, this concept has involved the belief that there is a final and absolute authority within the society. Applied to the problems that arise in the relations between political societies, its function has been to express the antithesis of this belief—the principle that internationally, over and above a collection of societies, no supreme authority exists. Nor need we be surprised at this antithesis. It is a logical consequence of the nature of this concept that in the international context it has denied the existence of the kind of power which, within the single community, it has been its function to sustain. The idea that there is a sovereign authority within the single community involves the corollary that this

From *Journal of International Affairs*, vol. XXI, no. 2 (December 1967), pp. 242–52. Reprinted by permission of the author and the publisher.

authority is one among other authorities which are ruling other communities in the same sovereign way.

In practice, however, this logical consequence was not recognized for hundreds of years. Neither the Romans nor their Byzantine successors, both of whom had developed the notion of internal sovereignty, ever applied it in its international sense. It was not until the end of the sixteenth century, when the theory of internal sovereignty was next formulated, that men first grappled with the problem of extending it to the relations between societies. And it was not until the eighteenth century that they finally solved it.

Men had to overcome great obstacles before they could conceive of the world as being composed of separate political communities, a prerequisite for extending the sovereignty concept. Thus, the evolution of Roman legal categories and, in particular, the Roman failure to evolve a true international law leave little doubt that the Roman and Byzantine failure to extend the concept to an international frame was due to the development of Rome from a tribal city directly into a successful conquest empire. The notion of the sovereignty of the emperor in Rome itself was extended to the provinces in harness with the imperial idea, which held that the provinces constituted a single world in which there was only one universal state and ruler, the state and the emperor of Rome. It was for this same basic reason that the concept of sovereignty within the separate community was not recovered until the sixteenth century, a thousand years after this Roman advance had been lost and forgotten except in Byzantium, and that, even after they had developed it in connection with the separate community, men still experienced so much difficulty in applying it to the relations between communities and states.

The drift of much recent writing on sovereignty has been to ignore or deny these early modern delays in an attempt to place the origin of the concept at an ever earlier stage of the Middle Ages. But the argument that even in its internal application this concept was advanced by any medieval mind is misconceived. It overlooks the fact that the sovereignty of authority is but one of several theories that may be proposed to justify or explain authority. More particularly, it overlooks the central feature that distinguishes the concept of sovereign authority from other such theories.

The other theories have been either absolutist justifications of supreme political power or denials that political power can be absolute. Sovereignty has been the "constitutional" justification of absolute political power. Historically, it has been formulated only when the locus of supreme power was in dispute, and applied only as an enforced compromise between those who claimed that it lay with the ruler and those who claimed that it lay with the ruled. It is the justification of absolute authority that can arise and exist only when a final power is considered necessary in a body politic, and only when the body politic and its government are considered necessary to each other.[1] If we bear this in mind, we will recognize that a sovereign theocratic authority—a sovereign pope, for example—is a contradiction in terms. We will also see why the notion of a sovereign king or emperor who is also king or emperor by Divine Right has been a confused compromise, never tenable for long. Finally, we will undertand why sovereignty, even in its internal form, was unknown to medieval Europe, not to mention medieval Islam or India.

There was, of course, continuous argument in medieval Europe about *authority;* but the political and social conditions in which it is possible—indeed, in which it is unavoidable —to conceive of authority in terms of sovereignty did not exist. Neither of the universal authorities—the medieval Empire or the Papacy—could be conceived of in such terms because their power, at no time more than a shadow of that which Rome had possessed, was inadequate for the task of making Christendom into a body politic. Indeed, we may say that it was settled as early as the ninth century that, should the idea of sovereignty ever reappear, it would not do so in relation to the universal but nonterritorial community of Christendom, but within the separate political societies of which Europe was already composed. Until the sixteenth century, on the other

1. For a fuller statement of this argument see F. H. Hinsley, *Sovereignty* (New York: Basic Books, 1966).

hand, the idea that Europe nevertheless formed a single community—an idea that was greatly strengthened when, under the pervasive influence of a revealed religion, a pope took his place alongside an emperor and the concepts of Europe and Empire were absorbed by the concept of Chistendom—remained sufficiently viable to give great ritual power to the universal authorities and to prevent the development of the notion of sovereignty around these separate territorial rulerships. Moreover, until about the same date—and this further helps to explain why the notion of Christendom, so weak territorially, could become so powerful ritually—the separate territorial communities were under theocratic rule because they were each as unintegrated as the community of Christendom, or the Empire of Europe, as a whole.

Since the idea of sovereignty could evolve only from the association of a cohesive community with a single rulership, these circumstances constituted an insuperable barrier to its emergence. We cannot be too careful about making certain distinctions when we contemplate the centuries during which they prevailed. It was one thing for men to claim, as claim they did in their quarrels about authority from the twelfth century on, that the separate component state in Christendom was independent even *de jure* of the emperor and the pope. It was quite another thing for them to argue that the independent state had or must have a *sovereign* power within its own community. Indeed, if only because of the segmentary character of that community, no government governed as if it pretended to this latter claim before the government of Tudor England; and no theorist, even in Tudor England, produced a clear formulation of the doctrine of sovereignty until after Bodin had published his *De la République* in 1576. Until then, men could claim that the separate state was *de jure* independent of the emperor and the pope *within its own community* without implying that it was independent of these universal authorities *in its relations with Christendom or with Christendom's other states.* Despite the fact that Christendom was a segmentary, largely ritual community, men still regarded it as a single community of some kind. If only for this reason, this implication was not seen.

On the contrary, if anything is clear about early modern Europe it is this: far from advancing to a statement of the sovereignty of the state in relation to other states before they had formulated the doctrine of sovereignty within the territorial community, men were unable to propound an international version of the doctrine for at least a century after Bodin had made them familiar with it. Even after the end of the sixteenth century, when the growing integration of Europe's separate communities and their states had made the concept of internal sovereignty a viable and even a necessary doctrine, there was a profound intellectual problem to be solved before it could be extended to interstate relations.

The idea that Christendom was a single political society had to be abandoned; but it had to be abandoned in such a way that it was not totally discarded in favor of the claims of the separate state, which was coming to be regarded as possessing internal sovereign power. It was a condition of the discovery of the international version of sovereignty that the notion of Christendom be replaced by a different understanding of international society—by one that was compatible, as the medieval understanding was not, with belief in the sovereignty of the state. For just as the evolution of the theory of sovereignty within the political community demanded some compromise between the ruler's superiority over the law and his continued subjection to ethical premises and political limits imposed by the ruled, so there could be no successful international application of the theory until the notion of the sovereign power of the individual state had been reconciled with the ethical premises and the political needs of an international community consisting of independent states.

We know that this was the problem because on no other supposition can we make sense of the views of those who concerned themselves with the question from the time of Bodin until the eighteenth century. For if it is clear that the problem was a live one from the moment Bodin's work was finished, it is equally clear that until the end of the seventeenth century the bulk of men's writings about it fell into two schools, both of which failed to solve it because they failed to see the need for this reconciliation.

The majority of men, unwilling or unable to discard the medieval notion of Christendom, continued to elaborate medieval ideas. They clung to the medieval understanding of international society as a single society in which the natural divine law imposed a network of common legel rights and duties on the component states. Some of these writers, especially those in clerical circles or in the German imperial area, took this course because of their conservatism. They still argued, as men had long argued, that the separate regional government had come into existence through the corruption of human nature. In their view, either the pope must have direct power over the emperor and the kings or the emperor must retain the *imperium mundi*. Others of this school—men like Leibniz and Fénelon at the end of the seventeenth century, and the peace-planner Saint-Pierre at the beginning of the eighteenth—remained in it for different motives: fear of the increasing anarchism of interstate relations and distrust of the growing Machiavellism and *raison d'état* theories that seemed to be encouraging that anarchism. These motives are understandable, for the second prominent school of thought, a school that included most of the advanced thinkers of the age, took up a position that did nothing to discourage anarchism.

This second school consisted of what have come to be known as the Naturalist and the Positivist positions in international thinking. The Naturalists, led by Pufendorf, held that there could be neither a political *societas gentium* nor any international law—at least any positive international law—between sovereign states in the state of nature, but at most the restraints of a natural, ethical bond. And some of them, like Hobbes, believed that the state of nature was a state of war in which no ethical bond or international law of any kind could exist. At the end of the seventeenth century, the Positivists reversed this attitude toward international law without abandoning the new emphasis on the autonomy of the individual state from which the Naturalists had derived it. They accepted the existence of international law but insisted that the only valid international law was positive law: for them the sole sources of international law were the practices and treaties of sovereign independent states.

We can see now that the main drift of this second and more advanced trend was taking its writers away from a solution of the problem as surely as was the conservatism of the majority of writers. The Naturalist and the Positivist schools of international theory, in their absorption with the new concept of sovereignty within the individual community, discarded almost all belief in the existence of an international community. Indeed, in their insistence that absolute legal authority within the political society must involve the absolute legal liberty of the state within the international society (and thus that what states agreed upon among themselves either could not properly be law or else could alone be law) their views were the equivalent in the international field of those notions of Divine Right absolutism that were currently distorting the internal theory of sovereignty to mean that a ruler who was above the law must also be above moral and political restraint.

We can see this all the more clearly if we now view a third stream of thought in this context. This third school had been intiated by Bodin, who had glimpsed the international consequences of his doctrine of internal sovereignty. Although rejecting the established belief in the inextinguishable unity of Christendom, he held that interstate dealings still required a legal and moral basis. His emphasis on this need was continued by Grotius, who in his *De Jure Belli ac Pacis* (1625) tried to combine the new notion of internal sovereignty with some residue of the medieval acceptance of the existence of an international community. It was along this route and by this reconciliation of old and new ideas that the problem we are discussing would one day be solved. But it was not solved yet. Just as nobody but Grotius understood the international significance of Bodin's thought until the middle of the seventeenth century, so Grotius's own significance was not fully appreciated, even by scholarly and legal writers, until the end of the century. This third stream of thought remained a subordinate stream until then.

One reason for this was the sheer intellectual difficulty of the problem, even for scholars. And the intellectual difficulty was compounded by the primitive international practice of the age. When we turn from the theorists to the practitioners of seventeenth-century statecraft, we cannot fail to notice that they faithfully reflected the two dominant trends in the world of thought. On the one hand, they clung to the medieval framework of Christendom, while on the other they emphasized the independence and sovereign power of the state to an extent that was inimical to the rise of a new international framework in place of decaying Christendom. After the beginning of the sixteenth century, the spectacle presented to us is a contradictory one. The growing integration of the kingdom and its growing resources, including the notion of its internal sovereignty, were being used by an increasing number of states to shatter the medieval basis of empire. But at the same time the revival of empire was ultimately, and perhaps also inexorably, the ambition of every state whose relative power rose above the average.

I say "perhaps also inexorably" because it is more and more apparent to me that it was not until after the end of the seventeenth century, even in Western Europe, that states developed beyond the primitive pattern of international conduct. This pattern prevails whenever the communities in an international system are basically segmentary. Its central feature is the search by each state for physical conflict with others. If a state is successful, the aim of this search does not stop short of consolidating all the communities within range into a single political structure. Although the European states had begun to become individually consolidated and sophisticated before that date in some ways, they did not escape this primitive international structure to any decisive extent before the eighteenth century. There are many indications in the historical record to support this contention. Of all these indications perhaps the most significant—and certainly the only one I can elaborate here—is the fact that it was not until then that even legal theorists succeeded in fitting the doctrine of sovereignty into an international framework. Indeed, they did not arrive at an interpretation of the international system that was fully compatible with that doctrine until the appearance in 1758 of Vattel's book, the *Droit des Gens.*

This was indisputably the first recognizably modern book on international law because it was the first to achieve this feat. Let us by all means emphasize that, like all products of the human mind, it had its antecedents and predecessors. Vattel borrowed from Grotius, whom he greatly admired, a central ingredient of his solution to the problem: the argument that it was necessary to attribute a legal character not only to the positive rules flowing from the will and practice of individual states, but also to the limits and injunctions stemming from the proposition that there existed a natural, if now wholly secularized, international community to which the individual states belonged. He borrowed from more contemporary non-legal writers—men like Montesquieu, Voltaire, and Rousseau—an understanding of this community of states that no longer emphasized either that the states were ritually or even politically a single *societas,* as some had gone on insisting since medieval days, or that they were utterly independent, as the Naturalist and Positivist attack on the medieval view had insisted. What these men were emphasizing after the 1730's was that Europe's states were politically sovereign organizations that had, however, been drawn together by contiguity and historical development into an international system that was a unity *sui generis.* It may be admitted that at least among writers this new conception of Europe had become commonplace by the time Vattel used it as the basis of his international law. Even so, it was Vattel who first compounded the existing elements into a modern statement of international law—a statement that founded the international system, as a system, on the sovereignty of the separate member state.

If one indication of the book's significance is that it is the first such statement that is readily intelligible to a modern reader, another is that it was the first to assume the need for an international law of peace as well as of war. Legal writers before Vattel, not only before the seventeenth century but also after Grotius, had merely sought to civilize conflict—to systematize rules for the conduct of war and the orderly transfer of its spoils. Vattel was equally interested in systematizing the rules that should govern the peacetime relations between states. And this suggests that he was influenced by changing conditions as well as by changing ideas. If it is right to concede that Vattel was able to stand on the shoulders of earlier writers, it also seems likely that he was reflecting the culmination of a major shift in the needs, and thus in the outlooks, of governments. In this connection, it is noteworthy that the *Droit des Gens* was the first book on international law to be used as a handbook by foreign offices. The French government was referring to it in the 1760's. It was venerated by the American government almost from the time of the Revolution as being the guide to "all those principles, laws, and usages which have obtained currency among civilized states." Soon after that, as is clear from their speeches, it had become the reference book for Fox and the younger Pitt. And by the outbreak of the French Revolution it was entering upon its long service in this capacity in most of the foreign offices of Europe, where it was now generally assumed that there was a well-known international law that Vattel had collected and written down.

It may be objected that no earlier compilation could have been used in any case, since organized foreign offices had themselves hardly existed before Vattel's time. The modern foreign office in England, for example, dates back only to the 1780's. But this very fact only goes to show that, if indeed a decisive shift had at last occurred in the behavior of states, it was largely due to the achievement of greater integration and more organized government within Europe's separate communities. It may next be objected that what might be called the victory of Vattel was followed before long by the Napoleonic attempt to return Europe to its older imperial frame. But this does not disprove the proposition that a shift had begun to take place. As with the resettlement of Europe in 1815, when the views of the Russian Tsar harked back to the federal projects of the sixteenth and seventeenth centuries because he was the ruler of the least developed of the great powers, this merely reminds us, if we need a reminder, that shifts of this order are finally consolidated with even more difficulty in practice than they are achieved in theory. Certainly if we ask which governments first based their policies squarely on an acceptance of the sovereign independence and equality of all states, we must give this reply: the governments of Western Europe, under the leadership of Great Britain, in the struggle against, and in the aftermath of, Napoleon. And if we persist, if we ask when the concept of sovereignty, with all its implications for international relations, became the central concept underlying the international conduct of *all* the states in the European system, the answer must be: only when Castlereagh's ideas had won out over Tsar Alexander's, only when the Congress system had given way to the Concert of Europe in the 1820's.

From that time on, however, so complete was the new concept's triumph that practitioners and theorists alike made the solution of all problems conform to it, as is customary when men have finally adopted a new fundamental idea. In Europe itself governments never again—until Hitler—so misused the concept of sovereignty as to abandon the conviction that they were members of an international community. At the same time, so great was their insistence that every political structure must be a sovereign independent state that they could not settle the international status of the Holy See without resorting to the device of establishing a sovereign Vatican city-state. And when this principle was utterly inapplicable to European circumstances and problems, they could conceive of no solution but the opposite of sovereignty, indeed its conscious negation: the negotiated neutralization of minor communities and of disputed or buffer areas.

Beyond Europe they likewise thought and acted solely within the categories of statehood and sovereignty except when they were overborne by the very extent of the inapplicability of these ideas to the conditions that prevailed there. We cannot fail to be struck by the rigidity of this approach when we see the representative of King William IV advising the natives

of New Zealand in the 1830's to form themselves into a state
to be called "The United Tribes of New Zealand"; or when
we read in a British report on the army of one of the Yoruba
tribal states in 1861 that it was necessary to give an account
of the "Constitution" of "this Power" before describing its
military forces; or when we study the difficulties that followed
when European governments, on the assumption that all
recognizable political authorities must be sovereign rulers in
modern communities, confused the powers of the Tycoon with
those of the Mikado, insisted that the admission of the Sultan
to the rights and duties of the circle of European great powers
would solve the Eastern Question, and made solemn treaties
with North American Indian tribes, Eastern potentates, and
African tribal leaders. Not a little light is thrown upon the
changing character of imperialism after the middle of the nineteenth century by the consideration that it was when the
European governments realized that the extra-European areas
were not ruled by sovereign states that they felt forced to
rectify the omission by the establishment of their own political
control there—by the expansion of formal empire. Even the
League of Nations could only be established on the basis of
the sovereign equality of member states.

We may be tempted to dismiss these attitudes as naïve. But
before we do, we should pause to recall that some of them
are still with us. Beyond Europe, and beyond the societies
that are its overseas offshoots, there are still vast areas that
have not developed to the point at which the concept of sovereignty, either nationaly or internationally, is relevant to
them, but which we persist in regarding as being under the
rule of sovereign states. In our views on the relations between
advanced communities, on the other hand, we are now naïve
in a different way. Having learned that sovereignty is not the
sole concept that states need in their relations with each other
—a sign of sophistication and progress—we long for the sovereign state to be superseded altogether. And forgetting that
sovereignty is only a concept, we seek to supersede the sovereignty of the individual state by superseding the individual
state itself. This is as sure a sign of confusion as was the

nineteenth-century insistence on applying the concept of sovereignty to areas that were not ready for it. For what would this program accomplish, assuming it could succeed, but the subjection of the most powerful structures the world has ever known to a single authority that would be incapable of controlling them, despite the fact that it would still have to be conceived of as sovereign?

Some may feel that this is a purblind judgment, that these latent dispositions of our day reflect not confusion, but rather a proper determination to replace the concept of sovereignty by a newer one that better fits the facts. To this I can only reply: distinguish between facts and aspirations.

In due course, under the continuous impact of economic and technological change and with the advance of communications, some of the territorial political societies that have made up the international system in modern times may be merged into greater political societies, as earlier the many regional segments of Europe were consolidated into fewer modern states. But we must not delude ourselves by thinking either that this process of reconstitution will obliterate any existing territorial community before the passage of many years, or that it will ever absorb all existing territorial communities under a single state. The facts are otherwise, and our aspirations should be guided accordingly. So long as there remains more than one territorial community, the quality of sovereignty in the individual state will continue to be an essential qualification, in law as in practice, for membership in the international community.

This will continue to be so, if history is any guide, for these reasons: the state is the territorial community's indispensable political mechanism once the community has attained a certain level of integration; the concept of sovereignty is the inescapable justification of the authority of the state in an integrated community; and so long as there is an international system it will be made up of territorial communities. Aside from the unlikely absorption of all the world's communities under one state, there is only one way this chain of consequences could be broken. It would not withstand a universal loosening of the bonds between communities and their states of the kind that set in when the territory of the Roman Empire dissolved into its tribal regions. Under modern conditions, however, we need no more expect the universal onset of this process—as opposed to its appearance in some undeveloped regions where it is only too likely to occur—than the achievement of the universal state. Moreover, its universal onset would be universally deplored.

It is perhaps important to end with a further thought. As I have already implied, to demonstrate that the concept of sovereignty will thus continue to be an essential concept in international relations is not to argue that it must remain the only concept. On the contrary, the question for the future is whether the sovereign community and state will learn to control themselves. To do so they will need the assistance of concepts other than sovereignty. Equally clearly, we can believe that sovereignty will continue to be a viable concept without denying that it will continue to fail to fit all the facts. In an international community increasingly composed of developed and undeveloped individual communities, it will indeed be surprising if it is not subjected to frequent distortion, as it has been in the past. We ought to remember, however, that in politics a working hypothesis is not necessarily outmoded because it fails to fit all the facts, since in politics no working hypothesis can ever do this. And we might even add that the concept of sovereignty will be less strained than any conceivable substitute. If the problem that confronts us is how to make the individual community and state control themselves, it is just as true that, the more they become advanced enough to do this, the more they are likely to think of themselves as sovereign.

CONCLUSION

W. J. Stankiewicz

THE VALIDITY
OF SOVEREIGNTY

Since the modern concept of sovereignty was formulated by
Bodin, many 'types' of sovereignty have emerged: political,
legal, internal, external, *de jure, de facto,* popular, coercive,
influential, positive, negative, absolute, and relative. The question arises whether such distinctions are justifiable or whether
they show that the term has no fixed meaning. Is sovereignty,
as Benn puts it, "a genus of which the species can be distinguished by suitable adjectives"?

Benn concludes that it is not. For him it is a "protean"
word, shifting its sense bewilderingly when one tries to establish its identity. Yet he admits that each of the six meanings
he mentions is appropriate to a particular type of study.

We know that for the jurists—who insist that they cannot
dispense with the concept—sovereignty is not only a fact of
social order but a logical necessity. Are we to conclude that
sovereignty is exclusively a juristic concept and that the political scientist might well dispense with the term? Clearly,
our analysis is faulty if we are driven to the conclusion that
while the specialized usages are valid, the concept itself is not.

The fact that sovereignty has multiple meanings is understandable. Any concept that is assumed to make a fundamental
statement about the nature of society will be adapted by special interest groups to serve their purposes; its application to
special areas will be investigated and attempts will be made to
fit it into other statements assumed to be fundamental. The
specialized senses that result are interesting because they re-

veal the interaction between various concepts and set limits to their meaning. Attempts to integrate the concept of sovereignty and the logical requirements of 'equality' or 'the rule of law,' for instance, throw a good deal of light on the limitations of these ideas. But we cannot test the validity of the concept of sovereignty by asking whether it can be accommodated into the concept of the rule of law or government by the people, for these are purely normative statements about what ought to be in a society made on the basis of certain assumptions. Nor can we say that the variation in the 'meaning' of sovereignty that results from attempts to adapt it to other assumptions makes the concept dubious because of the reulting multiplicity of meanings. The 'meaning' of sovereignty remains what it was before it was adapted to suit our special purposes. Indeed, it cannot be adapted unless we recognize that its meaning is not dependent on the adaptation but on something else, and that this is the core of the difference between studies of society and studies of the physical world.

The problem confronting the social scientist, or a student of human affairs, is that what he is investigating need not be as it is. Whereas the natural scientist on a certain basic level of experimentation as a rule makes the assumption that the regularities he observes are constants upon which he can build hypotheses, the social scientist must begin with the assumption that even observed regularities are not constants. Otherwise he commits himself to a determinist view of human behavior which the facts would seem to belie.[1] The incon-

---

1. As Nagel observed: "Human behavior is undoubtedly modified by the complex of social institutions in which it develops, despite the fact that all human actions involve physical and physiological processes whose laws of operation are invariant in all societies. Even the way members of a social group satisfy basic biological needs . . . is not uniquely determined either by their biological inheritance or by the physical character of their geographic environment, for the influence of these factors on human action is mediated by existing technologies and traditions." (Ernest Nagel, *The Structure of Science*, Harcourt, Brace and World, New York, 1961, p. 460) Unfortunately, he does not develop this point.

gruity of the attitude of deterministically-minded social scientists becomes apparent if one realizes that modern science is already moving away from strict determinism. Behavioralists are either unaware of the true nature of scientific revolution or unable to make use of it. Nor do they realize that the scientist's purpose is different from that of a student of human affairs. As F. A. Hayek has pointed out, science endeavors to group 'facts' regardless of 'appearances,' according to a recurrent pattern, and to reclassify them using the language of mathematics. The avowed objectivity of science involves ignoring the realm of man's reactions—comprising both thought and physical action—to things investigated.[2] Consequently the scientific (empiricist) approach depreciates the importance of both: ideas—as a factor in history—and social relations; in Peter Winch's words, they become "unsuitable subjects for generalizations." [3]

The behavioralistically-oriented social scientist can, of course, analyze society as a physical scientist analyzes the physical world, making observations of empirically distinctive behavior, but his classifications will be no more than generalized descriptions of particular phenomena.[4]

2. Cf. F. A. Hayek, *The Counter-Revolution of Science,* The Free Press of Glencoe, New York, 1964, Ch. II.

3. Peter Winch, *The Idea of a Social Science,* Routledge and Kegan Paul, London, 1963, p. 133.

4. The scientist's methods are not always appropriate to the social sciences. That the principles of scientific inquiry are of universal validity is a view which, although deeply rooted, is outdated. It reflects the obsolete tenets of Newtonian thinking that every phenomenon is explicable in terms of some fundamental concepts. This view—which prevailed for almost two centuries—has been found unsatisfactory. As Maritain said: "One can no more philosophize with non-philosophical instruments than paint with a flute or a piano." (*On the Use of Philosophy,* Atheneum, New York, 1965, p. 54.) To attach to the scientific method the attribute of universal validity is to ignore the modern, self-critical, skeptical trend which sees science as giving merely a partial knowledge of reality and as being not the only way of acquiring knowledge. The true significance of the modern scientific revolution lies in the realization of its own limitations. Empiricism may be still fashionable, yet in the words of Paul K. Feyerabend, it "is a fragment that cannot stand on its own feet." ("Problems of Empiricism," Robert

What is needed is a theory of society that makes empirically observable classes of behavior meaningful elements of a society: preferably, of more than one type of society. It is the ability of the theory of sovereignty to do this—to integrate into a meaningful complex a large number of distinct categories, such as coercive power, community, obligation, legitimacy, and authority—which determines the 'meaning' of sovereignty: not some normative statement that holds true of only one particular society, or some empirical observation about a single element in the sovereignty concept.

As previously indicated, the interaction between the concept of sovereignty and a particular ideology can serve the important function of revealing the limitations of certain normative statements. Thus the interaction between the classical concept of sovereignty and egalitarianism, which leads to the rationally untenable concept of the sovereignty of the people, goes a long way to undermine the relativist view that any ideology at all can serve as the credo of a society; that is, the purely normative statement of where power and authority ought to lie is in irreconcilable conflict with the statement about what is necessary to government. We cannot disregard the logical statement made by sovereignty in order to hold to the normative statement, unless we assume that 'reason' is itself only a norm having no greater claim upon us than any other norm. Nor can we 'integrate' the two statements to arrive at the concept of popular sovereignty. The logic of sovereignty denies that this is a possible way of looking at government in any society, even one theoretically premised on it.

Interaction of the above type, furthermore, cannot disprove sovereignty or be used to find its 'real' meaning or meanings. Its real meaning is its capacity to identify factors in social organization and integrate them into a rational, compre-

---

G. Colodny (ed.), *Beyond the Edge of Certainty,* Prentice-Hall, Englewood Cliffs, 1965, p. 147.) That modern science can recognize the need for an intuitional faculty does not change the fact that the method of science is limited to the study of selected or abstracted 'symbols' rather than 'reality.' The scientist who can bridge the gulf between 'symbols' and 'reality' resembles a speculative philosopher; he must transcend the method of science.

hensible system that resembles what can be empirically observed. If we ignore this and attempt to establish categories of sovereignty based, for instance, on empirically distinct types of 'power,' we are no longer dealing with the classical concept. No doubt there are different types of power, but this must not lead us to suppose there are different types of sovereignty; without the concept of sovereignty, the different types of power would be purely arbitrary classifications of phenomena.

When a case has been made for the validity of the classical concept of sovereignty and its critics shown to have misunderstood what Bodin and Hobbes really said, what has been established? What difference does it make whether or not it can be shown that many modern analyses are inconsistent with early theories of the state? Since acceptance of the concept in no way excludes the need for analyses of power relations, what (if anything) is changed? Does making a case for sovereignty achieve anything beyond a measure of tolerance for the concept?

No valid answer can be given to those questions unless the full significance of the concept is taken into consideration. If one accepts the concept as valid, the changes are far-reaching indeed, not only for the student of politics but also for citizens and members of the government.

Although the concept of sovereignty might seem too abstruse to be of any consequence to the citizen, it should be remembered that the classical argument was directed toward him. In this respect it was—and is—primarily a statement about obligation and the body politic. It is the sovereignty concept itself which explains why democratic governments are not acting as they 'should,' and it does so in terms that can be readily understood by the common man. The concept of sovereignty, moreover, is likely to be of much greater significance to the modern world than it was to the world of Bodin and Hobbes for, when it developed, modern democracy lay in the future, and could in many respects be viewed as a counter-statement to that made by sovereignty. Where sovereignty insisted on a hierarchy of power relations, democratic theory demanded equality. Whereas sovereignty required a clear-cut distinction between community and state, egalitarian theory demanded an identification: for it, the state must be a fiction. So long as men could be supposed to be literally equal, the argument for sovereignty must seem a device designed to deprive the people of their right to govern themselves. Sovereignty might profess to be an argument about social order, but if men are equal, it becomes an argument for a manifest injustice: namely, for inequality, special privilege, and an hierarchical structure which, if not absolutist in principle, at least promotes absolutism. Confronted by literal equality, then, sovereignty seemed an argument for order that was opposed to justice and all the writhing of philosophers was not able to make it seem both necessary and just.

Literal equality, however, can no longer be accepted except by the very naïve and the most rigidly doctrinaire. Egalitarian slogans only promote the modern malaise, the rebellion of disassociation: the feeling that although the government is legitimate, its practices are not, so that its legislation can be ignored whenever one can do so with impunity. So far as the common man is concerned, the government is not acting—as it 'should' act according to democratic theory—as the agent of the majority. Repeatedly and obviously it follows its own lights. This being so, the citizen follows his. He denies that he has duties or obligations to a government that does not behave as it 'should.' Instead, he pursues self-interest in the narrowest sense of the word. He abandons his role as citizen and thus creates a breach between community and state that leaves the government without the direction or controls that are necessary to its proper functioning. If the theory of sovereignty were substituted for the slogans of primitive egalitarianism, much would be done to restore the sense of community so badly lacking in our society: the sense that we have a common set of principles, and that it is the government's function to uphold and implement them, and act in accordance with them.

Recognition of the validity of the sovereignty principle must also have important consequences for members of the government, whose notions of what their office requires have been

curiously muddled by traditional democratic statements. Legislators soon learn that being 'public servants' and carrying
out the wishes of the electors is utterly impossible, but in the
absence of a clear statement describing the nature of their
function they tend to see their departure from democratic
requirements as expedients which must be concealed. Indeed,
intellectual and verbal dishonesty, a lack of frankness in relations with the public, and the concealment of intentions
behind clichés and empty phrases are rather common features
of democratic rule.

Yet these consequences of a government confused about its
function are not the only important ones. Perhaps even more
important is the fact that without a clear notion of the requirements of sovereignty, the sovereign power in a democracy
is left without principles of action. If public interest requires
the occasional ignoring of the public will as particular circumstances repeatedly make clear, what criteria are being
used to arrive at a concept of public interest? What principles
should the legislator follow when he is not acting in accordance with majority will? In the absence of a clear understanding of the concept of sovereignty, only two courses seem open:
response to circumstances without reference to principles, or
the avoidance of action whose course is not clearly indicated
by circumstances. The first produces the indecision and lack
of policy characteristic of many democracies today, and is
bound to lead to the disappearance of a society's value-order.
The second leads to the postponement of attempts to solve
difficulties until the society is faced with crises: to a policy
of 'brinkmanship' in regard to its political and social problems.

For the political scientist, the concept of sovereignty has
equally far-reaching consequences: it provides a number of
important criteria of analysis. The problem in any science
is how to decide when the classifications made are simply
arbitrary groupings having no significance except in terms
of the observer's perception of reality, and when they represent constituent elements of what is observed. In the social
sciences the problem has seemed insoluble, since human

beings do not appear to have a set nature. What some have called human nature seems to be largely the product of particular societies. Man's capacity to make choices seems to remove human behavior from the cause-effect assumption usually accepted as necessary to the method developed by the physical sciences, so that attempts to apply the method to the social sciences, as by the behavioralists, result in records of the particular behavior of particular people at particular times, rather than useful generalizations.

What possible defense, for instance, can we offer for behavioralist analyses of 'power'? We can, of course, postulate that 'power-hunger' is a part of human nature and proceed on that assumption: some assumption must be made. But if we apply this assumption to the kind of power found in society—which depends on organization and the submission of the many to the few—we are forced into a contradiction. Political power is possible only if men do not by nature have a power drive, as Hobbes recognized when he made it a response to the 'state of nature.' If on the other hand we proceed on the assumption that the possession of power—and perhaps its pursuit—is an empirical fact, it soon becomes apparent that empirically the 'facts' are of totally different kinds, none of which can be classified as members of a genus 'power' without a theory relating them one to another. This is the integrating role that sovereignty plays. It is difficult to see how, without it, an empiricist can justify his studies, and quite impossible to understand how he can suppose that his descriptions of types of power 'refute' sovereignty.

Power is not the only term which is given meaning by sovereignty. As has already been pointed out, a number of terms like community, obligation, legitimacy, authority, state, government, and constitution are integrated—and made meaningful—by the concept. Indeed, the most significant developments that are likely to come out of the sovereignty concept in the future will be related to its ability to make classifications of political behavior meaningful. Too much effort in the past has been spent on proving or disproving the concept and not enough on studying its potentialities as a tool of analysis.

INDEX

Absolute power: Bodin on, 45–46; 47, 51–52, 57

Absolutism, 64, 100, 166, 281; and concept of sovereignty, 7–8; Tudor, 172

Affaires de la Tunisie et du Maroc devant les Nations Unis, 161n

Allgemeine Staatslehre, 201n

Amitié Internationale, L', 167n

Anaxagoras, 47

Aquinas, St. Thomas, 43n, 62n, 163, 199, 200–1, 257n; on law, 254–56; and transmission theory, 254–56

Aristocracy: and transmission theory, 258–59

Aristotle, 43n

Asquith, H. H., Earl of Oxford and Asquith, 136

Austin, John, 44, 70, 70n, 94, 95, 100, 133, 138, 142, 170, 211, 225, 233, 236, 240; defects of doctrine of, 95, 101–2; on enforceability of law, 94; on sovereign, 67; on state, 170–71

Authority, 224–25, 243–44, 250, 275, 276, 277, 278, 281, 287; and coach-driver theory, 246–47; in democracy, 256–72; of the state, 287–88; and transmission theory, 264–65, 271–72

Autonomy, 56, 59; external, 52–53; internal, 52–53

Barker, Sir Ernest, 68n, 69n, 72, 72n

Begriff der Souveränität im modernen Völkerrecht, Der, 161n

Behavioralism, 33–34; its analysis of 'power' 298; in social sciences, 293–94

Bellarmine, Robert, 257, 264

Benn, Stanley I., **67–85;** 11, 12, 13, 14, 16, 17, 18, 19, 291; on legal sovereignty, 69–74; on legislative sovereignty, 74–77; on sovereignty as 'supreme coercive power,' 79–82; on sovereignty as 'the strongest political influence,' 82–84; on state sovereignty (international aspect), 77–79

Beyond the Edge of Certainty, 294n

Bodin, Jean, 4, 7, 9, 10, 11, 13, 15n, 22, 38, 43, 43n, 44, 44n, 47, 60, 61, 133n, 163n, 166n, 197, 197n, 198, 198n, 200, 214, 215, 240, 278, 279, 281, 295; on sovereignty, 15, 44–46, 197–98

Body politic, 50, 52–55, 169

Bosanquet, Bernard, 212, 215, 240

Bossuet, Jacques Benigne, 241

Bracton, Henry de, 139n

Brierly, J. L., 132n, 150, 150n

Bryce, James, Viscount, 70, 70n, 81n, 134, 134n, 211, 213, 220n

Cajetan, Cardinal (Thomas de Vio), 261

Cardozo, Benjamin, 94n

Cases on United Nations Law, 185n

Carnap, Rudolf, 204n

Castlereagh, Robert Stewart, Viscount, 285

Chamberlain, Neville, 136

Charles V, 50n

Chase, Stuart, 4n

Chauviré, Roger, 44n

Churchill, Winston, 187n, 259

Coach-driver theory, 243–51, 256; and democracy, 263–64; example of, 247–50; influence of, 246

Cochin, Augustin, 245n

Cohen, Felix, 94n

Cohen, Hymen Ezra, 41n

Coke, Sir Edward, 20, 103